The Unplanned Society

THE
UNPLANNED
SOCIETY

Poland
During and After
Communism

Edited, Annotated, and with Introductions by

Janine R. Wedel

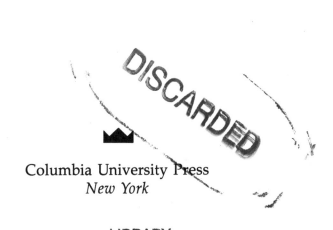

Columbia University Press
New York

10/92

Columbia University Press
New York   Oxford
Copyright © 1992 Columbia University Press
All rights reserved

Library of Congress Cataloging-in-Publication Data

The Unplanned society : Poland during and after
communism / edited, annotated, and with introductions
by Janine R. Wedel.
         p.   cm.
Includes bibliographical references and index.
ISBN 0-231-07372-0
1. Poland—Social conditions—1945–   2. Poland—
Social conditions—1980–   3. Communism—Poland.
4. Social networks—Poland. 5. Informal sector
(Economics)—Poland.   6. Poland—Church history—
20th century.   7. Poland—Moral
conditions.   I. Wedel, Janine.
HN538.5.U57   1991   91-29307
306′.09438′09045—dc20   CIP

∞

Casebound editions of Columbia University Press books
are Smyth-sewn and printed on permanent and durable
acid-free paper.

Printed in the United States of America
c 10 9 8 7 6 5 4 3 2 1

Contents

Preface

Over the past two decades a considerable body of literature has accumulated on task-centered practice—nine books and scores of published papers. This volume attempts to add to this knowledge base in several ways. First, and most important, it develops applications of the model for a range of problems frequently encountered by clinical social workers: difficulties of families and children, anxiety, depression, alcohol abuse, inadequate resources, and psychosocial problems associated with mental and physical illness. The focus is on how problems in these areas can be specified and assessed and how strategies consisting of tasks by clients and practitioners can lead to the alleviation of these problems. Although the methods developed enhance the task-centered model, they are designed for use within any practice framework. Second, the book updates and extends previous formulations of the model, while incorporating recent advances in task-centered work with families. Third, it articulates a relationship between the model and empirical practice and demonstrates how the model can be used as an exemplar of that mode of practice.

It is hoped that the book will be of interest to practitioners, educators, and students in social work and related professions. Practitioners who use a task-centered approach will be able to draw on the new formulations and methods presented in the book. Practitioners with other orientations should still be able to make use of the task-centered interventions that are linked to specific problems. Social work educators may find the book of value as a text in practice courses. Because it presents a form of empirical practice, including research techniques for assessing clients and for measuring practice processes and outcomes, the book may also be relevant to courses on clinical research.

In expressing my thanks to the many people who made this book possible, I turn first to my colleagues who took part in writing specific chapters: Julie Abramson, Anne E. Fortune, and Norma Wasko. Essential to this endeavor were the resources provided by three resourceful deans: Richard L. Edwards, Susan R. Sherman, and Lynn Videka-Sherman; I am deeply indebted to each of them. Consultations from experts in mental health—Larry Doyle and Henry Epstein—and in alcohol treatment—Barry Loneck and Linda Rotering—were most appreciated. I am grateful for the competent and patient services of Jean D'Alessandro, who typed the manuscript, and for the literature searches and editorial work so diligently performed by my graduate assistants—Janet Wheeler, Steven Press, and especially, Andree L. Heintz. Finally, I owe more than words can express to the many students and practitioners whose cases and ideas became a part of the book.

W. J. R.

Acknowledgments

Many people have been committed to this project. It is not possible to mention all of them, but I would like to thank some especially:

The contributors who helped to revise and update their articles and all those who offered materials for my review;

My friend Adam Pomorski for his generous assistance with conceptualization, organization, and later with translation and many aspects of this project;

My editor, Kate Wittenberg, for her kindness and steadfast interest;

Ernest Gellner for his thoughtful consideration and insights;

Agnieszka and Andrzej Wróblewscy and Elżbieta and Jacek Tarkowscy for their valuable suggestions on contributors and articles;

Timothy Dickinson, who helped with editing and indexing; Caroline Taylor, who also edited; and Dolores Wedel and Wiesława Dudonis who assisted with copyediting;

Elżbieta Goździak, Barbara Pomorska, Włodzimierz Rucewicz, and Michael Steinlauf, who helped with translation; and Michał Pohoski, Jakub Karpiński, and Grażyna Kacprowicz, with whom I consulted on critical parts of the text;

Martha Chomiak of the National Endowment for the Humanities for her moral support, and the National Endowment itself, which funded the project and did much to make preparation of the book possible;

The International Research and Exchanges Board, the Kosciuszko Foundation, and the Howard Belzberg Foundation, which also provided financial backing;

Lynn Featherstone of the International Trade Commission, without whose generosity in granting me leaves of absence completion of this book would have been more difficult;

My friends Michael Alexeev, Kathryn Kahler, and Jonathan Kwitny, and my family.

The Unplanned Society

Introduction

Whatever their similarities, no two nations take identical paths into the future. Nor can the experience of one be an adequate guide to another. For the nations of Eastern Europe, change has accelerated to an unpredictably high speed, forcing them to face complete overhaul of nearly all institutions—political, economic, and societal—almost overnight. It is tempting to read this story as a morality play climaxing with the end of Communism, then culminating in a predetermined, satisfying denouement. It is equally tempting to see Poland's period of "transition" as a messy necessity that inevitably will do away with the evils of the previous system.

Yet, as contributor Jacek Kurczewski has suggested, it is much more accurate to look at the developments of the "transition" as one responds to the clamor of events reported in a newspaper—events often complexly related, but not in ways obvious at first glance. Unlike a play, a newspaper must take account of past events, not merely selecting what best fits the story. And, of course, there is no foreordained outcome. The web of events continues to spin itself out, the final outcome elusive.

The tendency of many in the West to assume one particular outcome of the Polish "transition" arises partly from wishful thinking. Before the metamorphoses of 1989 turned Communist steel into scrap, the West cast the drama of Communism's failure into rewardingly "right" and "wrong" sides. Now equally simplifying and ideologizing phrases without adequate referents such as "civil society," "markets," "pluralism," and "transition to democracy" convey an equally reductionist view of the enormously diverse societies of Eastern Europe.

The conventional wisdom on "transition" also is flawed by its neglect of questions of social organization, a neglect that is by no means new. A generation of Sovietologists treated Polish society under Communism largely as a derivative case of the Soviet bloc. They tended to overlook Poland's institutions and social processes not defined primarily as political, and paid too much attention to such visible entities as armies, political parties, police forces, ministries, and state corporations. This conception of society could not adequately account either for variation among countries or for change from within. Twenty Poles here combine to address the relationships of social organization to political, administrative, and ecclesiastical authority and thereby to challenge this view. Our contributors show how Communist policies and prerogatives were less often obeyed or confronted than they were circumvented, supplemented, reinterpreted, or simply explained away.

Sovietologists have tended to gloss over the ways that linkages within and among institutions—and groups as influential as institutions—connect and transform them. Different kinds of linkages, responding to powerfully different contexts, facilitate different paths of development. The commentators here discuss how "social circles," social mobility, migration, networks and exchange systems, and institutions such as the Church and the Opposition[1] worked to arrange society in profoundly un-Communist directions.

Just as these processes were so vital as to reshape society away from Communism, it is reasonable to hypothesize that they might be even more vigorous in the new era, at least in the short term. Today it is apparent how far more long-standing informal groupings, rather than the much studied but marginally legitimate plethora of Polish political entities, move and shape community, policy, economic and political life. From within, we hear the voices of people who have paid their dues: Oppositionists on the Opposition and its use of foreign money; priests on the Roman Catholic Church and its theocratic ambitions. Poland's attempt to "return to Europe" after half a century's stagnation is likely to be as painful as the return of feeling to a frozen limb. Difficult economic choices and the impact of outside example and opinion have awakened constructive attitudes and new energies. But this means more painful adjustment.

The upheavals of 1989–90 had their prophetic echoes fifty years earlier when, under the German occupation, one-sixth of the people of Poland, including Jews, perished and city and village alike were bled and battered. In August 1945, on the heels of six years of occupation and world war that had devastated the Polish nation, the prominent literary critic Kazimierz Wyka wrote a powerful, still-disputed article, "The Excluded Economy." Neither Wyka nor his intellectual successors contributing to this book evoke the image of a nation of righteous resisters—Polish patriots against occupier-oppressors. Rather, like psychoanalysts, they seek to awaken a blocked memory, to bring to national consciousness a story of endless intrigue, manipulation, and accommodation in the name of survival.

When I first read Wyka's prescient article, I was impressed with the parallels between wartime occupation and Communist omnipresence. During the five years I spent in Poland in the latter part of the 1970s, the 1980s, and 1990, I saw heroes fighting a repressive government. Under the charged atmosphere of martial law, I experienced curfews, the internments of friends, and police harassment. But I also encountered a society in which the state and its rules were treated less as opponents to be brought down than as obstacles to be overcome.

Forty years after Wyka depicted the "social fiction" of an economy "excluded" from and functioning contrary to both the moral fabric of society and the commands of its formidable rulers, Polish observers of the 1980s have drawn an extraordinarily similar picture. The slow miseries and petty evasions of peace contrast with the adaptations dictated by the catastrophe of Wyka's time, but the fundamentals are the same. Although the overbearing, coercive Communist government cannot be completely analogized to the Nazi terror, in their daily manifestations both were overregulated systems of prohibition in which humiliation was the main instrument of social control.

Poland passed from being ruled by German conquerors, whose corruptibility offered defenses against many of their worst policies, to being subjected to an unpopular client government. Official power was deemed morally bankrupt and facelessly harsh, yet the day-to-day life of official structures was permeated by familiarity and face-to-face dealings. The sheer impossibility of operating the kind of system that communism claimed to be left a honeycomb of opportunities for the Polish people to finagle and "fix" their way through. Success in dealing with the state bureaucracy and economy depended on the ability to personalize matters and to impart an informal quality to one's relationships with the licensing bureau or the gasoline station attendant. Connecting with and often overshadowing the official economy, elaborate nonpublic networks distributed and even produced goods and services. Such networks gathered and passed on information through a grapevine critical to informally organized economic and political activity.

As during the Occupation, moral credibility was won within social circles by mutual aid: the individual's security rested on the family and social networks extending from and around it. The subversion of the work ethic became a downright patriotic duty; and a traditionally male-dominated society undercut itself further as women often brokered, cut deals, and handled business for husbands and families.

And, as during the Occupation, these practices have by no means vanished when the original desperate conditions that gave rise to them have disappeared. "Only now," warned Wyka, "are we paying the price of the Occupation." Wyka chided his readers that already there were too few who remembered what life in the Generalgouvernement had been all about.

Wyka stands out not only in the quality of what he wrote, but in his grave courage in speaking out. No other writer of the time confronted his contemporaries with such a clear exposé of the difference between dream and reality. There was then, as now, a tendency to dismiss everything evil or undesirable as retrograde, holdovers from the imposed regime, happily divorcing Polish society from any responsibility.

In 1991, a year and a half after popular discontent toppled Communist governments across Eastern Europe, a few unwelcome voices hark back to Wyka's sober combination of clear memory and ominous prognostication. As the informant for one of our contributors, Piotr Szwajcer, put it in "Opposition Against Society: In Pursuit of a 'Normal' Life": "We can handle the fact that people lived under Communism for 40 years. What is more difficult is that they unfortunately but naturally learned something from it."

Little though he may have imagined (or wanted to imagine) at the time, Wyka described the beginnings of a disruptive process that has lasted to the present day. Terror and devastation gave way to 40 years of social displacement, but also to social and material advancement, literacy, and educational achievement. Since the German invasion of 1939, Poland has endured permanent, unchosen change.

After the war, Stalin moved Poland's borders west, expelling millions of Germans and annexing disputed lands. One-third of the current Polish nation, both territorially and numerically, now sits on soil that once belonged to Germany. Poles from the eastern territories were resettled in former German lands; inhabitants of Lvov were relocated to Wrocław (once Breslau), residents of Vilnius (in Polish, Wilno) to Szczecin (formerly Stettin), and so on.

This westward—ever further westward—movement maintained its pace in the postwar period through four massive waves of emigration, in 1945–46, 1956–57, 1968, and the 1980s. During the 1970s about 20,000 Poles settled in West Germany each year, many of them from the Silesian and Masurian territories—formerly German lands. An estimated 120,000 people left Poland from 1981 to 1985.[2]

Another process reorganized those who stayed: the migration from village and farm to town and city. Although Communist governments monitored this movement economically and socially, it proceeded similarly to that of non-Communist countries. In 1946, 68 percent of Poland's population lived in the countryside; by 1989 only 38 percent.[3] As in the West, migration was related to "structural mobility"—the changing makeup of employment both in the creation of new kinds of occupation and also in changes in the numbers of already existing jobs.

The greatest migration and structural mobility in the postwar years occurred from 1945 to 1948, and was a function of the development and increasing numbers of the industrial working class and of bureaucratization. Despite the civil war that marked this period, Poland underwent a strong revitalization and rebuilding of its economy.

From 1949 to 1955, the Communists' "six-year plan" called for heavy industrialization, and changes in the structure of the labor force were achieved primarily through this. A process of industrialization superficially similar to that seen in Western Europe was more intense in Poland because it was concentrated in this much shorter period and was characterized by a narrower, more intense emphasis upon a few large developments rather than a broad spectrum of growth. The heavy industry built in the early 1950s was the locomotive of the wide-ranging structural mobility of 1950 to 1960.[4]

From 1960 onward the rate of industrialization generally slowed but continued in the same direction. The rate accelerated again during the 1970s due to the rising standard of consumption and of industrial investment spurred on by Western loans raised by First Party Secretary Edward Gierek. But in the late 1970s the standard of living declined sharply as the economy deteriorated, contributing to the emergence of the Solidarity movement in 1980.

In the official propaganda of this industrializing society, the most representative pattern of upward mobility was a farm laborer going to work in the factory or a factory hand or house cleaner becoming an office worker or bureaucrat. Some people moved up very rapidly through the enhanced opportunities provided by membership in the Communist Party: a quick and sure way for a talented village youth to scale the social ladder was to move to the city, get a higher education, join the Communist Party, and become a manager or apparatchik. Yet, as Antoni Sułek confirms in our concluding article, "Farewell to the Party," by the last decade of its supremacy the Party had ceased to be a rewarding career move for skilled workers, ambitious young people or others, who a generation ago might have signed up eagerly. Another path upward was ecclesiastical: through the postwar period, most priests, like most Party members, came from the village. As Father Andrzej Kłoczowski remarks in "Onward Exultation: The Church's Afterglow in Communism's Collapse": "The paradox is that . . . both Party members and bishops are sons of peasants."

Social mobility was perhaps most obvious in the particular organization of rural life—specific to Poland and not to be found in developed countries or in other socialist states. Many Polish peasants had been landless laborers before the war; in some areas there was an upper limit on the amount of land that even the most prosperous agricultural laborer could own. With the slogan "land to the peasants," the postwar government fomented a new social category of mobile "peasant-workers," who produced barely enough to feed their own families while working at state jobs in industrial towns. For example, many seasonal workers moved from the eastern farming region around Białystok to work in the southern Silesian steel mills during the winter. The long tradition of small family holdings, combined with the need for unskilled workers in a rapidly industrializing state, created the peasant-worker institution.

Under Communism, up to one-third of all farmers produced not for the market, but simply for subsistence. Small farmers tilled tiny plots, less than 5 hectares (12+ acres) on the average. In 1970, 27 percent of farmers worked patches with an area of less than 2 hectares; in 1989 the figure had risen to 30 percent.[5]

In 1991, many peasant-workers, although not starving because they live off farm produce, are losing their jobs as unskilled laborers; unemployment is widespread in areas where peasant-workers are concentrated. Rapid industrialization in the postwar years contributed to a social flux and reflux that has yet to stabilize.

Not only did Polish society undergo massive upheavals such as social mobility not directly attributable to Communist policy, Communism itself was in constant fluctuation. Each generation of change gave rise to new policies and new rules, to attempted "renewal" and to subsequent "crisis," to which the weary nation was constantly forced to respond, from the bitter Stalinist years, through the more enlightened but still depressing decade and a half of First Party Secretary Władysław Gomułka, to the euphoric expansion and consumer plenty of the 1970s under First Party Secretary Edward Gierek. The economy's sharp setbacks toward the end of the decade and the overbearing "propaganda of success" fueled an Opposition that forged links among the intelligentsia, workers and peasants, groups that were previously separated; and this helped to foment the Solidarity movement.

Few societies have so swiftly undergone so many transformations in so many forms as has Poland during the past half century. Few peoples have been so long and so relentlessly faced with such deep change and instability. Continuity was shown only in such facets of Polish life as Catholicism, aspects of culture, and personal relationships. With the disappearance of business, educational criteria became more important indicators of social prestige than financial and material tangibles. The state's lack of any final legitimacy and the relative ineffectiveness of the economy encouraged emigration, whether physical or psychological.

Forty years after Wyka exposed the social processes that shaped Poland under German Occupation, our other contributors—all contemporary scholars or writers living in Poland—set out to record the patterns of coping and compromise and initiative that structured the lives of those around them. Just as some of the processes that began during the Occupation endured, encouraged by the need to outflank Communist institutions, so in practice will the processes that flourished under Communism be either encouraged or discouraged in the new Poland.

More than half our contributors are sociologists. In Poland, sociology has been regarded as a relevant, all-embracing study of society. Many Opposition and Solidarity leaders were trained in sociology, as are many post-Communist government officials, advisers, and policymakers.

Contemporary Polish sociology draws on a long, distinguished record of scientific inquiry and ethnography, which boasts such eminent scholars as the anthropologist Bronislaw Malinowski and the sociologist-philosopher Florian Znaniecki. Both united philosophical and methodological considerations with meticulous fieldwork and made notable contributions to their fields in this century: Malinowski as the father of functionalism who would set off for years at a time to operationalize his holistic perspective among Trobriand islanders; Znaniecki for his contribution to the methodology of the social sciences and his five-volume work on *The Polish Peasant in Europe and America* (together with William Thomas).

Beginning in 1939, occupation, war, emigration, and Communist dogma paralyzed scholarship in the social sciences, and it began to reawaken only with the de-Stalinizing thaw of 1956. The late Stefan Nowak was part of this revival. Nowak helped to refound the Institute of Sociology at Warsaw University after 1956. He was known for his academic integrity and uncompromising stance both against Communist ideological influence upon academic discourse and specifically against government meddling in the affairs of his institute. I remember him as a widely respected man of character, who made his presence and discipline felt among his associates. (Sadly, Nowak died between Solidarity's 1989 landslide and the organization's entrance into office several months later; he did not live to take part in the self-examination Polish sociology would undergo in the new era.)

After 1956, Polish sociology developed unlike anywhere else in the Eastern bloc: Poles were allowed considerable academic independence and freedom to travel to Western universities. Prominent sociologists accepted invitations to Columbia, Stanford, Berkeley, and Chicago to study, lecture, and teach. The Communist government supported their endeavors and helped create official exchanges between universities. Aside from the obvious reasons of scholarship, sociology developed under the wing of the West partly through the unintended glamor of the opportunities it afforded scholars invited abroad.

Under Western influence, Polish sociologists worked out their own wide-ranging field of social science—often encompassing investigations that in the West would have fallen more readily under the disciplines of political science or economics. Such mainstream interests as social mobility, demography, prestige, and the study of institutions and occupational groups dominated. At home, sociologists were disillusioned with the government's propagandistic uses of Marxist theory and thus did not treat Marxism as an important contribution to the social sciences. Nevertheless, the government subsidized sociologists, often to produce papers critical of it or its policies.

Relations between the sociological establishment and Communist elites could be best characterized as an uneasy stalemate. Still, within the narrow confines of academic discourse and publication, almost anything could be tolerated. Even during the early months under the insidious influence of martial law, I witnessed astonishingly open class discussions. As a Fulbright Scholar affiliated with Warsaw University, I took part in a course on "The Mechanisms of Conformity" in which the participants spoke openly of the arrests of colleagues. During the latter months of martial law, underground tracts actually lay on Stefan Nowak's seminar table.

With these experiences fresh in their minds, sociologists began to look around them and not just to focus on topics that had more or less been dictated by Western sociology. They began to examine informal distribution systems, rationing, queueing, and resource pooling resulting from the decline of living standards and its corrosion of household budgets.[6] Because quantitative surveys and research methods were inadequate to these demands, many sociologists employed the participant-observation and interview tools of the anthropologist. Fieldwork in this anthropological mode slowly gained legitimacy through the late 1970s and 1980s.

Although interest in such field studies grew, the researchers' work was still considered novel, curious, tentative, and lacked a powerful school to lend legitimacy. For these reasons and the lengthy process characteristic of social science publishing,[7] much of this work was printed in small-circulation journals—scholarly booklets "for internal circulation only" in runs of a hundred copies—or in the underground press.

Underlying these new interests there lurked a wish, often almost subconscious, to examine the veracity of one particular social theory—one that the collected essays in this book show to be problematic. For the past quarter-century, many Polish sociologists have fallen under the influence of a theory developed by their eminent colleague Stefan Nowak—that of the "social vacuum."

Nowak's theory conceives of postwar Poland as an "atomized" society, its mediating institutions destroyed by war and imposed revolution. Family endures in harsh dichotomy to the state; an overgrown public sphere presses heavily against the private. People collide with rigid institutions. Nowak evoked this vision in a single dictum: "The lowest level is the family, and perhaps the social circle. The highest is the nation . . . and in the middle is a social vacuum."[8]

Polish society was thus to be construed as absolutist from the top and passive-evasive from below. The humanizing, mediating entities taken for granted in the West—voluntary, electoral, religious, or philanthropic—in Poland did not adequately offset or distribute centralized power.

The Poles' sense of social vacuum arose from a deep awareness that they had been prevented from forming open, independent organizations and their experience that society lacked predictable legality. Law was nothing more than arbitrary sovereign fiat, applied with complete caprice. In "Shadow Justice" journalists Ilona Morzoł and Michał Ogórek[9] outline the political-legal manifestations of the postwar era. The context is the dual system of authority where the Polish Communist Party, unlike the Soviet, could not be written into the legal code but in fact exerted control over it and could override and influence its functioning at any tactical juncture. The ambiguous and sweeping formulation of legislation, as well as the introduction of as many different overlapping statutes as possible, were crafted to lend the authorities almost total leverage. The law could therefore serve whatever political purposes were deemed necessary at a given moment.

Given the Polish national experience of suffering and sacrifice, it is understandable why so passive and victimized an intellectual model as Nowak's cast a spell over Polish sociology. The historic object of Polish comparisons is the (sometimes Catholic) constitutional West, not the authoritarian Orthodox East. A certain all-or-nothing disappointment at the comparison contributed to a denial that anything that could be seen as a workable mediating institution existed in Poland. But by a different logic, considering that other East European countries lacked the Polish legacy of Church and extralegal networking and put up less resistance to Communist rule, Poland should have been less likely to evolve such a model.

Models, rather than experience, are at work here: Nowak assumes axiomatically both the prior existence in Polish history of a classic civil society and such a society's ongoing survival in the West. He was right in that it is not easy to envision that a civil society could painlessly have been restored in Poland after the war. Given the magnitude of geographical migration and social mobility, disorder was not to be avoided. But Nowak goes on to observe that civil society in the rigorous sense remained lacking a generation later, and so judges his society to be guilty of vacuousness.

Nowak and his followers overlooked the degree to which their society had evolved alternate institutions because this fact would fit neither Western nor Eastern models. Perhaps most astonishingly, they virtually ignored the Roman Catholic Church, the most vital organizing agent of Polish society. The contributors in this volume exhibit conflicting views on the extent to which the Church serves as such an agent and the capacity of Church-rooted ties to offset the long fragmentation within other spheres of activity.

Father Kazimierz Jancarz reminds us in "Triumphant Religion" that during the most recent period of heightened confrontation, that of martial law of the early 1980s, the Church organized an extensive system of assistance for internees and their families. Father Andrzej Kłoczowski recalls the Church-sponsored theater and art exhibits— veiled protests against the government that could not have been staged on such a large scale by any other institution. Kłoczowski and Adam Szostkiewicz, Kłoczowski's friend, one of his flock, and a fellow contributor, herald the close-knit ties brought together by the Church and extending far beyond ecclesiastical to foster the Solidarity Citizens' Committees, politically active youth ministries, and a workers' university.

However, in "A Church Without Laity," Adam Szostkiewicz questions how widespread such ties are and alleges that the Church is a "spiritual bureaucracy" ministering to an "anonymous crowd" of petitioners. In "What Goes on in Catechism Class," Teresa Hołówka, a former catechism teacher, denounces the urban parish as a corporate entity differing little from state institutions such as schools. The Church, she laments, blindly enforces a "collection of prohibitions," and effectively discourages friendships and relationships outside the family.

Another problem with the social vacuum theory unrefined is that it could not accommodate the initiatives undertaken by citizens (including sociologists themselves) in a variety of arenas long before the authorities relaxed their prohibitions. Before Poland's recent steps toward democracy, quiet initiatives, unheralded in Western headlines, were altering at least some spheres of Polish society. Since the mid-1980s, hundreds of Poles, awakening from the helplessness into which the nation had been thrust by martial law, have turned away from explicitly political activities to reclaim control of their lives in business, housing, education, and the environment—areas for which the Communist state claimed exclusive responsibility. Hundreds of organizers sought (and many received) government registration enabling them to organize and operate openly.

The proliferation of voluntary associations attested to much more than a relaxation of rules. Although concerned citizens may have been meeting simply to discuss inadequate garbage collection or building maintenance, the very act of getting together implied a fundamental challenge to a government that asserted that what it offered was all anyone needed. In "Shared Privacy," Jacek Kurczewski argues that the energy poured into these groups (much like that which went into the Solidarity movement) was largely a reaction against individual passivity and anonymity. This revival of "civil society" was thus a backlash against the pervasive avoidance of responsibility and an attempt to reassert "self-responsibility." However, there is some disagreement among the contributors here as to the capacity displayed by these voluntary associations to expand beyond their originating circles. In "The Elitist Opposition," Wojciech Arkuszewski, himself a long-standing Oppositionist, likens the Opposition to "a closed religious sect."

Finally, if Nowak were completely correct and there were no "middle ground," it is difficult to imagine how bureaucratic systems, totally divorced from the community they allegedly served, could function at all, as clearly they do. In a society such as Poland's, many of the most vital institutions are publicly insubstantial and deniable. Internal discipline and pride in membership mean much more than acknowledgment, let alone official permission.

The Nowak model overlooks the fact that Polish society has long been organized by a complex system of informal relationships involving such forms as personalized patron-client contacts, lateral networks, and "social circles." It fails to acknowledge the labyrinth of channels through which deals and exchanges are made, both between people as "themselves"—private individuals—and as representatives of corporations, economic and social sectors, and realms of social identity or activity. Such relationships pervade the official state economy and bureaucracy and connect them to the community. Although not explicitly institutional, they are regularized and exhibit clear patterns.

The backbone of this system is the multi-functional *środowisko*—the "social circle" of family, friends, colleagues, and acquaintances brought together by some combination of family background, common experience, or formal organization that surrounds each individual.[10] In "Intimate Commerce," Wojciech Pawlik characterizes a small-town *środowisko* as the 20 to 30 individuals (sometimes more) linked by ties of kinship and friendship who maintain frequent social contact. In a larger town or city, the *środowisko* typically includes not only actual contacts, but also a larger array of potential ones—the approved people one can meet through the primary circle of already known friends and acquaintances.[11]

The *środowisko* is a pooling of possibilities and people's willingness to perform. It derives its power from putting together people who do not yet know one another, thereby creating new opportunities. It is more than a collective of actual acquaintances—it is an alliance against what is to come—an eliciting of possibility for oneself that is larger than oneself. Subjective criteria contribute to one's own and one's fellow's identity—whom one can invite to one's home for dinner, whom one marries, who has influence—and qualify people for membership in a given *środowisko*. The *środowisko* cannot be fully understood through objective criteria such as occupation, class, or status.[12] A *środowisko* verifies reputation to the outside world.

A *środowisko*, whether a drinking club that has expanded into an industrial brokerage or a high school clique that endures as a forum for deals among factory managers, is not an interest group. Nevertheless, it might be solidified by a desire to resist the Nazis, to offset the frustrations of early Communism, or to oppose General Jaruzelski's martial law. *Środowiska* (the plural of *środowisko*), like all human relations, are fluid and responsive to outside change. Over a period of time, new people might come to be included within the circle, and old members fall out.

Środowiska operate in many modes. Sociologist Jadwiga Korelewicz lists the following functions: the exchange of goods and services inaccessible through institutional means; mutual assistance in situations of injustice and difficulty; efforts to improve existing institutions (often connected with performing one's job); attempts to achieve maximum group benefits at the expense of ineffective institutions or other groups (such as those judged to be corrupt); and the exchange of information not published by the official mass media.[13] Members of a *środowisko* interact with other individuals within the circle on an individual basis and with groups of their fellows at multi-purpose gatherings in each other's homes.

Środowiska are responsive to, and crucial in, an environment of uncertainty and indeterminacy. A circle's internally stabilizing qualities of mutuality and continuity reinforce members' security against the often vulnerable and disorderly outer world. In sharp contrast to the fragmentation and contingency of life on the outside, participants in the *środowisko* offer unequivocal commitment and expect dependability. The circle's boundaries are determined by a protocol of assistance that dynamically balances those who ask for help with those who can give it. As Morzoł and Ogórek demonstrate, people's awareness that social pressure is the only instrument of countervailing power in a context in which there is no appeal to law serves to heighten the value of trust and to make binding the unwritten rules of loyalty.

The strength of the *środowisko* lies not in its separateness from public influences and resources, but in its interpenetration of them. Its strength lies in its ability to circumvent, connect, override, and otherwise reorganize political, economic, and religious institutions and authorities as powerful as them.

Środowiska and the relationships radiating outward from them are the mechanisms of social organization that underlie and enable "informal" economic activities—that private trading in information, resources, and privileges that arises parallel to, yet simplifies or outflanks, state regulation. Unofficial activities entail not only an exchange of goods and services outside the visible system, but also a second expediting bureaucracy within the state administration. State institutions depend on unofficial activities but do not authorize them. There is an enormous degree of complicity and avoidance.

Personalized relationships open channels for special, coveted forms of access. People call on bureaucratic contacts on behalf of family and friends, one by one, as situations arise. Under the Communist government, certain cliques of bureaucrats and Party apparatchiks had long-term understandings with one another in which substantial favors were exchanged. But even their advantages could not be pooled. Understandings had to be reached one at a time and face to face, not with wholesale efficiency. In post-Communist Poland it is still difficult to compound achievements: this system enables the most enterprising person to make deals but only to make similar deals over and over again. Although shielding, informing, and supplying their members, *środowiska* rarely can do more than help members compensate for the formal system's fragmentation.

Środowiska possess a double authority: like military elites and religious cults, they induce obligation and intense loyalty through shared ordeal. But the *środowisko* is also by far the surest source of dependable, continuing rewards. Sociologist Adam Podgórecki observes 'that loyalty sometimes degenerates into a community of "dirty togetherness," that tries to defend itself against the official 'hostile system,' in which it operates and which it supports perversely."[14] Circle members are compelled to ignore, circumvent, or, if necessary, sabotage official instructions if they threaten other members. Apparatchiks and bureaucrats sometimes subvert official instructions out of loyalty to the *środowisko*.

Even where "political" activity is one function of a *środowisko* and others define it by its political character, this is overlaid by the social dimension. In politically active *środowiska* (whether Communist or Opposition), a hierarchy makes itself felt in political work and doctrine. Elite *środowiska* have clearly recognized authorities. Jan Józef Lipski, leader of the Polish Socialist Party, was a moral leader in the Opposition. He retained such standing, whether he made decisions or shouldered responsibility for them, much as an aristocrat remains an aristocrat if others so deem him.

The *środowisko's* influence is one of impalpable but experientially intense pressure, positive or negative. During the period of resistance to the martial law government, for example, Oppositionists displayed their rejection of "traitors" by refusing to shake hands. A professor from a *środowisko* known for its university-Opposition standing was shunned by her circle because her husband appeared on a television talk show despite the Opposition's boycott of the propaganda-infused medium. Even though the husband spoke critically of the government, the very fact that he participated served to morally disqualify him and his wife as well. The "boycott" of the couple lasted several months. Such differences, although severe, do not usually cancel the lifelong fellowship earned through common endurance.

A circle's participants must uphold its rules by carrying out its rituals and standing up for its dignity. They must penalize transgressors with sanctions that range from the indirectly critical (gossip, pointed remarks) to systematic shunning. *Środowiska* deem members who do not join their fellows in whatever designated form of protest to be disloyal. *Środowiska* can form a common cause as part of the mobilization of a larger community (as often happened in response to government policies during martial law as in the television boycott), but it is *within* the *środowisko* itself that the sanctions are most categorical and can encroach on aspects of life not easily definable as "political."

Środowiska do not fundamentally set out to formulate and enforce rules; they are fundamentally about influence. They do not set out to cohere interest groups, consolidate class feeling, or bind together professional associations, although they may have come together from or drawn upon any of these contexts. The influences that *środowiska* exert differ from actual authority, in that authorities, by definition, must make and carry out decisions and accept responsibility for them. The *środowisko's* ascendancy over its members derives from influence, social pressure, and control, not from power or contract.

Florian Znaniecki, who observed Poland during a much earlier period of this century, was clearly influenced by the concept of the *środowisko* and discusses it explicitly in his seminal work, *The Social Role of the Man of Knowledge*. He writes that a person's social circle "grants him certain rights and enforces those rights, when necessary, against individual participants of the circle or outsiders. . . . He, in turn, has a social *function* to fulfill; he is regarded as obliged to achieve certain tasks by which the supposed needs of this circle will be satisfied and to behave toward other individuals in his circle in a way that shows his positive valuation of them."[15]

Polish society might be unplanned, despite the Communist-imposed ideology of central planning, but it is by no means unregulated. All entities, whether "grass-roots"—openly separate from the formal system—or invisibly, deniably, entwined with it, maintain their discipline and hence their credibility and dependability by developing the continuous capacity to monitor themselves.

In 1980–81, Solidarity mobilized and densified the society's social networks while fundamentally challenging the decency and fitness of the everyday "fixing" and finagling that existed to operate those very institutions. In "When Theft is Not Theft," Elżbieta Firlit and Jerzy Chłopecki document an elaborate repertoire of moral distinctions to account for these necessities. Wojciech Pawlik shows how people attempt to clothe deals, however secretive, quasi-legal, or illegal, in a cloak of legitimacy. Sociologist Andrzej Tymowski documents how "lifting," "side jobs," accepting gifts, and other such activities that in the immediate postwar years were considered dishonest, were tolerated and even accepted as "normal" 30 years later.[16] Yet "normal" has two meanings in Polish life: the way things *are*, and how things really *ought to be*. The expectation conveyed in the latter is often dashed by the reality of the former.

The system wrought both pride and shame—pride in having accomplished a difficult transaction and achieving something others could not and shame in being compelled to have done things that way.[17] To help bridge this duality, Poles developed an elaborate terminology to explain and to euphemize the world of transactions that operate in the twilight between the society's self-image of dignity and the day-to-day imperatives of survival. This preoccupation with moral integrity—dignity and honesty—that so characterizes Polish transactions may not be so strong elsewhere in Eastern Europe.

The Hungarian sociologist Elemér Hankiss suggests, for example, that "the craving for dignity—the curious mixture of pride and shame, of 'I'm breaking rules I haven't accepted'—is not so explicit in Hungary."[18]

In the postwar era, a more generic description has been applied to the social infrastructure of Eastern Europe, often styled the "second society." For Elemér Hankiss, a major proponent of this analysis, the second society consists of "two dimensions of social existence regulated by two different sets of organizational principles." The first society is defined by such criteria as homogeneity, atomization and vertical ties, bureaucratization, and official ideology; the second society by differentiation, horizontal attachment, and "nonideology" or alternative ideologies. The organizational principles of each sphere are different.[19]

A problem with this analysis is that linkage mechanisms and features typically ascribed to the second society also penetrate the workings of economy, bureaucracy, and formal institutions typically ascribed to the first society. The contributors to this volume present a portrait of Poland in which there are not two systems or societies or economies, but acknowledged and unacknowledged aspects of one in which institutions and groups are "integrated" far more extensively than official, romantic, or Oppositionist ideologies concede.

In Poland a long process of change made communism survivable, yet also led to its demise over the long term. However devastating its perennial internal troubles, the Party was thrown down by forces outside it. It did not fulfill the needs of the society while all other elements and institutions described in this book have come close to doing so, at least by the standards and in the context of the time and location. Although the exact timing of communism's downfall could not be foreseen, in a society so constituted, such a party had no place.

Once again, almost every aspect of life—from civic education through health care to the army—is up in the air. Today Eastern Europe is full of dreamers, but there are far fewer visionaries. Simplistic, easy answers are naturally plausible and welcome to a people finally released from the governments that trampled it for nearly two generations.

A year after the collapse of nearly all East European Communist parties, men once shadowed by the police now direct them from the Ministry of the Interior. Yet the atmosphere of the social world and even of many transactions dependent thereon as yet remain remarkably unchanged. In government buildings occupied by new ministers and administrators, the long corridors are still carpeted in red, the stately doors still trimmed in brass, and impassive soldiers still stand guard, having outlasted the apparatchiks who hired them.

In 1991 the pervasive sense of frustration and even danger under which Poles have lived for so many years has not dissipated. New uncertainties pervade life. People continue both to worry about how to survive the coming months and also to fear the growing economic and political isolation of their country and its long-term security, including the Oder-Neisse frontier with a united Germany. Virtually no one can escape nagging concerns about at least one immediate consequence of the economic restructuring begun in January 1990.

Some shortages and bureaucratic restrictions have disappeared. Ingenuity, creativity, and a certain capacity for navigating the system are still crucial in finding outlets for productive activity, both legal and illegal. While some of this creativity may ensure individual survival, it may prove obstructive to the development of the markets energized by the viable investment and impartial administration that the country's planners feel essential. Yet if these outlets are shored up by economic reforms, for example, by attempting to eliminate informal economic activities in workplaces (activities outlined here by Firlit and Chłopecki), the reforms will come into conflict with a long-standing way of survival at a time of declining living standards, thus threatening social explosion.

Whatever the outside world offers, the *continuities* of the *środowisko* will be critical in shaping Poland. *Środowiska* are responding dynamically, indeed helping to structure the new institutions. For example, membership in a specific *środowisko* is a criterion for appointment to many positions in post-Communist Poland, both in government and outside it. An acquaintance employed at the university recently received a telephone call from another member of his *środowisko*, now in public office, who was looking for someone to head a new project. When my acquaintance suggested putting a want ad in the newspaper to attract applicants, the official replied, "No, we're looking for someone from the *środowisko*."

Środowiska can seek influence over other social circles and within society as a whole. This is best understood as social struggle and not easily defined as politics, which would then be seen to lack those essential components of determining decisions and executing and shouldering responsibility for them. Under Poland's Communists, government after government was toppled by social crises of legitimacy, entailing disorder, and not crises of power, threatening revolutionary overthrow.

Politics is not likely to resolve these issues—at least not in those terms. Just as the toppling of communism was a *social* crisis of legitimacy, politics in the new era is equally social, viewed more as a series of dramatic confrontations than as a matter of issues that can be defined and debated. It follows that party politics are not likely to mediate between the community and the state, as in many Western countries.

The continuity of the *środowisko* and other such relational systems is the key to understanding how society is likely to respond to coming changes and how relationships among community organizations, political parties, and the state apparatus will develop in post-Communist Poland. These relationships will make possible certain options for "transition" and limit others. Thus, discussions of "transition" must not simply address themselves to transforming visible economic structures and institutions but to exploring how change in such entities is mediated through social processes and informal institutions shaped by Polish history and experience.

NOTES

1. The long-standing Opposition is made up of close-knit circles of dissenting political discussion and activity that evolved between 1968 and 1979.

2. *Rocznik Statystyczny* (Statistical yearbook) (Warsaw: Central Statistical Office, 1987).

3. *Mały Rocznik Statystyczny* (Abridged statistical yearbook) (Warsaw: Central Statistical Office, 1990).

4. These processes are detailed by demographer Michał Pohoski in "Interrelation between Social Mobility of Individuals and Groups in the Process of Economic Growth in Poland," *Polish Sociological Bulletin*, no. 2, 1964.

5. *Mały Rocznik Statystyczny*.

6. Some of this research came under the direction of the sociologist Jacek Kurczewski, Director of the Institute of Applied Social Sciences of Warsaw University and a contributor to this book.

7. The standard wait for publication of a book in state publishing houses was three to five years. To avoid this, some chose to publish in tiny university

presses allowed to print up to 100 copies of a book without submission to censorship.

8. Stefan Nowak, "System Wartości Społeczeństwa Polskiego" (The value system of Polish society), *Studia Socjologiczne* 4:75, 1979.

9. Of this husband-and-wife team originally from the Katowice region, Ilona Morzoł writes for the culture page of the daily *Gazeta Wyborcza*, while Michał Ogórek works for the weekly *Przegląd Tygodniowy*.

10. This concept has been catalyzed by many discussions with analyst Adam Pomorski. The workings of the *środowisko* are exampled in my book, *The Private Poland* (New York: Facts on File, 1986), and further developed in my essay, "Polish Society: The Ties of Legitimacy," in *Polish Paradoxes*, edited by Stanisław Gomułka and Antony Polonsky (New York: Routledge, 1990).

11. Although the concept of the *środowisko* is implicit in this volume, many contributors have not made it explicit. The book focuses on urban *środowiska*; comparatively little material on their rural counterparts is available.

12. The concept of the *środowisko* is similar to Max Weber's understanding of the "social state" (*sozialstand*)—roughly a group so fundamental as largely to define those who belong to it.

13. Jadwiga Korelewicz, "Social Differences—Feeling of Belonging—Belief in Oneself," in a study led by Edmund Wnuk-Lipinski under the auspices of the Institute of Philosophy and Sociology of the Polish Academy of Sciences, Warsaw, 1984, pp. 12–13.

14. Adam Podgórecki, "Polish Society: A Sociological Analysis," *Praxis International* 7:1, April 1987.

15. Florian Znaniecki, *The Social Role of the Man of Knowledge* (Oxford: Transaction Books, 1986), pp. 16–17.

16. Andrzej Tymowski, "O Przemianiach w Infrastrukturze Moralnej" (On changes in Morality), in *Biuletyn Towarystwa Kultury Moralnej* no. 59, 1979–1980.

17. This psychology is explained in my book, *The Private Poland*, chapter VI.

18. Conversations with Elemér Hankiss on October 14, 1987 and March 23, 1988.

19. Elemér Hankiss, *The "Second Society"* (Budapest: Hungarian Academy of Sciences, 1986).

Life as If

The Excluded Economy

KAZIMIERZ WYKA

Kazimierz Wyka, born in 1910, published "The Excluded Economy" in August 1945 in the literary journal *Twórczość*,[1] only a few months after the end of World War II in Europe. He had taken part in the literary and underground resistance under German occupation, and belonged to the same wartime intellectual circle as Nobel laureate poet Czesław Miłosz. Wyka's article, dripping with irony and challenging some heartfelt national stereotypes, not unsurprisingly provoked controversy about what really had gone on during the Occupation.

Wyka employs the terms economic "psychology" and "psyche" in the sense of mentality or collective attitudes. "Fiction" here is the *illusion* of a "very tight noose." Fictions are prohibitions shrouded in great pretension that nevertheless are manipulated for survival, although their violation ostensibly brings down an iron fist.

Wyka has made an important contribution to social history but has never before been published in English. Because of the classic character of the text I have left it uncut and have translated it quite literally. Some of the historic allusions may be lost on a Western reader, but I would urge the reader to focus on the *social processes* Wyka so skillfully illustrates and what they might portend for today.

Wyka's productivity did not stop with "The Excluded Economy." In 1945 he founded the influential and prestigious monthly *Twórczość* (Creativity), and in 1948 was a co-founder of the Institute for Literary Research in the Academy of Sciences. Under Wyka's direction from 1953 to 1970, the institute was a prominent intellectual center. Wyka spent his later years in Cracow until his death in 1975.

Whoever wants to understand the Polish economic psyche on the eve of the third epoch of Polish independence[2] must examine the economic phenomena of the Nazi Occupation. For this psyche confirms the dictum that psychological effects outlast their objective economic and social causes.

The problem I would like to examine here has twofold significance: as an account of very recent phenomena, yet little remembered or understood, and also of effects still at work in the collective psyche of our society, even though the economic structure of the former Generalgouvernement[3] has been destroyed. The past five years have afforded enough time for systematic and consistent obstinacy, which the Germans hardly lacked, to create conditions that left a profound imprint upon the Polish psyche. Especially since these conditions corresponded to many Polish hopes, unrealized until that time. We will only discuss the Generalgouvernement—for it was only there that the phenomena here examined could develop fully.

The Circumstances of German Economic Policy

What were the principles of German economic policy in the Generalgouvernement?

Two conditions give us a preliminary answer: first, the way in which the border between the Reich and the Generalgouvernement was drawn; and second, the rationing system of the Generalgouvernement as social and economic fiction.

The border was drawn to detach all industry, coal, and steel production from the Generalgouvernement. What remained had a purely agricultural character, and was therefore backward in comparison with every other European state with the exception of countries so bizarre and unnatural as interwar Lithuania, Latvia or Estonia.

Of course it was impossible to completely separate industrial regions from agricultural ones. Not even the Germans could recreate in the Reich the substantial industry of Warsaw, Starachowice, Tomaszów, Mościce, and Stalowa Wola.[4] But the principle was clear: the "independent" remnants of Poland were to be incapable of exporting anything except peasant women to weed beets, and, of course, the beets themselves. The only low-grade coal mine (Tenczynek near Krzeszowice)[5] that remained to the Generalgouvernement owed its inclusion to the selection of Frank's[6] residence in Kressendorf, which, of course, had to be located within the territory he administered. And in any case, every few months another alarming rumor about readjustment of the border circulated in the area, since the "Great Silesian" coal basin could not tolerate the existence of a mine not in the Great Reich itself, but in the *Nebenland*.[7]

Claims on Polish lands were nothing new to German appetites. During the First World War, when the German decree of November 5, 1916 aimed to establish an "independent" Polish state, the German General Staff demanded frontiers similar to that of the Generalgouvernement. Then, the Germans insisted on stifling the industry of the former Russian partition land they had conquered and intended the Polish state, under German auspices, to be a market for their industrial products. The Germans likewise intended the wartime Generalgouvernement to be an agricultural colony until the anticipated victory over Russia permitted a final solution: the Polish population, purged of its intelligentsia, deported to the banks of the Volga; the Russian population beyond the Urals. This time the ultimate goal was not concealed. It is not worth citing the relevant speeches by Frank. We remember without citation.

But until this final solution came, it was necessary somehow to establish relations with the native population. This was achieved through the second fundamental condition: *the rationing system as a social fiction*. The rationing system imposed on the native population was such that no one could manage to survive. Since all trade in agricultural products was forbidden, every German policeman who grabbed the butter out of a peasant woman's basket was acting legally. The Polish population was officially given nothing beyond an insufficient amount of bread. During the war I did not *legally* consume so much as one gram of lard, one drop of milk, one slice of sausage. Yet quite a lot of these foods came my way—and there were millions like me.

This fiction must be considered the basis of the economic changes within the Generalgouvernement. Even the most complex social-psychological processes are related to it. During the winter of 1939–40, the population under the Generalgouvernement faced a simple dilemma: to eat only what was permitted and die of hunger, or—*somehow to make do*. Naturally no one seriously entertained the first alternative, so the only important question was: *how to survive despite the regulations*. Each social class responded differently to that "how," with different conduct and collective reactions. We will describe these responses in detail, analyzing the psychology of the peasant, the worker, the intelligentsia, and the landowner.

But before embarking on such an analysis, there are two more questions we must examine: first, what could have motivated the

Germans to create such an economic fiction, and second, where was the gap in this system? I do not rate German obtuseness so high as to believe that they expected Poles to observe German economic regulations and quietly die of hunger. Even a nation of ascetic monks would have revolted. Such nonsense could only derive from extraordinarily vicious malice, the desire to torment Poles at any cost, and an impulse to bring home to them that they were *subhuman* in every respect. Moreover, such regulations gave the occupier a completely free hand in his subsequent maneuvers against the natives: since everything was forbidden, it was possible to loosen some restrictions and demand gratitude for doing so. Under the Occupation some working people actually received a pittance for their labor. Thus, inborn arrogance and whimsical benevolence combined to create an economic freak perhaps more densely stupid than anywhere else in occupied Europe. But Poles had to live with this freak and uncover its weaknesses.

Many became apparent. First of all, every law too severe has to compromise itself to be overseen and implemented. Even the harshest sanctions will not instill respect for it. If the punishment for illegal pig breeding is death, yet the activity is very lucrative and the German policeman doesn't visit the village for months, then nothing will stop the peasant's tender care for the sow. If on any train one may be arrested for transporting lard, but it is beyond even the most efficient police to guard day and night all the trains destined for a large city, then no one will prevent people from doing it.

Poles grasped these truths quickly and shrewdly, faster than the Germans noticed that their dam was scarcely even a sieve. When the Germans attempted draconian measures, it was already too late: society had adjusted to the fiction and was undismayed when the beast bared its fangs. This was, one might say, *a gap in the fiction from below*, opening a gap accessible to everyone, verified by experience, and inviting risk that usually paid off. In saying "paid off," I have two things in mind: risk was an unavoidable necessity of survival, without which the individual was driven below an acceptable standard of existence; but it also offered opportunities to learn how to be successful in business and to deal. I will return below to the consequences of the latter.

A gap scarcely smaller soon appeared *in the fiction from above*, at the system's very apex. This breakthrough was made, symbolically speaking, by whatever Pole it was who first had enough intuition not to be frightened by overbearing glares and sensed that *bribes*

were necessary and would be accepted: for this gap at the top was
German venality and corruption. Here let me recall my own experiences. When the first economic decrees were posted, I expected,
as one inclined to take official pronouncements seriously, that this
would be a very tight noose. I truly believed that practice would
find a way to loosen it, but through all my speculations and reflec-
tions, it never occurred to me that bribery could be a collective
defense—a kind of universal vaccine.

Today I know that I was naive. I simply trusted too much in the
Germans' appearance and apparent severity to sense the moral gan-
grene just below their skin. For that matter, no one in Poland sensed
the depth of the rot. But once we recognized it, we developed toward
the occupier that characteristic attitude of masked contempt that one
always entertains toward those whom it is easy to drag into the dirt,
but who in principle are supposed to stand aloof from it.

The Germans turned out to be fantastic bribe-takers. Everyone
was on the take, from petty officials up to Nazi Party bigwigs. The
system of bribery quickly evolved into a kind of contract, unwritten
but mutually honored. A pork butcher, baker, or miller who paid
regularly was not "done dirty." Bribery quickly became the cover
that shielded our economic life from the crushing fiction. But bribery
is a two-way street between giver and taker. To stop it, it is not
sufficient to cut off the taker's hand. The hand schooled in giving
is still there and will seek new recipients. We remember this and
observe it today—that ever-present little hand, discreetly prepared
to slip something into another palm.

Other factors also favored bribery. Already by the latter half of
1940, everyone noticed the development of new "price scissors," to
borrow a prewar term. This time, official wages and prices were one
blade of the scissors and real prices and needs the other. Before long
it became apparent that German economic policy attempted to maintain official prices and wages—those linked to war industry and
German needs, which were sucking the life juices out of the colony—
at the lowest possible level. But the Germans completely disregarded
real prices and how the "non-German population" would deal with
the progressive widening of the gap between the scissor's blades—
another bureaucratic fiction which inevitably would soon ramify into
further fictions.

What made the Germans hospitable to bribery? Only they had
wholesale merchandise and raw materials at their disposal, and they
were quickly faced by a temptation that no Nazi Party member

seemed able to resist. They were confronted precisely by the disparity between fictional and real value, the temptation to dispose of goods under the table. Potential profit was all the greater because money earned in such a manner had for the German not market value, which was low, but official value, which was high. Perhaps only in the final two years did the Germans have to resort to such methods to survive. The addiction to bribery itself began earlier and resulted from the uncertain status of the occupier, who demanded, despite official self-assurance, capitalization and investment of the capital in gold. Thus the ultimate recipients of the gold that poured out of Jewish hands into Polish society were, for the most part, Germans. I am not speaking, of course, of simple capitalization, consisting, for example, of ripping gold crowns from the mouths of murdered victims,[8] because that capitalization had an official state character within the German system.

The fiction of low prices and wages necessarily entailed a further official fiction, which this time worked to the advantage of Polish society, especially merchants. Under the official assumption that prices were no different from those of the prewar period, one could not impose additional taxes. Turnover and prices grew to multiples of those of 1939, but taxes rose only minimally. It was naturally possible to approve higher prices. Why the Germans nevertheless maintained the fiction of low prices transparent to all, I cannot explain.

Tax evasion was extremely important because of its effects on social morality. This is how economic life came to be, in the individual's consciousness, excluded from moral-economic participation in collective life. Poles under the Generalgouvernement quickly learned that the system, formally severe, was easily satisfied by fiction.

On the other hand, the Germans themselves began to patch the gap in the fiction in the simplest way possible: by printing paper money. As the war dragged on, the needs of the German army and industry rose. The Generalgouvernement had to pay not only with millions of workers deported to the Reich. Above all it paid with its own stomach, through the difference between earnings and the cost of living, and mainly by the hidden inflation of those years. No one can understand the apparent economic boom of the occupation years who does not clearly remember that it was a period of inflation with many effects on the collective psyche, of artificial excitement and vitality, of playing with easy money obtained no one knew where. This inflation was pleasant at least to the extent that "we were not responsible for it." We were like a child who has vodka poured into its mouth and thus can claim that it has to swallow. Now we are paying the consequences of such euphoria, and will continue to do so for a long while.

Indeed, so many were the fictions, consistent and inconsistent, in German policy, that it is difficult to explain them. Yet the explanation lies near at hand. One only has to assume that everything the Germans did under the Generalgouvernement was *provisional wartime arrangements*, concerned only to facilitate those economic processes for which there was immediate need: primarily to obtain the cheapest labor force both locally and for export to the Reich; next, to exercise absolute command over industry; third, to levy enough from agriculture to meet the needs of the army and German officialdom. Hence all this was ruthlessly carried out. Furthermore, the Germans exerted absolute command over raw materials in those areas of the Generalgouvernement vulnerable to their plunder. Their policy on forests and lumber followed from this. The occupier was indifferent to everything that did not concern these foremost objectives. For the sake of principle he meddled, but only lightly.

An economic system thereby arose, some of whose functions were *included* in a body foreign and indifferent to it: others were left to hang in the air, excluded from all social context, above all the individual's natural economic foresight and everyday concerns. In a word, the most fundamental psychological stimulus of economic life went disregarded. The subject of the Generalgouvernement, realizing that the occupier was in no way concerned about him, believed himself—and rightly so—to be freed of moral participation in this imposed social order. And because he was active and foresightful, there was much he could evade. As a result, society's attitude toward its own economic activities became governed by the conviction that these were activities apart, done on the side and for oneself, that anything was permitted and one *ought* to do whatever one wanted. The amorality of work even became a patriotic responsibility. This is how the social psyche, which I consider the central psychosocial phenomenon of the Occupation years, was created—*an economy morally excluded, separated from the state and society as a whole.*

It is now time to trace its manifestations among specific social classes.

The Worker

Throughout the Occupation, the situation of the industrial worker was undoubtedly the most difficult. Only the highest level of the intelligentsia, university professors, for instance, found themselves in similar straits. And they had various sources of assistance that workers lacked. Since the Germans needed a large and cheap labor force, their first decrees were designed to ensure themselves of this, both legally and practically. A broad and imprecise legal mandate requiring all Poles to work was introduced and served as the basis for all future decrees. The worker was tied to the enterprise where he was employed and prohibited from changing jobs. A system of work transcripts distinguished the trades, and each man was furnished with a document that, during the last two years of the Occupation, became as indispensable as a birth certificate. By these means a thoroughly legal basis for enslavement of the worker was created.

The work requirement, along with the difficulty of practicing the learned professions, and among youth the impossibility of continuing secondary and university studies, did much to alter the composition of the working class, a phenomenon whose psychological consequences for Polish society is still difficult to evaluate. Thus, it seems, there will be a few positive consequences resulting from the Occupation. For only a fraction of those with aspirations to the intelligentsia, dislodged from their prewar rung on the social ladder, were able through *handel*[9] and speculation[10] to assure themselves the privilege of not engaging in manual labor, a privilege heretofore considered essential for attaining higher class status. A larger portion, especially numerous among adolescent youth in the smaller towns, had to reinforce the ranks of the working class, go to the factories and stone quarries, and generally take up occupations entailing daily contact with manual laborers.

When independence is regained, all these people will abandon the ranks of the working proletariat. But the consequences of this restratification will probably be of a positive nature, especially for youth, who on the threshold of intellectual maturity had contacts over a long period with the worker and his class consciousness. For upward mobility among peasants and workers is a normal phenomenon, while the downward mobility of the intelligentsia as a result of the lowering of its social position that occurred during the Occupation generally is rarer, and this is why we emphasize it at the outset. Indeed, the entire conduct of the occupier towards our nation is exemplified in this lowering of social position: workers and peasants blocked from any path upward, while the intelligentsia were thrust below the position they already had attained.

The Polish slave would not have been as passive as he became out of necessity, were it not for the factors that made the evil of toiling in the Generalgouvernement an acceptably lesser evil. The tradition of traveling to Germany to work, the economic migration to "Saxon work,"[11] like all emigration from overpopulated countries, was readily recalled in Poland. It was known that one certainly had to toil very hard for several months, but one came back with a lot of money. Such migrations, as with all emigrations, had ceased almost completely during the period of independence after World War I, but they were remembered and became something of a lesser version of the myth of America and "American" earnings.

During the first months of the Occupation, the Germans rather skillfully exploited this legacy: "We have opened up the way for you, as for your fathers, to a wonderful livelihood—go to the Reich." The actual conditions under which money was transferred from workers in the Reich to families back home, at a time when it was not anticipated how high home prices would rise, did not look bad. Let us remember, moreover, the following trick, which few recall today: In autumn 1939, the recently opened *Arbeitsamt* [German Labor Bureau] paid unemployment benefits to anyone who applied, without checking their actual employment status. In my town there were queues in front of the *Arbeitsamt* longer even than those I later saw for vodka. But everyone who received a payment had to sign a receipt on the back of which appeared a clause stating that at any summons, they would depart for work in the Reich.

This anticipatory measure proved unnecessary at first. The initial groups of "departees" were not the fruit of street raids, but were truly voluntary—mostly poor peasants enticed by the myth of "Saxon work." Urban workers, more aware and politically mistrustful, scarcely participated, quickly understanding what this experience was really about. It was simple and readily apparent: *this is not the old Saxon work*. Not only was the promise that one might return home with one's earnings a falsehood, but also that one could help dependents remaining in Poland. For a bachelor this was no problem, but for a married man?

It soon became common knowledge that Poles were without civil rights and treated as miserable cattle marked with the letter P, and that compulsory or voluntary departure for work to Germany meant that one would not see one's native land until the war's end. Vacations were very rarely permitted because it was difficult to apprehend those who took them as an opportunity to escape. Furthermore, endless air bombardment of the Reich—while the skies over the Generalgouvernement remained absolutely calm day and night—made a stay in the Reich appear to be a permanent danger. Thus the following complex of attitudes arose: *the worst work in the Generalgouvernement is better than going to the Reich.* Here in the country one can always find a way to make a little something extra to survive through hard times, while going to Germany, especially for those burdened with a family, is a catastrophe. This, and not any foresight on the part of the authorities, was the reason for the Generalgouvernement's labor market being saturated, indeed ludicrously oversaturated. One fought for a work permit, especially for a good one, honored during street raids, as the most effective defense against being sent to the Reich.

It thus came about that the longer the Occupation dragged on, and more or less everyone learned to exist under its conditions, the greater the danger of deportation. The authorities had to resort to draconian measures: street raids to fill human levies—labor quotas. This was especially so since the *Arbeitsamte*, which should have sucked human material into the Reich, was hopelessly clogged by bribery. Of course, there were *Arbeitsamte* whose directors worked decently—from the German perspective!—and shipped out all superfluous labor. But these were a tiny minority. In general one could not find an institution more corrupt and less likely to conceal its corruption. Blackmail by threat of a deportation order was a daily occurrence, but was done to seize ransom. The spring and summer times of mass deportation elicited veritable flocks of geese, mountains of sausages and lakes of vodka. The paradoxical situation eventually developed that the German manager would threaten a recalcitrant employee with the ultimate punishment: "Off to the Reich with you." And to make an example, he would indeed occasionally send someone.

Thus the worker knew it paid to stay put even under the most miserable conditions. To stay, but how to live? As a class, the Polish worker survived, and for these reasons: first of all, especially outside the largest industrial and mining centers under the Generalgouvernement, the workers in many areas had not yet crystallized into a social class, a class entirely removed from the land and living solely by the work of its hands. The proletariat of the city of Łódz, the Dąbrowski Basin, and Silesia [industrial areas directly annexed by Germany] no longer manifested these transitional traits, and, as a class, operated strictly within the factory walls and controlled by the sign-up sheet at the gate. But in the areas under the General-gouvernement, the worker often still stood at the crossroads between his rural forefathers and the purely urban proletariat, still owned a patch of land, and often an inherited hut. Entire categories of work-ers—classically, Polish railway workers—had even strengthened their transitional status.

The majority of the population had to manage by means that unfortunately caused harmful psychosocial effects. To survive, it had to repudiate completely any work ethic. Before the war, a well-paid worker, faithful to his craftsmanship, did not lift goods from his factory, especially if he felt that inspection was effective. The factory guard did not shut his eyes to a suspiciously bulging pocket. During the Occupation the worker stole and had to steal. Neither inspection nor danger deterred him. Vodka was lifted, as were parts for weap-ons from munitions factories. When in about 1943 the entire staff of a Cracow cigarette factory was unexpectedly summoned for in-spection, the entire courtyard turned white in an instant with dis-carded cigarette cartons. There was no one to punish, since everyone was guilty.

But what can a worker employed, say, in a stone quarry, lift? To whom can he sell a block of porphyry? He has to resort to more complicated manipulations. Having spent the war in the vicinity of several large quarries I can offer an example of such operations. To live, one had to "make deals"; to make deals, one had to have two or three days of the week free, but free in such a way as to remain officially at work and not vulnerable to punitive deportation. To compound this equation, the worker labored under production quo-tas. How was this equation solved?

By working harder and by coming to an understanding with the supervisors on the job and in the office. One worked for four days at filling the quota for six days over which the supervisors agreed to spread one's work in their reports and attendance records. Two days remained for oneself. But the supervisors did not do this for free. They were rightfully entitled to a cut of these two days. The office worker especially—upon whom it was easy to check up and who had to be in the office every day—had to pay. Not everywhere was it possible to arrange this, which is why work sites where German control neither permitted such loose arrangements nor offset them with any opportunity for lifting, were treated as penal colonies against which the worker defended himself tooth and nail. In my region, "they assigned him to the IG-Farben"—to the quarry owned by this firm, was the equivalent of "they sent him to Płaszow"—to the worst of the forced labor camps.[12]

All the worker's efforts, therefore, were aimed at acquiring illicit goods of substantial exchange value or free time of similar utility to devote to "chasing goods," selling, and earning. When he couldn't go himself, he sent his wife. Here one should distinguish between those engaged in the petty *handel* induced by poverty and necessity and professional trade and brokerage. I know of no case of a worker who could turn petty *handel* into serious dollar transactions. Just about everything he earned he had to eat. An accurate picture of this economic process was the all-too-well-known sight on trains nearing Warsaw or Cracow, of the weeping woman stripped of five kilos of groats and a kilo of lard in Koluszki or Miechów,[13] sobbing that *this was for the children*. These were truly earnings that her children desperately needed. No writer attempting to describe those times could gloss over the sufferings and self-sacrifice of such women, their homelessness, sleepless nights, and endless slogging along bottomless roads. For let us remember that, except for gangs of bribe-defended untouchables, a single man rarely engaged in traveling trade, since he was too easy a prey for hunters. And that is why the "commercial" trains were filled with women, from fat hyenas in skirts to mothers for whom those five kilos of groats were a desperate necessity.

In no way do I affirm that the economic psychology of the worker during the Occupation developed properly or morally: I merely state that his resilience and ingenuity in dealing with the situation passed the test. But his psyche took very unhealthy forms. If it was less corrupted than in other social classes, then only because *the worker was not responsible for this corruption*. It was an elementary self-defense against the occupier's destructive labor system, a defense which nevertheless decayed and became gangrenous. The moral relationship between the worker and his work was broken. The worker toiling for the hated system labored as little and as poorly as possible. The classic example is that of the factory foreman who calls to the engineer's attention the faulty drawing of a particular part, which will not fit after it is manufactured. He hears in response: "What's it to you? Make it according to the drawing they gave you."

And both scrupulously get on with work that they know to be worthless.

The worker's "coat of arms" under the Occupation was the tortoise—embodiment of slowness—drawn on the factory walls. The Polish worker underwent this retrograde experience at a time when the workers of the entire democratic world were feeling a profound sense of the worth of their efforts, knew what kind of victory their sacrifice and toil were straining toward, and believed that their toil and privation were the price to be paid for the common triumph over fascism. The Polish worker was deprived of this uplifting and healing experience. For him, the moral exclusion of the economy from all other processes of collective life was particularly extreme and therefore particularly damaging to the psyche. For if a petty dealer plunders and grabs whatever he can, he is only carrying out his own shameful economic agenda. But by adopting a tortoise as his insignia, the worker contradicts his own economic principles.

It is with these psychological characteristics shaped by years of occupation that the worker enters the third epoch of Polish independence. Nevertheless, we are not pessimistic. We believe, and we see this from the first weeks of liberation, that if work is but given meaning, bad habits fall away. Yet we are still very far from actually abandoning them. Production figures, shocking if they are to be permanent, attest to this. They will not last, and that is why in the long run we do not fear that the addictions induced in the worker will endure.

Office Workers and Intelligentsia

Office workers and teachers had to report to the German administration and found themselves in an identical situation to that of the worker; the economic psychology of this intelligentsia forced into office work shaped itself essentially like his. But the situation and psychology of the free professional—lawyer, physician, pharmacist—was quite different.

The intelligentsia employed before the war at other professions and now put to work in offices, as well as employees of the prewar bureaucracy, were confronted by the same prospect as the worker: to die on starvation wages, or to somehow find a way to manage without quitting their jobs lest they be shipped off to the Reich. No one seems to have starved to death. Many were impoverished, but the majority managed fairly well. City dwellers remained well dressed, fashions changed over the years, pastry shops and places of entertainment maintained steady, though relatively small, clienteles.

A superficial observer who visited the Generalgouvernement after seeing other occupied countries would have said that here prosperity reigned. Germans of the Generalgouvernement, in their limitless stupidity, arrogance, and hatred, naturally took credit for this. Indeed one myth (the further from the Generalgouvernement the stronger it was) inverted the legend of Saxon work, and made it that the Generalgouvernement was a land flowing with milk and honey. This was a serious optical illusion. But whoever glanced superficially at our cities, whoever saw high-heeled shoes but did not notice posters listing the executed, whoever arrived on the Berlin express but not on the little locals from Piaseczno or Kocmyrzów,[14] was set up for this illusion.

Office workers and intelligentsia staved off harsh necessity just as did workers: through *handel*—but *handel* of a different sort, not so close to the dregs of misery and deportation. This *handel* depended on an extraordinarily well-developed system of middlemen, unnecessary under normal economic conditions. As soon as the source of the goods is legal and its destination also is legal, there is no need for so many middlemen. But both ends of the chain lay outside the law. As a rule, the source of the goods was a German, who was *forbidden to buy them*, its ultimate recipient a Pole, who all the more emphatically was *forbidden to receive them*. An extreme case was that of the *handel* in German weapons, which blossomed under the Occupation, in which the seller was a German soldier and the buyer a conspirator.

A typical commercial transaction would look more or less like this: on Sunday over tea at Aunt Pensioner's, her cousin, Mr. Middleman, a cashier at the Bank of Easy Earnings, learns from Mr. Percentage, whom he happens to meet there, that Mr. Percentage has a large quantity of, let us say, rosin. Mr. Middleman keeps this in mind, because in *handel* it always pays to remember. A few days later, Mr. Profiteer, a clerk in the firm Relay-Race Transport, mentions at the cashier's desk that he is looking for rosin. Mr. Middleman: "Sure. I've got heaps." How much? Middleman, who's no specialist in these matters, answers: "There's a different 'rate' now; please call me tomorrow." Mr. Profiteer also doesn't need the rosin for himself. He heard about it over vodka from his colleague Mr.

Homebrew, to whom he dashes with the news that *the day after tomorrow* he'll have some rosin. An extraordinary two-way transaction begins: Middleman looks for Percentage through Pensioner. Percentage finds his German with the rosin. Homebrew, armed with the news from Profiteer, looks for Sudsy, a soapmaker who needs the rosin. A little chain develops: from Percentage at the source through Pensioner, Middleman, Profiteer and Homebrew to the final destination, Sudsy. Each one, of course, takes a cut.

What does this mean less anecdotally? That under the pressure of illegality at both ends, *brokerage was beaten into a huge chain*, along which a disproportionately large number of people made a living. Around a little bone that a normal prewar dog could have carried between his two jaws, hundreds of ants now laboriously swarmed, and of course it must have seemed to the ants that they were extremely active. They truly lived from this activity, for the road from the higher than normal supply price at which the corrupted German official sold at the market price of speculators could accommodate many such ants. This is why all office workers engaged in *handel*. The office itself was only a meeting place from which people constantly rushed downtown to cut deals. Office phones were the communication lines of thousands of middlemen, whose sales and profits were beyond the easy control of any inspection apparatus. Amidst the easy money created by inflation, the illusion of an economic boom arose, and how many ants in offices now nostalgically reminisce about recent months when there was so much action?

The middlemen of the Occupation were the unimprisoned Polish officer; the engineer for whom working in a factory didn't pay; the wife of a university professor whose husband lacked business talent; the poet who discovered that he, too, had such talent; the secondary school student who started swapping postage stamps and came to the conclusion that studying was not worth his while; the typist and the bank cashier and the librarian and the janitor—human beings shaken and reshuffled in the most fantastic deals of the cards. Again I direct the attention of future writers to this theme.

Only a few free professionals, chiefly physicians and pharmacists, made a normal living from their work. Membership in these professions was particularly valued because, beside their assured incomes, they were protected against street raids and deportation—except in the Lublin area.[15] (A note from 1948—the reason for the postwar flood of students into schools of medicine, dentistry, and pharmacy may be found here.)

The rest of the intelligentsia either slipped below minimum living standards, sold their property and pauperized themselves, or survived by some ongoing miracle. Portuguese, Turkish and Swedish packages played no small part.[16] The coffee, tea, and sardines contained in them entered the bellies of the bigger financial climbers, thereby increasing the budgets of many intelligentsia families. Let us add to this the significant sums pumped in from London for political reasons, particularly to Warsaw, but distributed according to quite different priorities.[17] I call this source an ongoing miracle because it functioned entirely at the merciful whim of the occupier, subject at any moment to withdrawal. For I do not believe that the Germans did not know that Portuguese almonds and figs were a code between Polish emigrés in the West and their home country.

Among the forms of brokerage prevalent during the Occupation, a special place must be reserved for *handel* in hard currency and valuables. This was brokerage in which market orientation, the ability to seize the right moment to make a sale or a purchase, and understanding the customer's psychology, most approximated to a pure game—a kind of closed-hand poker. This was brokerage, moreover, in its purest form, a calculation of services and earnings. During the Occupation there was no lack of hard currency or valuables; they streamed in from many sources: restratification within Polish society, the tragedy of the Jews, and foreign support for resistance. And though *handel* itself was severely penalized, the possibility of earning money without touching it—just a whisper from table to table—and the frequently high profit margin, made the arbitrage of "hard" and "soft" currencies a daily buzzing in the brokers' marketplace of the Generalgouvernement.

As to currency, one should mention another kind, directly woven into the fabric of the collective morality of those years. For many reasons, women were the most active among office workers, intelligentsia, and the new merchants. It was they who brokered, cut deals, and handled business for husbands and families. It was they who were sent to the Germans, especially after work and during restaurant hours. A woman who found herself in such a situation quickly understood that another currency she brought to the deal was her body. Even when she became a waitress, a city woman understood that she owed the "right" to run around in a little apron to her well-endowed figure. Certainly, a good businessperson in skirts didn't pay out this currency for any old thing at each time of asking, but she nonetheless quickly understood how to treat her smile and the shape of her calf as small change for pocket money. When needed, she also extended qualities more highly valued in the masculine marketplace. And she extended them ever more frequently, thereby provoking complaints, common during every war, about the collapse of morality. Unfortunately, moralists lack the habit of asking what economic and social reasons cause morality to collapse, and so we will help them to understand.

Thus we put together a picture of office workers and intelligentsia whose normal functions were replaced, out of economic necessity, by a cancer of helter-skelter *handel* and brokerage. But a bureaucracy exists to create a control apparatus for collective life, to force individual processes into the general system. The disintegration of these processes, which characterized the economic psychology of the Generalgouvernement, nowhere reached a more extreme form, or one more pernicious to normal life—than in the bureaus of treasury and taxation.

We know that until 1939, the revenue office was the bugaboo of businessmen and manufacturers. Taxes were many and intricate, and it was difficult to avoid paying them. *During the Occupation, the most idyllic of relationships was that between taxpayer and tax collector.* This paradox stemmed from both sides' equal interest in cultivating the fiction that taxes reflected the actual level of earnings. The taxpayer cared for the simplest of reasons: he always wanted to pay as little as possible. The tax collector cared because he and his family were able to live, thanks only to his not interfering with this fiction, and supplying legal means of maintaining it. For this the tax collector received flour, sausage, and vodka and did not have to worry about the Easter table or his wife's birthday. And both parties were clear in conscience and conduct: together they cheated the Germans. One earned more than enough, the other managed with just enough. They forgot, however, that everything they did was a matter of indifference to the Germans: for when tax revenues fell too far, the presses began to print out fresh new faces on the banknotes.

In sum, we see that the economic psychology of the intelligentsia underwent a specific degeneration. This was less the result, as in the worker's case, of the threat of poverty. More accurately speaking, it was at first provoked by this threat, but quickly became an addiction with a life of its own—and, as such, more dangerous and lasting. This is particularly perilous for the state's tax-collecting agencies, which will have to be retaught their true functions. Nor does the intelligentsia, although reinstated in positions from which they had been displaced by the Germans, emerge with commendable, morally intact values. As long as the conditions and the discrepancy between earnings and actual needs continue to create temptation, the danger will endure. The cancer of brokerage, however, is already shrinking today, and will soon become only a memory.

Jews and Trade

The disappearance from trade and brokerage of millions of Jews undoubtedly remains a central psycho-economic fact of the Occupation years. Counting the survivors, we see that it is ultimate, definitive, and permanent. Less lasting, though equally important, is the passive and automatic entrance of Poles into positions from which the Jews had been driven. I call this movement passive and automatic because this entire process, to be brutally succinct, appeared—to those leaping into the vacuum—as the replacement of *the unbaptized by the baptized*, yet with all the disgusting psychology of the swindler, huckster, and exploiter. All the joy of the Polish "petit bourgeoisie" amounted in reality to this hope: "There are no Jews, we will take their places, *changing nothing*, inheriting all the negative traits that Polish moralists considered typically Jewish, but now the traits would become nationally lovely and taboo."

If this central feature of the economic psychology of the Occupation is not to weigh heavily on the moral health of the nation, it must be most carefully examined.

Let us state clearly that the misfortune of Polish economic life was not that Jews were everywhere in the forefront, from the market stall to the largest bank. The misfortune was that economic and commercial processes were excluded from the moral web of national life, joined to it only by taxation, and evaded by cheating and bribery. The petty bourgeoisie and the anti-Semites judged that this was precisely the fault of the Jews—a familiar tune for us.[18]

The Occupation demonstrated precisely the opposite. Jews were excluded, and a truly "national" merchant cadre finally arose. Did anything change? It turned out that what shaped the new situation was not the psychology of a group or nationality, but *the nature of the economic base within the totality of the system*. Since economic life was excluded from the realm of social responsibility as a consequence of specific German policies, since it became the conqueror's private feeding ground and a reservation for personal plunder, the psychology of the class that entered this feeding ground immediately emulated those of the class destroyed by the occupier. Before the war, other causes, namely, belated forms of economic liberalism, had created a similar feeding ground. And we know that bones always attract hyenas, never lions.

But there is a much more significant question. Were the ways in which our society desired, and continues to desire, to discount this economic replacement of Jews by Poles, either morally or objectively acceptable? And here, though I may answer only for myself and find no one to support me, I will repeat—no, a hundred times no. Those ways and hopes were shameful, demoralizing, and degrading. For the attitude of ordinary Poles to the tragedy of the Jews may be summarized as follows: in murdering the Jews, the Germans committed a crime. We would not have done this. The Germans will be punished for this crime. They have stained their conscience, but we—only we benefit now and in the future only we will benefit, not sullying our conscience, not staining our hands with blood.

It is difficult to find an example of reasoning more morally repulsive than this. May the fools who adhere to it understand that the annihilation of the Jews was only the first stage of the cleansing of the *Weichselraum*.[19] It was to have been our turn next.

A situation in recent Polish history repeated itself, this time on a larger, though purely psychological, scale. That moral heartburn of Polish society, created by the regaining of Zaolzie,[20] was, at the time, better understood by Churchill than anyone else: Poland pulled Zaolzie out of the rucksack of the German soldier occupying the Sudetenland. This time, from under the sword of the German butcher perpetrating a crime unprecedented in history, the little Polish shopkeeper sneaked the keys to his Jewish competitor's cashbox, and believed that he had acted morally. To the Germans went the guilt and the crime; to us the keys and the cashbox. The storekeeper forgot that the "legal" annihilation of an entire people is part of an undertaking so unparalleled that it was doubtless not staged by history for the purpose of changing the sign on someone's shop.

The methods by which Germans liquidated the Jews rest on the Germans' conscience. *The reaction to these methods rests nevertheless on our conscience.* The gold filling torn out of a corpse's mouth will always bleed, even if no one remembers its national origin. That is why we cannot permit this reaction to be either forgotten or accepted, because it contains a breath of mean necrophilia. Speaking more straightforwardly, if it has come to pass that there are no Jews involved in Polish economic life, then a new class of "baptized" storekeepers should not profit from it. *The right to profit belongs to the entire nation and state.* Jewish commerce should not be replaced by a Polish commerce structurally and psychologically identical to it, because then the entire process lacks all sense. This kind of commerce established itself during the provisional Occupation, and now believes that it will remain for all eternity. Let no one try to throw sand in our eyes by arguing that, after this brief experience of substituting the baptized for the unbaptized, "national commerce" has become something different.

But let us return to the Occupation. Did Polish commerce take advantage of this exceptional situation? Did a truly enterprising kind of merchant appear, a merchant with new horizons? Definitely not, and under the specific conditions of the Occupation he could not. During those years, the position of the merchant was shaped by two contradictory factors: *the necessity of risk and the security of passivity.*

Undoubtedly, the merchant had to take constant risks in order to circumvent official regulations. The success of his risk depended most frequently on the authorities' whims. The biggest fraud went unnoticed, while one was caught for petty swindles if the authorities' arrogance suddenly impelled them to be strict. This risk was diminished by the fact, already verified during the first year of the Occupation, that cash reserves always helped. The economic risk was inversely proportionate to the amount of capital one possessed: A novice dealer caught with bacon and tobacco generally wound up in a camp, while the wholesaler transporting entire wagonloads of goods "licensed" as military deliveries, was protected by the sheer size of the fraud, and, of course, by the number of interested, but silent, parties.

Moreover, the risk—formally so great that those unacquainted with the situation ask today how it was possible to deal in the Generalgouvernement at all—was in practice greatly diluted. But more importantly, this risk did not have the expected influence on the merchant's psyche. For this was not a creative risk, not a struggle with real danger, such as we find at the historical foundations of all great Western commercial classes. Initiative and entrepreneurship during the Occupation did not walk proudly and undisguisedly, but crept through the nooks and crannies of bribery, shady deals, fraud, and theft. It was, in a word, a posthumous renaissance of the petty and middle bourgeoisie at a time when, as we well know, liberal forms of trade belong to the past, and will be replaced by state-regulated industry and business. This is not the only example from the Occupation years, nor in our history, of the sudden development of a particular economic form at a time when it is obsolete in the general dialectic of economic phenomena. We will find a similar example in large agricultural estates.

The security of passivity was the second factor working to negate the potentially positive effects of increased risk. During the occupation years, the merchant could remain passive for many reasons, and therefore contradict "the normal behavior of a businessman." First of all, experience soon showed clearly enough that it was better to sit off in a corner than to show initiative, because then officials and inspectors required less of a cut. The merchant's prudence in business pushed the basic goods behind the counter into the back room, and dealings were transacted outside the store. Passivity also was encouraged by other factors: competition from Jews ceased automatically. Such free gain, like anything else attained without struggle, never inspires anyone to effort.

The final reason for passivity was the most demoralizing; and the nearer to liberation, the stronger its effect. This was the widening gap between the price the merchant paid for his goods and that which he received. If his goods—vodka and cigarettes—were acquired at official prices, then his passive profit automatically took on fantastic proportions. Rationed vodka acquired for about 15 złoty per liter sold "by the glass" yielded a profit of 500 to 600 złoty. A cubic meter of plywood costing about 150 złoty brought a return of well over 1,000, and so on. Naturally, this passive profit, accruing from *mere ownership,* was only fully attainable when a plentiful supply of goods could be bought at official prices. And this depended on good relations with the Germans. Business deals with them were the riskiest and the most passive. Investing in the right goods at the right time and with an appropriate profit margin permitted one to take a long refuge in one's peaceful nest behind the store and await new opportunities for plunder. It also permitted one to furnish the nest with new furniture and kitsch paintings, not to mention stocking the pantry. This therefore was not commerce but chasing after loot, punctuated with satiated purrs.

To bring our analysis to a brief conclusion: none of the factors that contributed to the exceptional position of the Polish merchant during the Occupation was either positive or permanent. The favorable position of the merchant resulted from the temporary and savage whim of the occupier. With German victory, this whim would have evaporated, and it was only the desire to keep people in the dark that resulted in abandoned stores not displaying signs, as were common in Gdynia, Poznań, or Łódz, *"reserved for front-line soldiers."*[21] The confidence with which the Polish dealer repaid the occupier for his merciful whim was extraordinarily short-sighted, a witness to the average bourgeois' being of a type most bereft of social and national imagination. Familiarity with conditions in the Reich—no secret to anyone—where the Polish bourgeoisie was completely eliminated, should have opened his eyes, as a parallel comparison opened the peasant's eyes. For the bourgeois it was enough security that he was still *dealing*, despite the fact that some fifteen kilometers away, no Pole could deal any longer.

Moreover, this conjunction of risk and passivity did not stimulate any impulses that were permanent and worth retaining. For this was the *psychological profile characteristic of speculation*, and not of true trade, which is based on large turnover and small profit. The speculative profile created a psycho-economic disposition that we continue to witness. The merchant became accustomed to having his actual sales and profits evade all control; he will have to surrender this habit. He became accustomed to having his goods make him an immediate profit, without any further service to a customer, and this he will have to forget. In a word, if the merchant who came to his calling during the Occupation is to continue to do business in the new Polish society, he must forget all about the easy life of those years.

The Peasant

Among all the effects of the Occupation on the psychology of the various Polish social classes, the economic psychology of the peasant during those years seems most paradoxical: the facts, if only they were decisive, *should have* evoked other psychosocial attitudes than those observed in the peasant of the Generalgouvernement. Economically, the peasant did better for himself than during the entire two decades between the wars. The shift in the prices of farm produce during the Occupation was permanent, though gradual. The peasant began to invest in his farm as never before. The first goods to disappear from the market during the winter of 1939–40 were agricultural machinery and tools. The Germans, looking out for their own interests, facilitated real progress in agriculture: farms produced more than before the war. The levy system, although severe, was not ruinous except toward farm animals, especially during the last two years. After contributing his share of the levy, the peasant still had enough for planting, for better eating than before the war, and for *handel*. It seemed that everything should have favorably disposed the peasant toward the occupier.

Yet the opposite happened. The village became politically conscious, consolidated itself with national consciousness, and mistrusted the occupier just as violently as did the worker. The worker's behavior, let us remember, had an economic basis. The village became the matrix of political guerrilla warfare, and no repression, even as cruel as in the Lublin region, was able to smother it. Does the psychology of the village contradict its economic base? Certainly not: except that the relationship between the economic base and its psychosocial response is most complicated here and therefore requires the most thorough analysis.

Let us return to the situation during 1939–40. The village reacted with typical—unfortunately only a German word expresses it—*Schadenfreude* [malicious joy] to the defeat of the prewar system, so hated by the peasantry, a hatred that peasant class consciousness extended to the city, to officials, and to the urban intelligentsia. Or to put it in peasant style: "You, masters, thought you were so smart, but just the same you were kicked in the ass." Simultaneously, prices of farm produce rose, and the Germans did not impose any levies during the first autumn and before the first harvest. The peasant reaction, which I repeat literally, having personally heard it many times, was: "At last a little sun is shining. We had to wait twenty years but it's finally come." Let us not be surprised or embittered by these reminders: the peasant, who from the crisis of 1930 on, had worked his land at a loss, finally began to make a profit from it. The overthrow of the hated prewar system, for the peasant a belated political liberation, coincided with long-awaited economic fulfillment.

What should surprise us, rather, is the behavior of the Germans, who were incapable of exploiting this opportunity to divide Polish society—an opportunity that had vanished by the autumn of 1940. All of us who observed the Polish village during the fall and winter of 1939–40, who took in the conversations occurring around us as if not intended for our intellectual ears, trembled at the thought that the Germans would strike while the iron was hot. In the village,

the stuff of economic prosperity and the fire of political disillusion-
ment were smoldering. What was lacking was the blacksmith. He
did not come. More accurately speaking, he showed up, but instead
of striking the iron, he turned on the peasants standing around the
forge and struck *them*.

It could not have been otherwise. A system pretending social
progress, a system in reality backward and reducing the whole
world's development to rending nationalisms, did not possess the
ideological tools that would enable it to penetrate such a complex
system requiring enormous moderation and psychological sensitivity. There was no room for such an approach in the stupidity of
Nazi social thought. The Polish village was too dirty and the Polish
peasant too poverty-stricken for it to occur to the Germans that social
changes of political significance were coming about. In general, the
Germans believed that the ability to think correlated with the
amount of soap used. They did not realize that it was possible never
to take a hot shower, yet still think and remember. They did not
even notice that the unwashed Polish village created an excellent
business opportunity for them. Instead the Germans dragged everything down to the primitive mythology of conflicting nationalisms. . . .

Instead of exploiting the opportunity, German economic and political policies began to destroy it. The basis for this policy was not
economic, but purely psychological. Although Germans have produced more treatises on psychology than has any other nation, and
pontificated with deadly seriousness about the transformation of
"Will" [*Wille*] into "Being itself" [*Selbst dasein*], it is common knowledge that they have never been good psychologists. But what has
not been sufficiently emphasized is the context in which this inborn
stupidity most affects their judgment, and that is *toward those weaker
than they*. The German in a position of authority does not notice at
all, from the heights of his power, what is taking place among his
subjects. And the greater his authority, the less he observes.

For the Germans, the Polish peasant was an ideal subject. His
patience was interpreted as acceptance of every whim. His reticence
and suspiciousness, which always permitted the other to express an
opinion before he expresses his own, were construed as lack of any
opinion. His inexhaustible perseverance in working for himself was
interpreted as an ox-like capacity to carry out the worst drudgery.
In a word, appearances sufficed for the Germans; they perceived
nothing of our peasant's real nature. Above all, they failed to per-

ceive his capacity to remember, his focused, silent ability to recall the wrongs, particularly economic wrongs, done to him.

They did not realize, moreover, that this man of few words valued himself no less than the urban intelligentsia or his land-owning neighbor. As if motivated by some instinctual death wish, the Germans assaulted precisely these two peasant traits—self-worth and long memory. The blacksmith, instead of striking the iron, literally struck faces at every opportunity. The peasant quickly realized that the German fist was worse than the pre-1939 policeman's rifle butt. This is not to say that he longed for the rifle butt. But he saw that submitting to collaboration with the occupier was no less dangerous than collaboration with the prewar policeman.

Let us further remember that the worst excesses occurred during the first two years, when the Germans were completely intoxicated by their own success. The peasant reacted to the outrages with silence, knowing that he could not respond any other way. The German does not understand silent rebellion; only a wide open mouth restrains his raised fist. He took the silence as proof that he had broken his opponent. So he struck him again, struck him in demonic and foolish frenzy until the last weeks of the Occupation, when the peasant already carried on his back and face the marks of that profound knowledge of things German won by prolonged experience. Perhaps the German struck only to inscribe the experience, forever and ever amen, upon the mistreated peasant, and thereby create a class which, unlike Polish dealers or landowners, would not have to be taught who the German really was in democratic Poland.

At the same time the Germans did so much to nourish the peasant's long memory. No one remembers unfulfilled promises as well as the peasant, and few respond so directly and intensely to straightforward facts. The first and only wave of voluntary departures for the Reich, which turned out to be a fraud, came from the village. The village remembered this once and for all. It later supplied the largest proportional share of laborers of any social class, but these went at gunpoint. It was the village that received the first impact of the resettled refugees from the Western Territories, and remembered poignantly what awaited each household.[22]

Finally, the levy system, which, although pure economic exploitation, inscribed itself least in the peasant's memory. In terms of quantity, this system was not ruinous for the village itself, not to mention the rest of our economy. But over the years it came to be perceived by the peasant as an economic injustice consciously directed against him. The differential between the actual prices of grain and meat and prices paid for the supplies levied was not met by the worthless bonuses the Germans offered, and the more the price scissors drew apart, the more aware the peasant became that he was being wronged. The scissors opened increasingly under the Occupation. The gap between the blades was covered only by colorful propaganda images of the happy, smiling peasant hurrying along to the provincial cooperative with a piglet under his arm, then returning through a pretty meadow bent under the weight of heaps of horseshoes, bottles of vodka, and sacks of sugar received in exchange.

Such a poster was supposed to teach the peasant his true good fortune, but when displayed too close to the border of Reich and the Generalgouvernement, it collided with another image, no longer a poster, but the actual picture of what awaited the peasant. This was the boundary strip separating the fields of his own village from those of the one next door, no less Polish than his, whose ownership had never before been in question. Turning his plow at this strip, the peasant saw his own not distant future in the event of a German victory. On the other side there were no longer any Polish peasants, and if any remained, they were slaves of German farmers.

This instructive sociology was carried out with a mad consistency characteristic of the Germans alone. Any other people, only slightly more sensitive, would undoubtedly have created some sort of neutral zone to prevent peasants from imagining so vividly the fate of lands annexed to the Reich. Words simply lack the power of what confronted the peasant's naked eye at this frontier of two worlds. The peasant turning his plow around at this border strip knew what awaited him. From the border village word spread to the one beyond, and further still. And even very far from the border, where word might not have reached, the foresightful Germans undertook agricultural colonization and deported all the peasants, especially from the Zamość region [far from the German border],[23] to prevent the experiences of the lands around Koluszki, Modlin, or Częstochowa [near the German border] from being forgotten.

As a consequence of such foresightedness, the peasant clearly felt—and it is to the credit of his sober sense of reality that he could not be fooled by any verbal tricks—that his relative prosperity was only provisional until the moment of Nazi triumph. For all these reasons, the peasant defended himself relatively well against moral corruption.

Nevertheless, his defense varied with the class structure of the particular village. Indeed, we would be mistaken to treat the peasant's psychosocial reaction to the Occupation as identical throughout the countryside. It was above all the small farmer and the poor farmhand who remained least corrupted. These categories of peasant bore the brunt of the obligations that the village had to provide for the occupier. A cow levied from a large farm was a small loss. The seizure for a pittance of the cow that nourished an entire family was an irreparable misfortune. It was generally replaced by a goat, aptly called the poor man's cow. Furthermore, demands for local corvées as well as forced labor deportations fell principally upon such poor peasants, who were unable to raise the ransom needed to redeem a deportee. On the other hand, the improved standard of living derived from high agricultural prices barely compensated such families for years of prewar poverty. Nor was this improvement of such a degree as to permit the small farmer to engage in speculation, which was dependent on the clandestine breeding and slaughter of animals.

And since at the same time the poor peasant drew down the harshest blows precisely because of his ragged attire and ramshackle hut, he was held in contempt and considered to be subhuman. It was he who was the prime victim of the no longer concealed Saxon myth, he who was the worst sufferer and the most bitter hater of the occupier.

With the wealthy peasant it was quite different. He gained most from the price rise, from the demand for lard and meat. He could breed animals secretly. His stash of cash and supplies gave him an excellent chance to reduce the risks of being "caught" by authorities. Finally, he was able to shield his family against labor deportations, and therefore his farm was never short of laborers. During the Occupation speculation reached the village primarily through the instrumentality of the wealthy peasant and reinforced his class egoism.

The degree to which the excluded economy penetrated the village demands a more detailed analysis than the present sketch. Although it is impossible to trace its full scale, I will at least point out the ulcer of the most naked speculation, the most certain profit, and of unceasing bribery of the Polish and German police: the country mill. It was easiest to evade quotas on milling at a secluded mill. The miller demanded good pay for taking on the risk, since he had to "give" lavishly to the authorities in turn. Yet he shared a relatively small portion of what he received. All local authorities knew perfectly well that the millers were getting around the rules, but the authorities had no intention of using this knowledge to their own disadvantage, of plugging their source gushing with vodka and piled high with sacks of the purest wheat flour. And therefore, whoever wants to trace the effect of the Occupation in the countryside at its most glaring, let him set his story at a tree-shaded mill in a secluded corner of the village, amidst a sodden November landscape. It should be nightfall, and tipsy policemen and *Sonderdienst* should be slumped in a wagon. Under the seats, vodka and sides of bacon are heaped.

Returning from this secluded corner to the village, we realize that the economic dealings of the wealthy peasant were most excluded from the imposed system. He lost just as everyone lost, but proportionately he lost much less, and what is worse, *the peasant could recoup his losses only at the expense of his countrymen.* He did not seek buyers; buyers came to him, to the most decrepit village, and paid any price. It was not he who sustained the greatest risk in *handel* during the Occupation—that of transport—but the urban trader, professional or amateur. Similar processes develop during any war; the situation was similar at the end of the war of 1914–1918. But this time, German efficiency developed these phenomena to a particular intensity. As a result of the wealthy privileged conditions, prices became hypersensitive, a situation lasting until today. Prices swept up all too easily and on any pretext, particularly so the price of bacon, as sensitive as mimosa. But only sluggishly, with great difficulty, did prices return to normal; mimosa-like bacon suddenly became as tough as agave.

Our peasant, indeed like every other, was insensitive and hard, his insensitivity exacerbated by peculiarly Polish survivals of the age-old peasant misery of his class. This is the kind of peasant Poland inherits from the Occupation.

Large Landowners[24]

The relationship of the German toward large landowners cannot be explained from any of his explicit decrees, but only in German visions of the future of the *Weichselraum*. Except for the "model"

German settlements in the Zamość region and in the Radom district, the Reich's designs for the agricultural structure of the Generalgouvernement cannot be discovered in the conditions there, but only in the changes in the annexed territories, and above all in the changes in the area lying between the Russian-German-Austrian border of 1914 and the border of the Reich and the Generalgouvernement, a strip of land from Żywiec to Mława, widest along the Kalisz-Koluszki parallel.[25]

The agricultural structure of Polish lands was to be maintained despite the colonization system of the East. Colonization here meant the resettlement in every village of a number of German farmers, nearly all from Bukowina and Siedmiogród.[26] The land belonging to the village was divided among them, thereby creating large farms of the type and size that have long existed in the Poznań region. The original inhabitants were assigned to the colonists as farmhands on their own land. Those not required for this task, a sizable number given rural overpopulation, were deported to factory work in the Reich; the more politically active were sent to death camps. Cruel and ominous as this was, it was still doubtless only a transitional stage. With German victory, the native Poles, dangerous because sentimentally tied to the land, undoubtedly would have been replaced by workers taken from other countries. The transitional system of serfdom would have regressed, in accordance with the entire economic logic of fascism, to the conquering feudalism of the Norman invasions: knight and imported slave.

The Germans treated the rural economy of the Generalgouvernement as provisional, to be exploited for maximum profit during wartime and, only after victory, transformed according to their colonization scheme. Only in this context can we understand the agricultural policies of the Germans in the Generalgouvernement: the transitional stage of enslavement to a master race was to be held up at its borders until the unrealized final victory. Thus *the Germans were uninterested in any progressive social changes in the agricultural system.* In general, the political economy of the Generalgouvernement sanctioned only unavoidable passive changes: for example, Polish trade that "leaped" at the chance to replace Jewish *handel*.

In the Germans' perspective, the most reasonable immediate policy was to maintain the agricultural system for the time being, particularly those elements of it that most lent themselves to colonization. Thus it was undoubtedly easier to dispossess an individual landowner and divide his property among several German farmers than to integrate tiny plots in the overpopulated villages. That is why the Germans did not turn over large ownerless properties to the villages for cultivation, but kept them, under the provision of the *Liegenschaft* [landed estate] and trusteeship system, in the form in which they were acquired.

I encountered an excellent example of this in Krzeszowice, on the old Potocki estate[27] taken over by Frank. The estate contains scarcely 200 hectares[28] of arable land and meadows. The farm buildings, though old, served the property quite well. Despite this, at a cost of many millions, the Germans constructed stables, barns, and storehouses for chemical fertilizer on a scale appropriate to serve thousands of hectares. In about 1941 a rumor spread that the surrounding farms were to be incorporated into the Krzeszowice estate, to be followed by the peasant plots. The alarming whisper was quickly silenced. Yet development of the farm continued, and to the attentive observer there was no question that the would-be feudal sire of Kressendorf was making the preparation necessary for annexing the lands of peasants, landowners, and convents after victory. Nor was there any question that the silenced rumor had been the premature revelation of a careful and consequential plan.

This reluctance of the Germans to divide large estates was due to another autonomous psychological reason—the craving for feudal authority. The Germans, particularly high Party officials, were undoubtedly impressed by the life of the landed nobility. They felt very good amidst well-spread tables, fireplaces, and reminders of golden heritage; and each of the Party elite, whenever he was able, modeled his lifestyle on the Polish squire's. These financial climbers with retrograde social imagination luxuriated in such surroundings. Extraordinarily amusing was the sight of Frank on a fine spring day touring his estate in an open carriage pulled by a team of horses, or in autumn receiving a harvest wreath from his farmhands. Even more comical was the sight of his assistant rebuilding an old farmstead on the strict model of a manor house, and plundering birchwood, sabers, and battle-axes (all authentic). The difference was that his manor was equipped with modern facilities unknown to its originals. I suspect that, in the event of a German victory, these same masters would have had galleries hung with paintings of alleged forefathers, castellans in full dress and bishops in senators' chairs.

It was in this way, albeit in the milder psychological climate of Poland, that the lifestyle of the Prussian aristocrat, a long-standing model for the German rulers of the East, was realized. Yet the Prussian aristocrat was as ascetic as a knight-monk of the Middle Ages. But now an entirely different type of lust for power manifested itself, brutally revealing the moral and social decay of Nazi Party leadership, *entirely hedonistic and oriented to enjoying* life. This Party leadership created the illusion for itself that hedonism was possible under such conditions. The illusion: the subjects' trust and love of their masters, pathetically served by the little harvest wreath, the master's gracious mingling with the people, and the farce of mutual confidence and trust. These fantasies mingled with Nazi order and undisguised layers of Nazi stupidity, hypocrisy, and cynicism.

The backward social character of National Socialism, therefore, revealed itself nowhere more openly than in these psychological impulses. The Germans despised the peasant, whose nature they completely misunderstood. They hated the intelligentsia, and only concern for their own interests restrained this hatred. They half envied the landowners and half secretly admired them. It should not be surprising, therefore, that such a willing attitude evoked a symmetrical response: it is difficult not to be courteous to a notorious brute who is courteous *only toward me*. And so the highest proportion of those inclined toward limited collaboration was found among the landowners. (The social background of the leadership of the Central Welfare Council[29] is in this respect extremely instructive.) The landowner's vision of how the agricultural system would change in the land once liberated from the Germans strengthened his relations with them.[30] His awareness that it is possible to live while delivering levies—even while counting bribes—also played its part.

The Germans favored all agricultural investment. The landowner, generally better versed in it than the peasant, could implement his expertise and meet the authorities halfway while protecting his own interests. In agricultural production, which the Germans most valued and awarded with large bonuses in goods, the manor was essential: beets for sugar refineries, potatoes for distilleries, oleiferous seeds.

This convergence of factors, some emerging out of the objective though temporary economic situation—such as the high demand for the rape plant and beets—others out of the conqueror's mind-set, resulted in high agricultural prices, and therefore, finally, to the manors doing well for themselves—doing well for themselves at the moment of their ultimate decline.

This feeling that the landowner's prosperity was the last ray of an irrevocably setting sun, expressed itself characteristically enough.

Until the war years, Polish landowners had been the main pur-
chasers of works of art. During the Occupation the manors ceased
to buy paintings and fine furniture, for such things are only for those
who have faith that their homes are permanent. The newly rich
merchant acquired paintings by Wojciech Kossak, Wierusz-Kowalski,
and Brandt.[31] It will remain his secret why he believed his home
would endure.

When it came to fulfilling collective responsibilities, one must
admit that the majority of the large landowners acquitted themselves
decently by harboring refugees, and not displaced relatives only:
very many Polish *prominente* survived the Occupation only because
the landowner understood the implicit responsibility that came with
prosperity. This belated prosperity also characterized Polish *handel*
during the Occupation. In both cases, our backward economic development resulted in a situation in which the enlargement of consciousness brought by material prosperity came too late to the different social classes and was, in the economic dialectic, backward
and paradoxical.

Further consequences flowed from this, becoming apparent in the
first months of liberation. Success always leaves behind a residue
of yearning for what used to be and an aversion to the forces that
did away with it. Certainly no one claims that the landowners longed
for the perpetuation of German rule. Yet anyone can see that they
did and would do so for a long time because of the benefits that
the Occupation brought them. Such yearning is a social mistake.
The attitude of the Germans toward large landowners was like a
smile on the face of the beast gathering to pounce but for a moment
restrains himself. A smile of delicious anticipation that *this tidbit will
be the tastiest of all.*

Our Mortgaged Independence

It is time now to summarize our analyses and to reflect upon what
our conclusions hold for the future.

Polish economic psychology during the Occupation years was
shaped by factors that excluded economic life from any creative,
and at the same time moral, participation in the design imposed
upon it. The very exclusion of the most important processes of collective life from responsibility and active participation necessarily
provoked a profound moral corruption, a corruption generally not

intentional, but resulting from the very necessity of surviving within a system based on falsehoods that served those in power, on injustice as a principle. In many cases, nevertheless, this corruption was intentional and conscious, well-understood and entered into by those participating in economic life, particularly those engaged in *handel* and brokerage. Finally, in another facet of the problem, facts that were in themselves apparently positive, such as the rise of ethnically Polish small *handel* and the revitalization of agricultural mechanization, appeared too late to be able to become the embryo of future economic development.

Most significant is the resulting common psychology that seems ready to endure into at least the first years of independence. Polish society inherits from the Occupation the half-conscious but deeply rooted conviction that the most important element of modern economic life is *handel*—*handel* conceived in the most individualistic manner possible. Let us recall the reasons for this: the elimination of the Jews; the passive entry of Poles in the places thus vacated; the participation in *handel*, prompted by the need for survival, of classes that heretofore had no contact with it, such as industrial and office workers. *Polish society during the Occupation lived from and survived through handel.* Given the backward Polish economic system, society undoubtedly took a step forward. But such a step, the rise of individualistic *handel*, would in the context of world development have been progressive in the era of the rise of the world bourgeoisie—not today, in the period of its decline. Because society survived through *handel*, it concluded that, in the emerging economic system of independent Poland, the situation would be the same. This is a mistake, excusable psychologically as an echo of the past, but inexcusable if it is a vision and forecast for the future.

Yet for the time being, one can predict that the situation that arose within the Generalgouvernement will, in the coming months and perhaps for longer, infect the Western lands.[32] When one crosses the border between these two areas—I am writing this in March 1945—and travels through cities that belonged to the Reich during the Occupation, one is struck by the conspicuous absence of all those street dealers whispering, "Buy, sell, cigarettes, dollars." One is struck by the absolute lack of crowded displays of all sorts of goods, from perfume to bacon. Polish *handel* does not exist there. But one can predict with absolute certainty that those women and their accomplices active at the very battle-front [in March 1945] will introduce the practices of Polish *handel* into areas where they were un-known. I traveled with them on the same train from Oświęcim [Auschwitz, in the Generalgouvernement] to Katowice [in the Reich] where one can deal with great profit due to the amazing naivete of the Silesians unaccustomed to the *handel* of the Occupation. (In June 1945, I can attest that this indeed has happened.)

But predictions do not change evaluations. The expansion of *handel* was a cancer metastasized only through a morally riven economy, imposed without the least concern for the most basic needs of a subjugated nation. *Handel* was the temporary self-defense. All of this happened during a war, which was won not only by the courage of soldiers, but even more by sacrifice and *the stubborn struggle of work* as the statistical curves of production output show. This war was won by nations that inculcated a high level of economic mo-rality, the morality of work. For the losers, only the capacity for such an exertion outweighed their preposterous ideologies. Poles only read about Russian factories, evacuated with their employees over thousands of kilometers, rebuilt in remote areas, and resuming normal production within several weeks. They only heard about shipyards in which a new ship was laid down and launched, all in a week. They heard about roads cutting across entire continents, from Senegal to Ethiopia.

Poles heard and read, but *did not participate in any comparable effort* as conscious actors. They do not know and cannot feel the weight of sacrifice, exertion, hunger, and foresight concealed in these facts, whose ultimate and fantastic fruits are now their own. What was taken from them, denied them, and erased from their experience was perhaps the most important lesson of the war: *economic processes are woven into a nation's moral fabric.* This is no idealistic morality, but one deriving from pragmatic goals drawn from direct experience. Polish society did not learn this great historical lesson.

For such a lesson did not arise through the petty cunning of the "baptized" dealer or the shrewdness of the peasant skilled in skirting every regulation. It grew where it did because the econo-my's place within the life of other nations became a moral com-mitment—so moral because so responsible. Yet the excluded econ-omy of our nation has left behind a residue difficult to cleanse and eradicate and all too likely to continue in the new state and society. Yet, if nothing else succeeds, the residue must be torn out of the psyche of our society *even if it means losing some skin along with it.* Otherwise the moral corruption is bound to last longer than what is still forgivable and acceptable as the echo of circumstances that no longer exist.

This psychosocial residue attains various depths in various spheres, most profoundly in commerce. We understand why: its temporarily privileged situation came about without the responsibility and participation of those who benefited from it—a gracious gift of fate. Also, the state's normal method of control—through taxation—was most unreal here, creating a situation that has outlasted its origins. Many therefore still hope for a taxation system lastingly fictional, for a lack of state inspection, for passive black market profiteering. And many factors still encourage such hopes. The new Polish merchant, if he is not replaced by a system of state-owned stores, must now learn to make a living from normal business profits. This is why the role of merchants must be carefully controlled and bad practices eradicated in our new state.

Next in severity is the mind-set lingering among large landowners. The enactment of land reform does away with this class' social significance and hence the problem. Yet the economic foundation of the village is sound and resilient. The irritation and opposition that developed in the villages during the Occupation stemmed more from psychological response than from the denial of the state's right to intervene. In a country that is industrializing its economy, higher agricultural prices will maintain themselves, thereby removing the main source of dissatisfaction in the village. The settlements in the west create an escape valve for the overpopulated villages. The levy system, if judiciously applied, reasonably well-paying, and above all, carried out without bureaucratic pilfering, can be maintained without alienating the village, for the peasant understands its necessity.

Handel, then, is obviously weighty, while the village is a lighter burden on our mortgaged independence. But the problem remains complicated and difficult to solve. At its core are the workers, the urban intelligentsia, office workers, and managers in state-run enterprises. It is complicated because the economic bases that corrupted morality under the Occupation still largely survive, and unfortunately in many cases will continue. These bases resulted from the discrepancy between the actual standard of living, people's financial needs, and the actual income of industrial and office workers. The discrepancy continues and it is clear that rather than eradicate the practices of the Occupation, the new system often favors them and will continue to do so.

Above all, temptation has grown. Economic transactions and the distribution of goods, which still have and will long continue to have two prices—an official and a market one—have now passed into Polish hands. *Bezugscheine*—German ration cards—now lie on the Polish bureaucrat's desk. As a result, all those opportunities for "legal" fraud that were within German reach are now between Polish fingers, along with the well-learned practices of six years of occupation. The consequences are well known, and it will be a long time before they come to an end. We understand that it is difficult to eliminate this discrepancy immediately: if it is not to fall into the vicious cycle of an economy patched by paper money, the state cannot pay inflationary salaries or increase its services. But on the other hand, if the new Polish state is to survive, it cannot settle for make-believe taxes and requirements. It must demand revenue in proportion to its needs, and at the same time sanction relatively high prices in order to collect equally high revenues. It must give as little as possible, and take as much as possible.

It is necessary to take these steps, but for the time being the ongoing temptations and discrepancies are encouraged, and with them an economic psychology that evades moral considerations has still not lost its base. That is why we must scrutinize our mortgaged independence carefully. Until economic development and state policy eradicate this discrepancy, we should not conceal it behind pretty speeches. This particularly applies to journalism, which should call a spade a spade. The worst evils are concentrated in managing planned industry, in the planned distribution of goods, in administrative intervention in economic life, and above all, in fictionalized earnings.

An economy morally excluded from the life of the nation has left behind calamitous psychosocial practices. The Nazis were aware of these practices, but cared little about them as long as they benefited. Moreover, such corruption applied only to the despised Poles and that was handy for the Germans. Ultimately they regarded everything that occurred in the Generalgouvernement as provisional; it would end with the day of victory. But the new Polish state feels the full weight of these practices and social distortions. Only now are we paying the price of the Occupation. To cope with it, we must first become aware of it. The present remarks are intended to serve that end.

NOTES

1. The article was reprinted in 1959 and 1984 in Wyka's book, *Życie na Niby: Pamiętnik po Klęsce* (Life as if: Memoirs after defeat), with very few changes.

2. According to this vantage point on Polish history, the "first epoch of independence" was the time before the partitioning powers—Russia, Prussia, and Austria—completed their carving up of Poland in 1795 (the Prussian territories being assimilated into the Bismarckean German Empire in 1871). The partitions lasted until the end of World War I. From 1918, when Poland reemerged as a recognized state, until the German-Russian occupation of 1939, was the second. The third epoch began after World War II.

3. The regime and territory that the Nazis occupied and placed under their administration. Occupied territory included central and southeastern Poland and the cities of Warsaw, Lublin, Kielce, and Łódz; Cracow became the administrative capital. The occupied people were treated as *untermenschen*—"subhumans." Poland's western and northeastern provinces (formerly under German partition) were directly incorporated into the ethnic German Reich, and the ethnically Polish people of those territories classified as German (most spoke the language). They were conscripted as Germans into the *Wehrmacht* and granted privileges *"nur fur Deutsche"*—"for Germans only."

4. These towns represent the highly developed region of the machine and chemical industries, which was built in the second half of the 1930s.

5. The Germans knew Krzeszowice, a small town near the city of Cracow, as Kressendorf. The Nazis Germanized it and many other place names, including the names of streets, under the Generalgouvernement.

6. Hans Frank (1900–1946), the Nazi Governor-General, chose Kressendorf as his headquarters. He was sentenced to death by hanging for crimes against humanity at the Allied tribunal of Nuremberg.

7. The Upper Silesian coal basin was incorporated into the Reich, and the German owners and administrators of the area hoped to monopolize coal production by incorporating the only remaining mine in the Generalgouvernement into the Reich. *Nebenland*—the border territory—was the German propaganda term for the Generalgouvernement, which bordered on the Reich. The term implied an ideological and cultural, not only geographical, closeness.

8. People murdered in the gas chambers under the direction of the Nazis had their gold teeth removed. The gold became the property of the German state and was sent to the Reich.

9. *Handel* connotes informal trade tinged with cunning and legerdemain through private exchange often unregulated by law, yet governed by well-recognized rules. Although *handel* usually is "half-legal," the term is rather

pejorative. A *handlarz*—someone who engages in *handel*—is not looked upon favorably, in contrast to a *kupiec* (merchant) who is respected.

10. Speculation (*spekulacja*) is the private resale of goods with the intent not of using them but of selling them at higher prices.

11. "Traveling to Saxon work" ("*na Saksy*") is a slang term that refers to employment in Germany—the closest country with a strong economy. During the second half of the nineteenth century many Polish peasants went to Germany for seasonal or temporary labor.

12. Camps were located in or outside nearly all major towns and cities. Of the German IG-Farben's 43 factories and plants located in Poland, 28 manufactured chemicals and other products necessary for the war effort or poison gas to exterminate people in the gas chambers of Auschwitz and other concentration camps. IG-Farben owned a plant outside Auschwitz in which inmates were worked to death.

13. These towns are railway centers near the cities of Warsaw and Cracow, respectively, where German police searched trains and confiscated goods from Polish smugglers.

14. Small towns near the cities of Warsaw and Cracow.

15. The intelligentsia was exterminated as part of the Nazi plan to turn the Lublin region of eastern Poland into an agricultural colony. Armed partisans were extremely active in this area, resulting in particularly severe reprisals.

16. Poles abroad could send packages to Poland through these neutral countries.

17. London was the headquarters of the Polish government-in-exile. The money was sent to keep resistance going but, in a desperate, demoralized society, often went astray.

18. Much of the energy of Polish right-wing nationalist parties before 1939 went into the struggle to force Jews out of their supposed leading role in the economy, and replace them with a "native" Polish middle class which, it was theorized, would labor for the common, that is, Polish good.

19. The basin of the Vistula River that runs through the heart of Poland.

20. Zaolzie was a small "ethnically Polish" piece of disputed territory between Poland and Czechoslovakia that Poland had demanded during the interwar period. In the months after the Munich Agreement of 1938 Hitler seized first the Sudetenland of western Czechoslovakia (with its German majority), then the predominantly ethnically Czech Bohemia. The Polish forces "conquered" Zaolzie. Wyka indicated, as did many other Poles, that Poles should be ashamed of their part in the partitioning of Czechoslovakia.

21. These cities were in areas directly annexed into the Reich.

22. Poles were deported from the Reich in the areas of Poland annexed to it, and their property expropriated.

23. Under the direction of Heinrich Himmler of the SS, the Germans experimented in creating an agricultural colony and Germanizing eastern Poland, including the Zamość region, known for its especially fertile soil. This entailed huge deportations of peasants out of the area.

24. Before the war, about 65 percent of the Polish population lived in the countryside. Peasants owned small plots or worked as farmhands for large landowners (*wielka własność*) or the upper peasantry.

25. This was a railway junction where German police checked for smugglers and confiscated food.

26. German minorities had long lived in Siedmiogród (Transylvania)—a territory disputed between Romania and Hungary—and in Bukowina on the Ukrainian-Romanian border.

27. The Potocki family was one of the wealthiest and most prestigious of Polish noble families.

28. One hectare equals approximately 2.5 acres.

29. The Central Welfare Council (*Rada Główna Opiekuńcza*), a charitable organization by and for Poles permitted by the Germans, was under the leadership of the Polish aristocracy.

30. Landowners feared they would finally lose their properties to agricultural reforms that had been in the works since the independence of 1918 but which had been continually postponed.

31. These Polish painters, known for their depictions of historical battle scenes, were almost compulsorily fashionable among the large landowners.

32. The Western lands were territories directly annexed by Germany during the war.

2

Shadow Justice

ILONA MORZOŁ AND
MICHAŁ OGÓREK

> Indeed, so many were the fictions, consistent and inconsistent, in German policy, that it is difficult to explain them. Yet the explanation lies near at hand. One only has to assume that everything the Germans did under the Generalgouvernement *was provisional wartime arrangements.* —Kazimierz Wyka, 1945

Over the 45 years of People's Poland, a steady flow of legislation was enacted to create and to punish new crimes. Ideologues tirelessly conceived of new categories of "public enemy" for whom appropriate punishment had to be devised. Laws were drawn ambiguously and imprecisely of set purpose—the better to apply arbitrarily. One could not rigorously ascertain whether someone was guilty of a given offense or whether a given act was criminal. The whole system was set up so as to make it possible that anyone subject to the system could be convicted or acquitted of one charge or another, at the complete discretion of state power. As a popular saying went: "Give me the person, and I'll find the law [that he broke]."

In postwar People's Poland, punishment alone defined which activities were illegal, and just *how* illegal they were. What did the law hold to be the most heinous crimes during a given period? What crimes were punishable by the most severe sentences? Crime Number One was violent assault, if carried out against the wrong person. Members of the National Council (the then Polish Parliament), state and self-government functionaries, and trade union members enjoyed such protection. Assault on a member of a political party was especially punishable—provided the party had been legalized. The memorandum of judicial instructions that accompanied the code emphasized that the ideological stance of the organization did not matter, just its legal status.

The only legal organizations were those under the control of the Communist Party.

The introduction of new statutes, even where many prewar statutes remained on the books, created some muddle. For example, the prewar act affording special protection to the president was not repealed but supplemented by a parallel postwar act. The two codes remained equally binding; and thus an assault on the president was punishable with two death sentences.

The same legislation laid down that not only was an assault on a Polish army unit punishable, but an assault on a unit allied with Poland was equally punishable. This clause raised certain difficulties, since it could not be explicitly written that this meant the Russian army. And so it was glossed: "The notion [of an allied army] is understood as meaning organizational ties between the Polish state and the ally expressed in a formal alliance. The mere fact that the armies fought together against a common enemy is not sufficient."[1]

The so-called abridged legal code[2] introduced some innovative classes of offenses: sabotage, organizing or leading a criminal conspiracy, and a new crime of "nonpublic dissemination" of false information: before the war one could only be punished for publishing falsehoods in the press. Now all one had to do to be guilty of this crime was to talk with friends. The state determined what was false.

An entire page of judicial instruction was devoted to constructing the doctrine of criminal conspiracy: "a particular form of collusion with permanent organizational ties." "A criminal conspiracy," said the last sentence, "is a so-called gang." Another outlawed organizational form was the armed gang. If one wanted to start one, better to do it with only one other person. Any kind of collusion or action committed by more than two people was deemed more harmful and hence became punishable with a harsher sentence.[3]

Spying, illegal possession of weapons, and forgery of Polish or foreign money could entail capital punishment. But even the most trivial crime could incur the death penalty if the court decided that one was "acting to the detriment of the Polish People's Republic." Under this provision of Article 1, Section 1 of the "Summary Justice Act" of November 1945, the number of potentially capital crimes thus became limitless. Moreover, something not criminal according to the abridged code might fall under some criminal category of the Polish Code of Military Justice, from 1945 to 1955 also applicable to civilians. The three articles most often applied were those punishing attempts to deprive the Polish state of its independent existence, to overthrow the organs of the highest ruling authorities, and to change the political system. All were deemed high treason.

Crimes against the communist state—the Polish People's Republic—were considered more serious than any other. Those against human life and private property ranked much lower. Only "the use of a weapon" displaced such an offense into a higher category. Murder and theft fell into greater or lesser violations, depending on the political status of the victim.

In 1945 a new type of crime was created: economic sabotage. Legislation brought into being the Special Commission for Corrupt Practices and Economic Sabotage, an unprecedented legal body, and endowed it with broad authority. Such sabotage could be understood as intentional damage to the economy—not only attempting to blow up a factory, but also petty theft and the failure to fulfill state-established production quotas. The act introduced a new punishment: for the first time in Poland hard labor camps were created to which "saboteurs" could be deported for three years without the formality of a prison sentence. The most serious economic crime under the new dispensation became "dishonest swindling."[4] It became illegal to sell something "if the price was evidently too high," as determined by the judicial system. From 1944 to 1947, this restriction even applied to commonplace items of the most trivial value.

In 1947 the law of supply and demand was made totally illegal. If a customer bought something for too high a price, the (private) seller from whom he had bought it "[could have his] shop temporarily shut down [and undergo] up to five years of prison and a fine of up to 5 million złoty."

In 1949 the interpretation of these laws was administratively expanded without revising the statute to radically intensify the status of such activities, many more of which became classified as sabotage, a crime that could only be committed against "state institutions."[5] Many branches of industry had been taken over by the state and so the category of state institutions had greatly expanded. According to the act's accompanying judicial instructions, "factories, steel works, mines, etc., previously serving the interests of their private owners, now come under the protection of this law."

The instructions selected brickyards as an example of "public enterprises and services"[6] while excluding "factories that produce gramophone turntables." Charges of economic sabotage were usually brought in sectors of the economy producing such goods deemed essential to the socialist state as bread, steel, and tractors. Turntables were a luxury. But the instructions did afford the hope that as the country developed, acts of sabotage might be committed in these factories as well: "In the future when the essential needs of the masses are fulfilled, it might become possible even for turntables to be included on the list of basic articles." At the same time certain institutions "whose activities could not be geographically specified such as the Headquarters of the Textile Industry," glided under the state's particular protection.

Farmers also—whether private or collectivized—could easily find themselves found guilty of sabotage, however unintentionally. Wasting agricultural products or achieving a lower crop yield than called for by government quotas were naturally sabotage. A saboteur did not have to do anything; it was sufficient, glossed the instruction, that "the perpetrator, given his position, profession or military service, was supposed to carry out certain activities and did not do so."

Yet it proved necessary, even with all these regulations and expansive interpretations, for the courts to extend them yet further. The Supreme Military Tribunal drew out the fine structure of categories embracing those particularly protected against violent assault: "By members of trade unions, political or social organizations the regulation means activists. Undoubtedly a worker, a farmer, an office worker or a 'champion of labor' [an exemplary worker] who is not a member of such an organization but fights for the strengthening of the people's authority with his active involvement in his professional and social work, may be considered such an activist." According to the instruction of the Supreme Court, participation itself in anti-state conspiracy was yet a further crime.

To a suitably vigilant authority, "anti-state activities" could manifest themselves in so many ways. One need not belong to an anti-state organization to be guilty; but if one did, it was not necessary to have engaged in any "anti-state" activity—membership was quite enough. Judicial instruction was explicit: "The very fact of joining a criminal conspiracy, without undertaking any activity, is to be treated as committing such a crime." The only difference was that active criminals—distributors of leaflets, speakers at meetings—got a double dose. Teachers who created an "anti-state attitude" among their pupils were considered to have attempted to change the nation's political system by force.

It became dangerous to be a passer-by. "A passer-by," ran the instructions, "may become a participant in a crowd by joining it consciously. The fact itself that he remains with it may be an expression of his support for it. It is enough that the person does not walk away, but remains with the crowd and is aware of the crowd's intentions to commit a crime."

Each fiat covered a wider area, even than first glance disclosed. The ideal situation under this legal system was to make the same crime punishable by as many different statutes as possible: if one regulation did not fit the "guilty" party, another one surely could be found.

In 1948 the penalty for an illegal attempt to cross the state border rose from one year's imprisonment to three. On April 19, 1950, malice became a crime. Another window was opened into men's souls: the courts could impute "malice" pretty much at will, and soon were sending people down "for persistent and malicious avoidance of employment." Employees who missed work for four days were taken to court on the fifth, usually to lose between 10 to 35 percent of their wages for three months. Should they not take up the job assigned, they went to prison for five months more.

On the other hand, employees were not supposed to go to the other extreme and take work home: they faced ten years in prison for removing documents from the office. To lose such documents was high treason.

Agricultural work was also riddled with criminal opportunities: the act of July 10, 1952 regulated compulsory grain deliveries and imposed three years' jail for those "delinquent" in their obligations to deliver specified amounts to state procurement centers. Three other acts applied the same penalties to farmers failing to fulfill comparable deliveries of potatoes, milk, and animals. Poor harvests became a crime.

In 1953 theft suddenly rose in the hierarchy of crime. One activity took on many faces—misappropriation of funds, fraud, or "seizure in any other form."[7] All these elaborate measures operated only to defend state property. Every category of the violation of state property, however minor, was regulated by a separate act. Stealing an item worth 300 złoty, such as a man's jacket, could bring a year in prison.

The currency act of 1952 made the very possession of dollars a crime. Someone caught "dealing in foreign currency on a particularly large scale" could be certain of lifetime imprisonment. Again, no initiative was required. It was equally illegal to have savings in foreign currency. According to the act, "Unlicensed possession of foreign currency on the territory of Poland is punishable by prison." If the amount was sizable, up to ten years in prison.

The act of 1953 passed to protect customers in retail and wholesale trade carried its vigilance to the point of subjecting those who hoarded petty goods to ten years in prison. The act prescribed sentences for crimes it could not yet predict, that is, "other acts that could destabilize the market."

One could construe the significance of an activity in terms of its severity as a crime by the number of years in jail one could get for it. The areas of life not subject to any punishment became ever fewer: unlawful emigration closed in degree of enormity with common assault; undeclared dollar wealth crept toward equality with murder.

Beginning on September 10, 1956 absenteeism ceased to be criminal. Sabotage was thereafter construed as directed to harm the state, not merely as before, say, "misappropriating [public] ball bearings (from work) for private use." Crimes against an abstract "common good" were no longer rated so harshly, while crimes against other human beings were weighed with increasing severity. The worst period of Stalinism had passed, but the way people lived was subject to more stringent regulation. Vagrancy and brewing alcohol at home rose in the hierarchy of offenses. Special legislation passed against such conduct carried a maximum penalty of five years in jail.

From 1958 on, the greatest menace to the state economy was deemed to come from those who worked for it. Breaking into a factory was treated no more or less seriously than before. But stealing the same things from inside could result in a life sentence.

The act of January 21, 1958 intensified the protection of the State, and only the State, against depredation. Political organizations and parties were considered public property. Judges were instructed: "For example, property of a political party; a party wing or an association, although actually not public property, is understood by this act as public, since such organizations fulfill public functions." It "was understood" that to offend the Party was comparable to offending the common good. A loss was considered large when it exceeded first 100,000 złoty, later 200,000 złoty. (The average monthly salary was then about 3,000 złoty.) The moral aspect was, however, more important—whether the crime created difficulties in fulfilling the central economic plan.

Theoretically, economic life was based on *not* making a profit. The act of protecting a customer's rights made a villain out of a spiv or a "speculator"—a wheeler-dealer selling goods for personal benefit. The biggest crime a retailer could commit was "to sell goods with the intention of further sale for profit." Polish citizens were also "stained" by getting involved in business with foreigners, and for this could receive three years in prison. Tax evasion was also punishable with three years and a fine of up to a million złoty. As a result, the only legal way to run a business was to bankrupt it.

It was still far more blessed to be poor and sick than rich and healthy. From 1960 on, those who "possess prohibited foreign currency on the territory of Poland" got off with a mere two years or less in prison. Dealing in foreign currency, platinum or gold was punishable with three years in prison and a fine of up to a million złoty, as was taking hard currency out of the country. Smuggling out złoty was punishable only with a fine.

On April 19, 1969, all crimes were reevaluated without specific prompting by political events. The new code defined the most contemptible crimes as being those against the basic political interests of the Polish People's Republic.

First in order and in gravity was treason, an attempt to overthrow the system by force. Previously, to become a spy one had to seek to betray a state secret. This was no longer necessary. Judicial instructions conceded, however, that a foreign press agency was not an intelligence operation, for "its purpose is to gather information, but with the intention of making it known to public opinion."

The code became stricter in that the number of people considered as personifying the state increased. It became a serious crime "to assault a public functionary or a political activist." It could not, of course, be explicitly written in the code that these protections covered only Communist Party activists. But that, of course, is just what the statute meant. In 1973 the instruction covering the article on assault against a public functionary or a political activist was elaborated by this rider: "The article also applies to political activists considering the fact that the word 'functionary' does not include persons who do not take any of the enumerated positions but whose role in the state is outstanding, such as local Communist Party committee officers." Later commentaries bring drivers in the state bus company within the category of functionaries. To assault any such person was to commit a crime "against the basic political interests of the Polish People's Republic."

Economic sabotage was treated with somewhat less severity. Only acts of "larger significance" qualified, said the instruction. "It would not be considered an act of sabotage (but rather an ordinary crime or not a crime at all) if a hairdresser closed his shop (the only one in town), even if his intention was to foster an atmosphere of general discontent."

All crimes committed against an "allied country" were treated identically as if committed against the Polish People's Republic. An allied country, the code elaborated, was a socialist country—the first time in the history of the Polish People's Republic the code entertained the notion of a "socialist state," by which, however, was understood only the countries belonging to the Soviet bloc.

From 1969 on, counterfeiting was no longer punishable with death, but at most with 25 years behind bars. The crime of possessing unlicensed weapons fell most radically of all in status, from a capital offense down to five years, the provision itself being demoted to the final article of the code.

Those who wanted to engage in racketeering should have done so before 1969 when, legally speaking, it made the big time. The judicial instructions explained that "as a result of relatively numerous swindles in which employees of state enterprises (in catering, the meat trade, leather tanning) have embezzled funds, such a crime is introduced into the code under its own head, as a crime not only against property but also a crime against the basic economic interests of the Polish People's Republic." It was particularly important not to get involved in such activities in a state enterprise, which could earn one 25 years in prison and especially not to be one of the organizers for whom the death penalty was lurking, though rarely enforced. Burglary carried a much lower opportunity cost.

Those planning to smuggle something across the border should choose only one partner. Three people make it a smuggling scandal punishable by 25 years in prison.

Until 1982, it was wise not to steal property worth more than 100,000 złoty, (300,000 złoty after inflation began to bite). One still should not kill anyone, but if one really must, better to do so only "under the influence of strong emotions" to get a lighter sentence.

Generally speaking, prospective criminals were better off committing unprecedented outrages: the severity of sentence was related to the frequency of the crime.

It did not pay to be caught in speculation after 1981, when the authorities' fear that people would speculate in scarce goods and sell them at much higher prices than those set by the state greatly altered the application of the law. Matters that had previously gone unprosecuted—such as selling goods without a proper license, or concealing goods from customers for one's own private exchange or speculation (resale for higher than official prices), could send offenders to prison for two years. A new category of crime appeared: defrauding the state by taking undue ration cards—and it carried up to five years in prison.

When martial law was declared on December 13, 1981, new laws were introduced as of December 12. One could no longer belong to the organization one legally had belonged to before. The laws mandated "up to three years in prison for a member of an organization or trade union [Solidarity, of course] whose activity has been suspended, who does not cease his participation in this sort of activity." Those who wished to take part in a strike had better not do so as organizers.

The proclamation of martial law assumed that disseminating "false" information—and false was a matter of the state's judgment—could undermine the defense of the Polish People's Republic. It became a crime to incite public unrest. Across the board, every crime became more serious. There were only three penalties for more than 90 crimes: court martial with death, 25 years in prison, or more than three years.

These penalties endured only briefly. The acts pertaining to them were in effect for a year, then forgotten, and finally repealed when martial law was lifted, although the Trade Union Act of 1982 providing prison sentences for the organizers of illegal strikes remained.

Under martial law in 1982 the legal code was changed, mandating that crime had to be paid for with ever larger fines: for 1,000 złoty—5,000 złoty, for 5,000 złoty—20,000 złoty, for 200,000 złoty—600,000 złoty.[8]

Still, the martial law authorities considered the legal code too light and proclaimed a farewell special statute in 1985 that remained in effect until 1988. If one stole goods, the fine was exactly the amount of the stolen goods. If one speculated, the fine was just twice the value of the goods sold. If one accepted a bribe, the fine was ten times the amount extorted. . . .

NOTES

1. According to the latter definition, Poland's allies would have included the United States, Great Britain, and France.

2. The abridged legal code was that part of the prewar code incorporated into the postwar judicial system. The code enacted in 1945 was termed "abridged" because intended to be provisional. However, a code to replace it was enacted only in 1969.

3. The term "gang" ("*banda*") was used by the communist state in the 1940s in reference to anticommunist resistance groups following the war. This was how later political resistance became classified as criminal. The law was conceived to meet all eventualities and to deal with all possible forms of gathering that could present a threat to the state.

4. "Dishonest swindling" ("*nieuczciwe machinacje*") sounds as strange in Polish as in English because it is tautological, far from ordinary legal terminology and conjures up images of street speculation.

5. So-called social property (*własność społeczna*), all "social enterprises," was de facto state property.

6. Like "social property," "public enterprises and services" were de facto state property.

7. Again, these terms are somewhat ambiguous, not precisely specifying an activity but alluding to an entire range of activities, thereby conferring considerable discretion upon the court.

8. Curiously, the graver the crime, the less proportionately was the penalty intensified.

PART II

Enterprising Inner Circles

Introduction

In 1991 the explosion of non-capital-forming *handel* of the kind that
Kazimierz Wyka describes is the most dynamic phenomenon in the
Polish economy. In the lax climate of deregulation, a backlash
against the entanglements of communist intervention, the sidewalks
of cities and towns are choked with freelance traders selling everything from bananas to cosmetics to bathroom fixtures. Residents of
a Warsaw street overwhelmed by farmers hawking chickens and
beef cuts out of trucks—in the summer heat without government
inspection—could not find administrative relief at any level.

Handel is not only a Polish problem. From Berlin to Stockholm
to Lvov, Polish peddlers strain their country's relations with its
neighbors. Singer Janet Jackson canceled her summer 1990 promotional tour to Poland because "pirate cassettes" of her music—
mass-produced in violation of international copyright agreements—
sold thousands of copies not only on Polish streets but also in Swe-
den.

These traders—mostly workers, small-town residents, farmers,
and young adults—have expanded their activities and urged their
legalization both as a ticket to survival and as a libertarian remedy
for the nation's economic ills. The traders' economic clout has transformed them into a political force. They comprise that one-fourth
of the voters who cast ballots for the Canadian businessman
Stanisław Tymiński, who suddenly appeared out of 20 years' ex-
patriation to run for president in late 1990, with the aim of toppling
Poland's prime minister, and wrenching many of Lech Wałęsa's potential supporters away from him. Tymiński might have come from
nowhere, but not so these workers, small-town residents, and farmers, the object of three intense studies in the 1980s by our contributors.

As Wojciech Pawlik, sociologist at Warsaw University's Institute
of Applied Social Sciences notes, people "arranged" goods, services,

and information during the scarcity-ridden early 1980s, simply to make ends meet.[1]

Today, finagling may no longer be necessary to buy premium meat, well-made shoes, or furniture. Yet for a family in need of an apartment, an unemployed person looking for work or to emigrate to Chicago, a businessman wanting information, suppliers, or simply to get started, and those needing speedy outcomes to any number of administrative matters, "arranging" remains the way of life. The problem-solving networks joining community to the state economy and bureaucracy, especially visible during the shortage-ridden 1980s, have not dissolved. Change will entail more than eliminating shortages or introducing "bureaucratic rationality": people accustomed to turning to their friends and acquaintances for help are not inclined to operate otherwise, even when "otherwise" becomes theoretically possible.

Despite the Poles' inclination toward *handel* and taking matters into their own hands, for 45 years they were trained to be beneficiaries of the state. With Lech Wałęsa at the helm in 1980–81, Solidarity fought for workers' rights and the implementation of promises made by the socialist order—guaranteed employment, subsidized health care, housing, and social security. Public opinion surveys show how many Poles still endorse these values.[2]

One feature of socialist work was the informal benefits derived from the workplace. Elżbieta Firlit and Jerzy Chłopecki, sociologists in the city of Rzeszów, show how often workers treat their jobs as a basis to qualify for social insurance benefits and as sources of orders and free materials. Continuous interaction is this system's heartbeat, which also works to "democratize" a class-bound, hierarchical society: the less important people gain standing; the prominent must get off their pedestals. Reciprocal favors between workers help to humanize and "integrate" the life of work.

But like so much of Polish life, attitudes toward work and its informal earnings are being thrown into uncertainty. Greater discipline may be introduced and thus low-paid state workers, if they still have their jobs after plant closings and consolidations, may not be able to continue to supplement their earnings through illegal "side jobs."

So, in addition to the shattering of socialist guarantees and the drop in earnings relative to prices, workers may no longer be able to fall back on the old standby informal economy. The informal activities so widespread during the 1980s are becoming a political football in the 1990s. Workers are frustrated—a frustration that, as Stanisław Tymiński demonstrated, can be skillfully tapped. More than 50 percent of all manual workers who voted cast ballots for Tymiński in 1990's presidential election, while only 30 percent supported Lech Wałęsa, who in 1980 had emerged as the guardian of the working class.

Small private farmers, too, have been at odds with the government, which they blame for its ill-executed farm policies of decontrolling prices and raising taxes. Farmers have found beef production for state distribution centers unprofitable, reports Joanna Śmigielska, a sociologist at the Institute of Applied Social Sciences, preferring to bypass the centers and any middlemen via direct sales.

Profound rural dissatisfaction has issued in protests, including a sit-in at the Ministry of Agriculture, where farmers bitterly denounced the post-Communist government ("Is this what we fought the Communists for?") as a fundamentally urban movement engaged in exacerbating the traditional Polish rift of city and countryside. What began with the occupation of the ministry has so far crested in fervent opposition to Solidarity's economic programs and authority and support for Stanisław Tymiński.

Ironically, Solidarity's original constituents, who poured their energies into the movement in 1980, sometimes at the risk of their lives, may, at least in the short run, be the biggest losers in the Solidarity-inspired reforms of the 1990s.

NOTES

1. The government's Central Statistical Office estimated that, in 1987, the scale of private, unregistered profit-making activity was about 1.9 billion złoty, or 25 percent of people's total income. This estimate does not include informal exchanges of goods and services among friends, and much of the hard currency turnover. Some $2 billion was held in private accounts, and total private hard currency reserves were estimated at between $4 and $6 billion.

2. Interviews with Stanisław Kwiatkowski, head of CEBOS, the government's public opinion research institute, and his colleague, Piotr Kwiatkowski, 1989 and 1990.

3

Intimate Commerce

WOJCIECH PAWLIK

> The economic bases that corrupted morality under the
> Occupation still largely survive, and unfortunately, in
> many cases will continue. These bases resulted from
> the discrepancy between the actual standard of living,
> people's financial needs, and the actual income of in-
> dustrial and office workers. The discrepancy continues,
> and it is clear that rather than eradicate the practices
> of the Occupation, the new system often favors them
> and will continue to do so.
>
> —Kazimierz Wyka, 1945

In the early 1980s shortages of basic goods encouraged an array of
unplanned secondary processes that resonated throughout social
relationships. Shortages were by no means unknown in Poland, but
their pervasiveness through the 1980s encouraged all kinds of
"quasi-legal" activities: people stepped up trading of professional
services, scarce goods, and information about where and through
whom to get them, and developed personalized exchange relations
with clerks and bureaucrats. Social conventions changed: to offer
soap, stockings, chocolates, and even "monetary gratuities" became
customary in situations in which, not many years earlier, flowers
would have sufficed.

In studying a small town of about 15,000 residents from 1982 to
1984, I took part in its everyday humdrum. I grew up in a small
town myself and eased into community activities to the extent that
I was able to tape interviews without creating undue suspicion. The
town, which shall remain anonymous, is accessible by bus and elec-
tric tram from a provincial capital. The townspeople I came to know

are employed primarily in small factories and service enterprises located in the community or nearby city. Most residents have completed primary or secondary vocational school. The men most often work in factories, the women in administrative or service occupations, or as housewives.

I was impressed with how almost everyone participates in the informal exchange of goods and services: a multiplicity of imprecise and ambiguous expressions refer to these transactions.[1] Their equivocalness is actually a functional advantage: it enables people to avoid elucidating how they get scarce goods and services. The terms *wynosić*—"to lift" (literally "to take out")—and *kombinować*—to scheme up an ingenious, often illegal solution involving what outsiders might define as theft—by no means imply criminal behavior. Not so *kradzież*—"theft."

Innumerable expressions mask possibly shady or even illegal deals: *załatwić coś*—"to arrange something"; *pogadać z kimś*—"to chat with someone" in order to work something out; *coś przynieść*—"to take something" from the workplace; *zrewanżować się*—"to return a favor"; *odwdzięczyć się*—"to return thanks" by reciprocating a favor; *opić coś* "to drink something over" with someone in order to arrange something; and *przyswoić sobie*—"to make something belong to one" so that one can lift it.

Of course, people use these terms to talk about their own activities. When the speaker is the object of such transactions, the same activity might be described as swindle, trickery, theft, and the like.

Most workplaces offer opportunities for income beyond formal salary. It is a widespread and deep conviction that wherever one works, in a factory, school, or office, there inevitably is a sphere within which one can *kombinować*. Not only can one solve problems in this sphere, but one's "accomplices" in such problem-solving also can achieve their own, often illegal, remunerations.

Different workplaces offer varying opportunities for exchange. As one informant, a 32-year-old private store manager, put it: "I live according to one assumption—that today you can't 'arrange' ['*załatwić*'][2] anything without gifts, money, and so on. In Poland this is the one law of the universe."

A 25-year-old foreman observed: "Everyone has some 'in' ['*dojście*'][3] somewhere, regardless of his occupation. One has more, another has less. Everyone 'takes' [bribes], except for fish [ruling elite]."

A 30-year-old mechanic added, "In every trade there's an opportunity [to make money on the side]. If you can't steal, then you can take bribes. Even the director, who doesn't trouble himself with production, steals: he 'arranges' something for someone, 'takes' from him in return and this is really stealing from him. Maybe that is an even worse crime than stealing from society, since society as a whole gets robbed [by the Communist state]. But that director robs an individual."

For the townspeople, the "perks" tied to a particular occupation are as important as the salary itself in evaluating its desirability. Services, stores, and the state's bureaucracy and regulatory agencies often provide opportunities for receiving "gifts" and bribes. Opportunities for "dealing in" merchandise produced at the workplace and rendering informal services are available to mechanics, drivers, and construction workers. It is beneficial to have such professional skills as those of physicians, nurses, and dentists, as such skills provide one with access to scarce and attractive goods and services.

My informants divide their occupations into those in which one "can earn" *money additional to one's formal salary* and those in which one can not.

For townspeople looking for work or thinking about changing jobs, their ability to earn additional income in a prospective job figures prominently in their decision. Often people turn down a position involving a much more attractive formal salary because the illegal income tied to their current employment far surpasses the visible increase. Many drivers pass up the opportunity to be foremen to avoid the additional responsibilities that would preclude "side activities." Drivers supplement their incomes by trading gasoline on the side. The power to dispose of such assets is invaluable in the network of unacknowledged trade and an important factor in keeping certain workers, poorly paid on the books, on the job, and sometimes even in keeping them from retiring.

People believe that everywhere, in every situation, it is possible to earn a little extra "on the side." This assumption is so widespread that they include such earnings when calculating their "real" salaries. Among workers employed on a piecework basis, such earnings attain a normative status. Among low-paid workers subject to forced lay-offs and work stoppages (due to lack of materials or resources needed to continue production), non-legal earnings are regarded as a regular part of salary, and calculated into the household budget as a simple necessity.

"When I'm paid less," says a 26-year-old worker, "I go to work on the side or the entire work crew earns extra. Otherwise I couldn't survive. I treat this as part of the salary that I have to bring home to keep the family going. As for *fucha*,[4] that's when I don't take money but vodka instead. That's become the custom, vodka as pay for side work."

Strictly speaking, "*fucha*" is an informal earning that exceeds the minimum needed to maintain one's family, and that the worker may feel entitled to keep for himself.

Townspeople's daily experience reinforces their sense of the prevalence of informal dealing; many are in a position to offer a service, access to which often involves violating regulations. Daily involvement with such activity not only fosters the sense that such transactions are all-pervasive, it also weakens disapproval of them, particularly if they are one's own.

By the same token, people perceive that *kombinować* works to lower society's moral standards. Over and over again one hears "we all are robbing Poland." Nevertheless, people lubricate their activities with a handy supply of euphemistic idioms that soften the ethical and legal appraisal of a given activity and dilute its negative connotations. They tend to rationalize their own activities in practical, worldly terms: "After all, you can't survive on just your salary," or "You have to do what others do. You can't stand out from the crowd."

This informal way of doing things acquires an objective reality; it becomes, ethnographically speaking, one of the elements of the natural world, just as common as talking, going to mass on Sunday, or watching television. Although complaining about dishonest bureaucrats or poor television programs (since there are only two television stations and program selection is limited), townspeople nevertheless consider it natural to enter into exchange relations with the same bureaucrats or to watch an inferior program.

The residents of a street slated to have their road paved feared the work would be put off indefinitely, so they formed a committee to collect money from fellow residents. They then delivered the "gift"—vodka and cash—to the construction workers and the bureaucrats who would decide when the project would begin. Although most residents resented this "hustling," they nevertheless acknowledged that it was the only effective way to accomplish the task. Interestingly, they were more contemptuous of neighbors who were reluctant or slow to pay their share toward the common venture than they were toward the workers and bureaucrats. Residents accused their delinquent neighbors of shirking responsibility—of not living in the real world.

The "naturalness" of such informal activity is so taken for granted that giving up or turning down standard customary gratuities elicits more amazement than accepting them. How "normal" people regard this activity is indicated in how state television, praising state services, suggests that patients will be admitted to hospitals without patronage, regardless of who they know, and that nurses and physicians actually will turn down patients' offers of money and gifts.

The Switchboard

Most transactions are not realized through occasional and incidental contacts, but within the more stable *środowisko*. The *środowisko* encompasses some 20 to 30 individuals (sometimes more) who maintain frequent social contact and are brought together by familial and friendship ties. The *środowisko* is fundamentally about social life; daily encounters cement the relationships that form the backbone of each group of "ours" (*"swoi"*).

Simple proximity facilitates many of these contacts: brief meetings in the street while returning from shopping or work encourage a continual updating of information about circle members' health and domestic and financial situations, while exchanging the latest news about what may be purchased, from whom, and for how much.

A complex web of family and social ties is thereby transformed into an efficient switchboard. News of an offer or a request for goods or services goes around the *środowisko* within a few days, and can most often be dealt with by "one of ours" right away. When people say "the matter remains within the family," they mean the family will "take care of" the problem—that is, in that particular instance they do not need the help of others in the *środowisko*. If not, then the information begins to spiral outward, the circle of acquaintances expanding as far as it takes to locate someone willing to *załatwić* the issue at hand.

Although all *środowisko* members engage in such activities, some do so more frequently than others because their occupations provide access to goods or services constantly in demand. This also applies to incoming information: certain individuals, or even homes, are permanent communication channels. They have the best knowledge of who can do what, and let others in on selected information "in a disinterested manner"—without necessarily expecting something in return. They thus serve as middlemen to the whole *środowisko*'s ongoing search for services and goods.

I suspect that the most important factors determining an individual's position in the *środowisko*'s communication structure are such personal qualities as the capacity to mediate interactions that are at once familial, social, and commercial in character. Adept players maintain "open houses" with an intimate, not purely commercial atmosphere. Guests drop by at any time of the day or night without needing to forewarn the host. They chat with everyone present, exchange information, and if an opportunity arises, "arrange" a matter.

Important gathering places other than private homes, of neighborhood rather than family character, are private businesses and service centers. One initiates business transactions while sitting in the back room; it is also there that one "drinks to a deal" to finalize it. Such business toasts are usually given by and among men. Between close friends and relatives, the ritual of toasting the deal, paid for by its beneficiary, is the *only* acceptable way to ratify a favor. But between people separated by more distance, toasting is independent of material and financial reciprocity. In any case, drinking together is a "stamp of approval," a symbolic gesture that seals trust and transaction.

For many townspeople, especially those who are single, divorced, or in difficult family situations, these centers of private activity also function as a second home. Their proprietors are natural middlemen. Well-acquainted with town life, they frequent the "open houses," facilitate the flow of information, and arrange many transactions.

Little is kept secret; interaction is continuous. Information circulates about participants in transactions, their individual strengths, and the rates and rules of the informal trading game. Townspeople know not only what can be "arranged" and with whom, but also manage to retain a personal flavor when entering into dealings with "strangers." These encounters come about not through chance, but through references from mutual acquaintances.

"If a customer I don't know approaches me," a 26-year-old saleswoman in a clothing store told me, "I immediately reject the proposition because I know the danger. You simply have to have your own trusted people, and this happens on the principle that your acquaintance sends his acquaintance, because it's known that in such a *środowisko* everyone knows everyone else. So things can be 'arranged,' but only among those you trust."

From the strict legal point of view, there is no difference between a "thief" and one who "takes something" home from work. But common usage makes a marked distinction. The idea of thievery never applies to public and state property—only to private property. Employees "take away" goods of little value from the workplace without concealment and even with the foreman or manager's knowledge. But one can never "take away" something from a private home, even a stranger's. This would be theft.

The unwritten principle of "disinterestedness" governs relations in the *środowisko*. This means that it is improper for one to accept from members of one's circle money for goods "lifted" from the workplace if the goods are of little commercial value or less than the official market price. Given the constant circulation of reciprocally rendered services, these little generosities at the collective expense come around to each individual, and their cost should rather be counted as profit which could have been gained from dealing with "strangers." This cost is repaid through services and the shared consumption of certain donations.

For example, a driver offers his relatives the fish, fruit, or preserves that he transports and, in return, is invited to a meal at which fried fish or jelly doughnuts are the main attraction. Clearly, reciprocity in rendering services is not the conscious motive for such activity. Although townspeople emphasize the importance of this principle, the dominant motive in day-to-day activity is disinterested goodwill, based on offering those goods and services available within "our" own professional competence to "one of ours."

"You don't take money from your family," says a 29-year-old driver in a state enterprise. "It makes you feel foolish. You work here, so you have enough of something, more than enough, so you give it to people you care about, like the director, the mechanic, those you depend on, and the rest you cram into the so-called free market."

Because there is little respect for public or state property, and because security at workplaces is ineffective, workers "lift" ["*wynosić*"]—albeit in individually small quantities—nearly everything that can be of any use to them or "ours," that is, most of the merchandise and services available in their workplaces. Such activity generally occurs in workplaces engaged in manufacture or reprocessing. I was unable to confirm cases of pilfering in retail enterprises. In the latter case, workers also lifted merchandise, but always after first paying for it, and then usually offered it at the same or minimally higher price to family members or friends. One can well imagine that in 1982 the list of such scarce items was very long.

Within the circle, exchange is based on the reciprocal rendering of services, characterized by lack of concern for financial gain. Exchange with strangers more often involves some calculation of profit and the offering of different forms of service. While exchange within the circle generally revolves around small household matters, transactions with strangers often entail valuable goods and atypical services. Although conducted relatively openly, such transactions must nevertheless be cloaked in greater confidentiality than the preceding forms. The warehouse worker selling paint and solvents, the clerk accepting bribes thereby enabling someone to purchase scarce merchandise, and on down along an almost infinite line of participants, often take advantage of the brokerage of family and friends. The transactions themselves, however, are concealed from the eyes of the curious, becoming an open secret about which little is said. This is because such deals often involve criminal activity, and the townspeople so engaged know this.

Individuals able to dispense desirable services on a steady basis frequently prefer to enter into exchange relations with "others" than with members of their own circle. This is at least in part because, as we have already seen, exchange does not pay off equally well for all, so that for some members it is more worthwhile to conduct a few lucrative exchanges with strangers than innumerable profitless "disinterested" transactions with "one of ours." A store employee, therefore, prefers to sell shoes or clothing to strangers, since he thereby realizes a greater immediate profit than when he exchanges with a group member. Similarly, the owner of dollars or *bony*[5] is more inclined to seek buyers among distant acquaintances than among "his own," since he fears that should he offer them to his circle at free market prices, he will be accused of seeking to "make money off his family."

Despite this, a certain portion of the services rendered to members of the *środowisko* is treated as an obligation. If one prefers to deal with strangers, one conceals such transactions from members of one's *środowisko*: they would be displeased. A relative equilibrium in relations is therefore a necessary condition to keep "disinterested"

exchange at concert pitch. Too great an imbalance in this respect
leads to valuable objects being discharged into the world of the free
market through safety valves by which privileged individuals re-
move a portion of their services from circulation within the *środowisko*. Relatively less well-placed *środowisko* members are conscious
of this and therefore try not to abuse the "disinterested" services
offered them and frequently express their gratitude for such services.
"I benefit from this," explains one 32-year-old technician, "but I
can't pay them back with some other marketable merchandise. I can at most pay with regular money. So only I profit from
this, and they in reality are losing, because if they traded their merchandise elsewhere with someone else, they might make more
on it."

The Store as a Last Resort

Another issue arises with respect to disinterestedness which, as
we have seen, is mandatory in relations within the *środowisko*. The
possibility of obtaining certain services gratis within the circle leads
townspeople to attempt to meet their needs in this manner before
turning to formal means. If one therefore needs certain kinds of food
or services, one first tries to acquire them for free or cheaply from
within the *środowisko*, or lift them from work oneself. Only when
such opportunities do not exist does one actually try to buy them
in a store. Taking into account the great number of things unavailable
in retail stores, it is easy to understand the economic pressure that
leads townspeople down these at first glance time-consuming paths.
Townspeople's inclination to seek bargains and opportunities grad-
ually institutionalizes itself, and many prefer these means over official ones, even if the latter method is intermittently cheaper and
more time-efficient.

An interesting dialectic develops: on the one hand, townspeople
invest effort in justifying their own behavior—"If these screws and
this cement were in the store, then certainly no one would lift them
at work." On the other hand, they invest energy in searching for
informal access to goods and services that are available in the most
completely legal manner. The dialectic of this process is interesting
because the majority of my informants tended to see it as moving
in one direction only (pointing to the system as a kind of "original
sin"), while they perceive their own activity at worst as a factor

contributing to the dysfunction of an already dysfunctional economic system. This mechanism tends to reduce the psychological tensions arising from the contradiction between one's own activities and one's judgment of it, and facilitates "getting used to" the activities.

Although exchange within the *środowisko* is generally free of financial considerations, deals of considerable commercial value nevertheless require that one "reciprocate by giving a gift," most often by toasting the deal's success. The cost of this return gift often approaches and even exceeds the value of the services received. Treating those involved to vodka is also the accepted repayment for small but frequently rendered services. This method of balancing accounts encourages the exchange of services within the circle, deters its members from the temptation to deal with strangers, and at the same time intensifies group bonds. Quite obviously, drinking fulfills an entirely different function in transactions with strangers. It is a customary activity that emphasizes the personal character of an exchange, but because of its occasional nature, does not necessarily create more lasting social ties. Nevertheless, drinking is how they often begin.

The Budget Fight: Fashion or Booze?

The worlds of women and men differ in the division of household labor, the type of employment, and also in the division of funds. "Side jobs" and *boki* belong to the men, while household funds are managed by the women. Consequently, a large portion of the informal income is spent on men's meetings, the cost of which does not usually infringe on the household budget, assuming, of course, that such meetings are not too frequent.

Those in the *środowisko* can gauge the approximate magnitude of income acquired through informal activities. Nevertheless, the precise amount is jealously guarded by the individual, who considers it his personal capital, or *boki*, so-called "pocket money" earned under the table. The household budget is most often the responsibility of mothers and wives, whose objectives differ from the husband's. Family members play an intricate game: the husband shields as much of the additional income as possible for personal use; the wife tries to increase the size of the household budget.

"I give everything to my wife," boasted a 27-year-old driver. "For myself only scraps, that is, various little moving jobs. For example,

Mrs. Zosia asks me to move a sofa from one place to another. On the other hand, I also get money from selling gasoline from my truck that I take from my job, and from driving passengers I pick up in it [many truck drivers supplement the chronic deficiency of taxis]. All *this* goes for my amusements, that is for cigarettes, for some little treats. The wife doesn't know about this *boki* [side income]. Oh, she knows it exists and where it comes from. But how many jobs, and how much, she doesn't know."

Who calls the shots in the family determines one's reputation among family and *środowisko* members, and at the workplace: those who devote all or most of their additional income to the home or to family savings acquire a reputation within the extended family as good providers. Yet among co-workers their status is low; they are called henpecked husbands.

In many families *boki* in its entirety is allocated for collective family needs. Women, who generally have fewer opportunities to earn such *boki*, almost invariably incorporate it into the household budget. Sometimes, if the financial situation permits, the wife spends it to enhance her wardrobe or home furnishings. It happens just as often that at least part of this income evades family control and is consumed as alcohol.

However, the high level of alcohol consumption by men is not a direct drain on the household budget. The rise in the price of alcohol is at least partly offset by the increase in the number and prices of informal services. With the exception of family and social get-togethers financed from the household budget, the majority of so-called men's meetings over vodka are financed from *boki* that plays no part in household finances. This can partly be explained by the small-town patterns of leisure activity. Women and men spend the majority of their time in the company of their own gender. According to a 28-year-old driver:

> Drivers drink, a great number drink and amuse themselves with the money they make on the side, but many also bring the money home in the proper way, but again, it's all from stolen goods. So drivers drink up the extra money, but they hand over their salary to their wife—to the penny [even showing the pay slip that blue-collar workers get] to keep her from thinking that they're spending their salary.

The contradiction here is that goods and services sought for household use are paid for out of household funds, managed by women from the principal portion of family earnings, and therefore in the last analysis, "nest eggs" arise at least in part as monies transferred from specific household budgets, managed by women, to personal funds, controlled by and egoistically consumed by men. I stress "in part" because a good portion of these incomes arises from funds put into circulation by self-employed workers (taxi drivers, mechanics, and artisans purchasing gas and raw materials from state enterprises). Such funds constitute investment capital, so to speak, connected to their professional activities. Therefore, goods and services stolen from enterprises and sold to private households and individuals do not directly increase, on balance, the actual incomes of the majority of townspeople. The monies realized are only in part saved or used to augment one's own household possessions, while a significant portion goes for alcohol and thus ends up in the state's tax coffers. (It is estimated that 10 to 15 percent of the state budget is financed through vodka taxes.)

Mutual Theft

In people's consciousness, there is no strict distinction between state coffers and those of individual state-run enterprises. Hence the common stereotype that reduces the relations we have described to a competitive zero-sum relationship: "The State robs me, I rob the State, and it all comes out even." Yet a more adequate scheme would involve five "spheres" among which money and merchandise circulate: the sphere of state property, belonging to state enterprises; the sphere of money and merchandise acquired from the illegal sale of appropriated goods and services; two spheres of recipients, "one of ours" and "others," forming a consumers' market and leading to the creation of illegal incomes; and finally, the state's coffers, into which a portion of these incomes, as a result of these government policies, is deposited.

The laws governing the informal circulation of goods and services do not, however, operate uniformly, and vary with the type of social ties linking participants, their needs, the type of merchandise at issue and opportunities for acquiring it. Relations within one's family and środowisko are frequently described as "altruistic," proportionate to the degree of intensity of social bonds. But profit is the basis of deals with "strangers," who aspire to negotiate the highest possible payment. Here the traditional term "handel" is appropriate. The latter type of exchange establishes and nourishes social bonds, which are created and strengthened through unceasing material exchanges and symbolic offerings, whose principle is their participants' deliberately incomplete formalization of mutual responsibilities.

Exchange interactions among "ours" occur according to this very principle—that is, they are subject to the rule of reciprocity, so that exchange equivalence is based not only on marketable value and the objective exchange of goods, but incorporates a symbolic and subjective component of reward such as gratitude. In addition to its purely practical function, an unintentional, hidden function of this type of incompletely defined interaction is the integration of one's *środowisko*. Exchange contributes to a significant "warming" of relations within the circle, as daily collaboration in resolving everyday problems widens the realm of cooperation to areas of life beyond the economic.

Daily collaboration and the network of social ties built within it are not, however, as simple a category of phenomena as might at first appear. For beyond that behavior which the townspeople discuss using the deliberately imprecise euphemisms described earlier and through which they become aware of the mutual dependence of their own actions and those of their partners, is an entire realm of activity not subject to this principle, or at least not perceived in these categories by the actors. This is behavior toward one's closest relations, sometimes toward one's friends, which townspeople describe as disinterested assistance, and also behavior that they define as fulfilling moral responsibilities toward those close to one.

Although I usually knew all parties to transactions in the town I studied, I often found it difficult to judge the value of an informant's declaration of altruism in offering certain items to a relative or neighbor.

The ambiguity of the participants' intentions is heightened by the use of conventional expressions that emphasize the noncompulsory nature of the transaction, be it a question of goods or even money. Phrases deprecating the financial value of a gift and expanding on its affective aspects may reflect the actual motivation of the giver but also may mask his interests and intentions. Such an approach facilitates a safe retreat under the guise of having misunderstood intentions, or, if the offer has been accepted, permits continuation of the transaction while retaining all the verbal pretenses of its properness.

The following excerpt from a 26-year-old saleswoman illustrates this manner of communicating mutual expectations:

I say that I'm from Doctor So-and-So, and that I'd very much like my child to be operated on, and that I'll certainly repay the favor. When later I bring him a bottle of cognac and flowers, and probably also something from a clothing store, he acts a little reluctant for the sake of principle. I say, "I wanted to thank you," and he replies. "No, I thank you, I did this purely as a favor, I did it for T's sake." To which I reply, "No, this is simply my way of expressing my appreciation." From experience, I know that I have to give, because if not, my child won't get the surgery he needs.

In colloquial language, customary expressions such as "this is of great concern to me" imply almost explicitly that "if you arrange something for me, I'll provide something in return for you." Saying "really, it's nothing" or "it's a trifle" is a safe way of initiating and continuing interactions. But words alone do not reveal the hidden meaning of the interaction. Gestures, intonation, and other discreet means of communication facilitate interpretation and permit one to gauge one's partner's offerings and expectations.

If one accepts an exchange partner's assurances that his intentions are "disinterested," one has a convenient alibi for one's own behavior. Many interactions are undertaken and continued precisely because the contradiction in defining the situation is never realized, or at least never made explicit. The "alibi" suggested by the initiator diminishes any conceivable moral inconsistency and allows one to remain convinced of the disinterestedness of one's own behavior. Only a disturbance of the interaction, for example, unfulfilled expectations consequent upon accepting a gift, reveals the concealed rules governing the interaction.

In explaining the motivation for their own actions, especially with respect to close relatives, people readily invoke altruism and disinterestedness. But in describing the activities of others, they more often employ a lexicon of motives in which gratitude is mixed with other concealed interests. Many interviewees find it difficult to fully accept a disinterested offer and impute to their exchange partners motives that may have been entirely unrelated to their actions. Perceiving one's actions as "reciprocating" for past favors, or as intended to create an appropriate climate for later approaching someone with a proposition (what is known as "working a guy"—to do everything possible to make him "one of ours" ["swoi"] in order to get something from him), allows one to avoid the unpleasant feeling that one is someone's debtor, and to feel of equal worth as a partner in an interaction.

As an illustration of how complex and imaginative the process of "explaining" such activity can be, consider the experience of this 36-year-old construction technician.

> I arrive just as he [the proprietor of a kiosk, that is, a vendor of newspapers, cigarettes, and small household items] has just put out his newspaper. No queue. I take some papers, walk inside, look to see what he has, shampoo, laundry detergent, razor blades or what, and say: "Please sir, might I?"
> "Certainly, no problem, just take what you want, and for nothing."
> All the time I'm waiting to hear what he's going to want from me, whether I'll be able to take care of something for him. There's some kind of debt of gratitude I've got to him. Stupid business, the guy doesn't want anything, that is, doesn't suggest that I do anything for him, that is, to the extent I might be able to. But a person has that debt of gratitude. I don't know, finally I put up his kiosk for him. I happen to have the ladder with me, and they'd set his kiosk on the bare ground, so he asked if I could lend him the ladder for a bit to pull up his kiosk a little and stick some boards under it . . . but the whole thing just took 15 minutes!

The question, "Why is he doing it?" which participants ask themselves in the course of their mutual contacts, aims not only at discovering the reasons inclining someone toward a given action. It also is another form of the skeptical query, "What's in it for him?"

Reciprocity is most often understood as a payback for past services; its significance is to express gratitude and the willingness to continue interacting in the future. The act of expressing gratitude through reciprocity may be an incidental, short-lived interaction, or may also solidify interpersonal ties, creating a dense network of mutual expectations and responsibilities within the *środowisko*. In either case, the circulation of goods and services as reciprocity is treated as a qualitatively different phenomenon from calculated, mercantile forms of informal remuneration such as bribery.

In interactions in which reciprocity is "voluntary," when, for example, payment for services is not clearly defined, people tend to describe and even perceive their actions in terms of disinterestedness and gratitude than in interactions in which payment, agreed upon in advance, clearly motivates activity. This contrasts with transactions such as bribery, in which equivalences and definitions of mutual responsibilities are understood more or less explicitly. A 24-year-old nurse explains:

If someone proposes to me "take care of this for me and I'll repay the favor," then I sense that if I arrange something for that person, he'll repay the favor by doing something for me that only he can do. But a bribe is just simply, "take this and give me that." That person may not repay the favor until 10 or 15 years later. Maybe I'll find myself in just the situation he was in. So there's a difference. This, I feel, is on the level of a kind of mutual goodwill, a kind of assistance, while bribe is an ugly word and generally an ugly business.

A 48-year-old female clerk further distinguishes between reciprocity and bribery:

I treat reciprocity in this sense—I take care of something on my own initiative, voluntarily, often without that person knowing, and that's why I consider the box of candy as reciprocity. While a bribe is something I set up in advance: "If you please, sir, if you take care of this and that for me, I'll give you such and such." That's why I treat a bribe as something arranged.

The transactions I have been discussing are based on fixed, observable rules of exchange. Participants' explanations not only mask these truths and rules of interaction, but frequently also project them.

Social pressure within the *środowisko* ensures that its members provide each other with at least some services and goods disinterestedly. The further the ties outward from the *środowisko*, the more the principle of profitability applies, or at least an equivalence of mutual returns. A continuum of symbolic to material rewards, and of altruism to reciprocity to profit, parallels the continuum of exchange relations from the family to "others."

NOTES

1. The words cannot be rendered into English without context and therefore will appear in quotation marks.

2. "*Załatwić*" embraces the accomplishment of serious objectives, from reserving a place in a hospital or kindergarten or getting an apartment or telephone—often by skirting the system. *Załatwić* entails "arranging," or finagling commodities, services, and privileges unobtainable the state economic or bureaucratic institutions. *Załatwić* and *kombinować* are to some degree interchangeable, but *kombinować* is shadier in connotation and can refer to larger-scale wheeling and dealing.

3. *Dojscie* means "ins" through connections to bureaucrats or officials who can deliver privileges or services.

4. *Fucha* can refer to *any* extra earning acquired informally, but also to what one so earns and hides from one's wife to buy vodka or beer to drink with male colleagues.

5. Paper certificates used as dollar stand-ins in the Pewex shops where goods are sold for hard currency only.

4

When Theft is Not Theft

ELŻBIETA FIRLIT AND
JERZY CHŁOPECKI

> Polish society inherits from the Occupation the half-
> conscious but deeply rooted conviction that the most
> important element of modern economic life is *handel*—
> *handel* conceived in the most individualistic manner
> possible. —Kazimierz Wyka, 1945

The terms "informal" or "parallel" economy, "black market" or "black labor," although each stresses a slightly different aspect of the same phenomenon, refer to a problem that arouses vital interest in the West. The problem has finally ceased to be a taboo subject in Hungary and in Poland, the only Eastern bloc countries in which research on it has been undertaken by official institutions for more than a decade.

Western writings about informal economies in socialist countries are characterized by an optical illusion, largely the consequence of Westerners' limited access to information, which they generally derive either from the official mass media of East European countries or from immigrants. An equally important limitation upon these analyses is their distinct tendency to treat informal economies in the socialist countries as primarily engaged in "lubricating" ineffective mechanisms of the centrally managed, planned economy. It is true that some aspects of informal economic activity play this role, namely, many forms of service activities, goods produced through so-called side jobs, and certain kinds of *handel* (private exchanges unregulated by law, but by well-recognized rules, and tinged with cunning and legerdemain). "Speculation" (the private sale at high prices of goods originally procured from state stores) also flows naturally from a shortage of many market goods.

The basic difference between the informal economy in the West and in the socialist countries is the fact that in the West, informal economic activities are marginal, while in a socialist planned economy, they are a fundamental part of the activity of state-owned enterprises—a difference with far-reaching consequences.

Western analysts make the mistake of imposing upon our reality typologies of relationship that obtain in the West. They tend to impose a clear distinction between the first and the second economies; the term "parallel economy" frequently appears in their literature. But the relations between the two economies are not based on their "parallelism": informal activities are actually integrated into the official economy, interconnected to it by specific crossovers.

Western researchers mistakenly assume that in the socialist countries informal economies only undergo additional reinforcement, that is, that socialist informal economies simply compensate and compete with official economies to a greater degree than in the West. They suppose that here, as in the West, informal activity competes with the official economy, filling both a compensatory and complementary role in response to shortages. Nothing of the kind!

The interdependence between the two systems in Poland is determined first and foremost by the fact that the principal components of the informal economy operate within the activity of state-owned enterprises and are carried out for personal gain by the people employed in the socialized economy. The informal economy is not a "second system," but, to a greater extent, simply a constituent part of the first, that is, the official economy, to which its relationship bears a parasitic character. This view has been strongly confirmed by our fieldwork.

We base this article on our own observations and those of student fieldworkers employed as factory laborers. The study was carried out in five state-owned enterprises located in as many southern voivodships. No one at the factories knew the students were keeping detailed notes; some of the enterprises are not fully identified so as to protect sources.[1]

For Personal Gain

Each of us knows very well without any research at all that in many factories things are stolen, that time on the job is used to serve personal needs, that bribes are taken, and that various kinds of "side jobs" use factory machines and equipment. Knowing that such phenomena exist would not justify studying them.

The significance lies in the wide variety of forms that these activities assume and the fact that those engaged in them assess each manifestation differently. Even more important, each activity has a different function in the workers' community, forming a continuum from offenses in the strictest criminal-law sense of the word through imprecise infringements of the rules to activities only to be judged as proper or improper organization of work. On the ethical level, the continuum ranges from what is commonly condemned, at least as a matter of form, to what is openly justified or even acclaimed by public opinion. Going by the range of activities we observed, we find that such opinion makes it necessary to distinguish among theft, lifting, "arranging," doing favors (for no pay), exchanging services, *handel*, "side jobs," and bribery.

At first glance such a classificatory scheme might seem to be hairsplitting. But a closer review reveals that each of these activities has a different social meaning and implications. In our classification we do not stick to terminology deriving from official economic divisions or the social division of labor but address ourselves to conceptualizing it in light of the public and cultural contents that saturate these manifold adjustments to the system and to the open and, more often, hidden—in the sense formally deniable—functions that they assume in the factory community.

Theft

In our culture theft is traditionally strongly and unequivocally stigmatized. But in the contemporary mind-set, such a judgment no longer applies to public property, for only something that is someone else's private property can be stolen. This analysis is too simplistic and it probably owes much to the belaboring by official mass media publications that all too often have suggested that attitudes toward public and private property are governed by different moral codes. But the matter is not so easy.

Only once in our research did we come across the term "theft." It was in a clothing factory where two pairs of pants vanished from a parcel ready to be mailed to the purchaser. While they were being looked for, one pair was found—probably returned in secret by a thief with frazzled nerves. The other pair was not located, and people commented that the article, *stolen* by somebody, would never turn up. It is significant that the goods in question were paid for and ready to be mailed. The recipient was known, it was his property.

It is worth noting that shoplifting, even from a state-owned shop, and lifting by an outsider to the workplace, are always considered theft. The fact that shop clerks are responsible for keeping track of goods (and therefore liable for them if these are missing) does not fully explain this. An inventory clerk also bears financial responsibility. In the clothes factory we studied, people often said that inventory clerks also traded away stored goods in the same quite uncondemnatory tone in which they described how drivers who worked for the factory sold gas on the side to state-owned gas stations. The network of private acquaintances in a socialist enterprise is much wider than in comparable enterprises in the West, and so it is not unusual that the seamstress probably knows the driver personally and certainly has heard stories about him, even if the two have had no formal dealings. Nobody referred to these transactions as theft.

Would we be justified in speculating that goods in a warehouse are still "ours" while those prepared for mailing are "ours" no longer, because they have a definite addressee? The explicit term "theft" deals with the taking of an object not only "not mine," but possessing the crucial additional attribute of belonging to an identifiable other. The owner does not necessarily have to be a private person: such identity is in fact secondary because the lack of our ownership rights with regard to what is undoubtedly "not ours" is self-evident. The "rationalizations" people offer will become more convincing after comparing "theft" with other forms of activity for personal gain.

Lifting

While theft is a secret act, always a violation of principle, lifting is open and utterly sanctioned by custom. Lifting is not held at bay by moral but only by material considerations—namely, is there anything to lift? When we asked a worker "What can be lifted?" he simply replied: "Not much, apart from nuts and screws. Only plaster is of some use, but you can't lift much of it because there simply isn't much." In another factory, a worker said that "he could always use everything: bolts, screws, plastic pipes, some scraps." When the observer asked why he lifted things that cost so little and that could be bought in any shop, he replied with surprise: "Why the hell should I buy them, if I have them free here?" Lifting was reported in all but one fieldwork site—an industrial service enterprise where there was probably nothing to lift. Characteristically, in none of the plants where lifting did occur, did anyone call it "theft," a usage apparently confined to a few official newspapers and "scientific theses."

In three of the factories studied, lifting was limited to small items. In the industrial construction company, however, lifting was carried out on a huge scale, both in the quantity and value of goods lifted. Two factors were undoubtedly decisive: the range of possibilities— not only the presence of a lot of attractive, expensive, and hard-to-obtain goods, but also the organization of work, which permitted and even promoted an almost unrestricted wastefulness; and an exceptional degree of demoralization among employees. We encountered the term "theft," indeed, but in a curiously characteristic and significant context applied, for instance, to a worker's taking panel boards, already prepared for lifting and hidden away by another employee. The worker who found the goods missing remarked, "Some scoundrel stole them from me." Lifting something is not theft, but taking something prepared for lifting, and thus "privatized," is theft. The distinction, in this case, was that the action was performed against a specific individual.

These two forms of the pursuit of personal gain—theft and lifting—deserve more consideration. If there were a radically complete, workable distinction between private and public property and this were reflected in the attitudes toward activities against property such as vandalism, it would mean that the state-controlled economy is mainly "an economy excluded from the moral life of the nation"— as Kazimierz Wyka wrote in "The Excluded Economy." Our perspective is slightly different, as we regard some mass forms of activity for personal gain, such as "lifting," as an important part of the informal economy and as a pathological consequence of property being publicly owned.

The idea of public property blurs the distinction between mine and not mine (someone else's), a distinction ever-present in the moral consciousness, even when we cannot say whose property something is: it is enough to know that it is not ours. Therefore, shoplifting from a state-owned shop will always be considered theft, because goods lifted from it are goods that may become "mine" if I pay for them. Lifting something from a factory where one does not work also will be theft.

In a state enterprise, many factors operate to blur the boundary between mine and not mine (someone else's). The worker's paradoxical role as simultaneously employee and co-owner is particularly important.

Equally important is the scale and range of waste in tools, materials, and practically all elements of production, including wasted work time, about which we will write in more detail later. We cannot ignore the rationalization that both explains and absolves lifting: "It'll get destroyed and wasted anyway." Also, the peculiarity of the offsetting of loss and gain, profit and cost, further blurs the boundary. In all those kinds of activity for personal gain discussed here, one thing is clear: some known person stands to profit, while the loss, the bearer of which is not really known, is abstract. "All this is reckoned into the building costs anyway," the inventory clerk explains to us, as he siphons materials off to remodel his own home.

Favors

Favors are services to other people carried out by employees within the scope of their professional duties. Unlike a service, a favor is free, and is not associated with expectations of reciprocity. The world of favors is sustained not by the anticipation of a specific benefit returned but a much vaguer assumption that what goes around, comes around. The reasoning is not that "Today I'll help him, tomorrow he'll help me"; but "Today I'll help someone, tomorrow someone will help me." In the industrial construction company, the construction manager gives the inventory clerk several jars to be filled with emulsion paint for one of the clerks from the administrative office. Our fieldworker himself received 1.5 liters of oil-based paint, 1 liter of primer, and a bottle of pigment from the same inventory clerk—all for free; the inventory clerk could not really expect anything from the fieldworker, whom he knew was employed only temporarily and would have practically no opportunities to return the favor.

A separate group of favors refers to evading formal work discipline. A worker who "skips out for a short hour," which turns into most of the afternoon, is shielded from the boss by his colleagues. A power-shovel operator in the municipal construction company wants to use the shovel to level the ground in front of an acquaintance's house. The foreman gives his approval, warning him only, "Don't take too long, 'cause after the lunch break the boss might drop by." The foreman knows very well that he has no choice. If he refuses, either the operator's shovel "will go out of order" or the operator will work so slowly so as to leave no doubt that the foreman's attempts to impose discipline are not effective.

The fact that the exchange of favors is universal plays, it would seem, an important although pathological function of "humanizing" interpersonal relations, of soothing frictions and tensions in teams of workers that otherwise would lack common goals and interests. In no factory did we ever see a favor refused and so we know nothing of the public reaction to such a refusal. We presume that a worker who refused to do favors, justifying himself by saying that it is in fact an act against the factory, would be considered antisocial, a "disobliging" person, or at the very least, legalistic and square.

Services

Unlike favors, services are not free, although they do not involve cash payment, or immediate and direct reciprocity in every case. Unfortunately, we were unable to observe many such transactions, especially in services whose payback was not immediate. The only case we heard about in detail was in the metalworks factory. A mechanic fixed the shop director's private car during work hours, using state-owned tools and materials. The director paid him and also promised to let him use the metalworks factory tractor for his own purposes.

In relations between fellow employees, the most common form of payment for a service is a "treat"—usually drinking a bottle of vodka that one person brings to consume with his cohorts. Alcohol functions as an honorarium, a more subtle gratuity than cash.

In our discussion of services, we exclude transactions with people outside the factory, which our culture classifies as *handel*. In *handel*, goods have a price set by unwritten, tacit agreement and controlled by practice or contract; and the relations between the person performing the service and the person commissioning it remain at a purely commercial level. The fulfillment of the contract brings nothing new to the parties' reciprocal relationship. But services between employees, and particularly the exchange of services in the factory community, lead to greater leveling in relations between people who occupy different places in the factory hierarchy.

The director having his car repaired talks to the mechanic differently when they discuss this service—both what he says and how he says it are different—than he does when giving an official order. The dependency relationship between them, although not reversed, becomes more nearly equalized. Now the director also might feel dependent on the worker, at least as long as his car needs repair. But their reciprocal relationship will be enduringly established. Normally, this director might be arrogant toward subordinates, stressing his superior position in everyday contact with them. But in "private business" dealings with a worker he will be a shade less arrogant, more equal and partnerlike. Normally, the worker acts deferentially towards his director, but this is not as much the case after he carries out the contract. It is not even a question of the director's gratitude or the worker's awareness of the director's being obliged to him. It is rather the worker's imperceptible feeling that he has the director "in his hands," a fact that the director also will keep in mind.

The literature on informal economies, particularly that which deals with the exchange of services, emphasizes that exchanges expand into a complicated network of reciprocal dependencies, often multilevel ones, based on the principle, "Today I will arrange something for your colleague, in return for which you will arrange something else for my colleague's colleague tomorrow." The dearth of goods and services and the scale of bureaucratic barriers and impediments encourage the extension of services exchanged (even paid ones, but above all those in which money is not a sufficient equivalent) between people not only of different professions, but of different positions in the social hierarchy. Given the markedly hierarchical nature of our society, the exchange of services plays a leveling and democratizing function. As a result, the less important people gain stature, while even the very eminent descend from their pedestals.

Arranging and Organizing

Under the "the economics of shortage" (to cite the landmark work of the Hungarian economist János Kornai),[2] the category "to arrange" claims its place in life and language at the expense of the term "to buy." Many goods are not bought, but "arranged" or "organized." These words define processes broader and more complex than just a simple contract of purchase and sale. It is impossible to avoid entering into relationships dominated by "arranging." This is the case not only when an individual purchaser wants to buy an article in short supply for his own private use, but also when he wants to "assure" his procurement of resources and raw materials and all things necessary to fulfill the state plan. And this much we learned even without observing the management level.

"Arranging" in an open and complex community such as a town or city is different from "arranging" in a relatively closed group, such as a team of factory workers. In the latter case, "arranging" is primarily "a game with a bureaucratic control and record system," and not a social interaction between partners of different but equal possibilities.

The industrial construction company supplied most of our observations on this subject. One could get the impression from the inventory log that the opportunities for lifting tools and materials were limited only by the availability of resources. But it turns out that, in order to lift something, in some cases one had to "arrange" the lifting, to legitimize it in some way. First of all, the inventory clerk is doomed to play "a game with the books."

The construction company inventory clerk was an exceptionally efficient businessman as well as a very generous giver. When asked how he copes with shortages that must arise in the warehouse, he replied: "That's why I sit up late at night so often writing reports, making calculations, sometimes giving them to someone who is drunk for signing, or treat this someone [his superior] to vodka." It's normal to write off tools that have been "lifted home" (lifted and taken home) as scrap.

Someone who wants a new tool can take something from the scrap heap and exchange it for a new one at the warehouse, or bring an old one from home. This interchange applies mainly to expensive tools such as drills.

Economizing one's time, so as to be free for private matters, or simply to earn extra money, is one form of "organizing" in a factory that is specific to activities for personal gain. Work hours may be fictitiously extended to get overtime pay: if the factory does not pay overtime, one simply works fewer hours.

Free time clearly has a different value than work time, for it is authentically prized, while work time—already paid for—has a low value, or none at all. Work time is regarded as time wasted, except by those employed at piecework. In the metalworks factory, our observer noted that "you can sleep" when the consignee of the goods does not show up. But it sometimes happens, he reports, that more trucks come; and one has to work overtime. "Today we worked till 16.00 (an hour longer)—so we put down that we've worked till 18.00." Some other days "we stay half an hour longer, but we put four hours overtime in the register."

It is also worthwhile to mention another mode of "organizing" time in the industrial service enterprise, which affects not workers, but drivers from other state-owned enterprises responsible for picking up goods there. (We cannot describe the essence of this activity in more detail without revealing the enterprise's identity.) A driver picking up tools could get some an hour or two before the allotted time but then he would receive tools of poorer quality. But if he did come earlier he could have free time later. Employees were not permitted to give out defective goods or to release goods before the stipulated hour. But it was worthwhile for the drivers to bribe the employees to pass off inferior goods on their factories in order to win time for their own personal gain.

Bribes

We described the previous case from the drivers' perspective—for whom "organizing time" is the main concern. Let us now examine it from the point of view of the workers in the supplying enterprise. About 40 vehicles arrived there each day to collect goods. The fee for giving out one item in advance to the driver was 100 złoty. Most workers were familiar with this, and most took advantage of it. One of our fieldworkers wrote: "All the drivers coming to collect goods wanted was to load up at the earliest time possible and to drive off. There were bribes in kind—sausages or other cold meat products clearly lifted from the drivers' factories—sometimes offered instead of money, sometimes in addition to it.

"The manager of the warehouse," reported our observer, "often left work with bags full of bribes." The observer could not find out what the manager took the bribes for, but says that it is known that the manager could not have been bribed for the same services as the employees. One might assume, then, that he took bribes so that his warehouse would actually deliver any service to a customer, or to put the delivery ahead of its turn. So we may presume that the drivers were acting in such a way that their factories paid double the cost for shoddy but ready goods. Furthermore, they thus required more frequent servicing, since they lengthened the queue in front of the enterprise and indirectly created the need to pay even higher bribes to the manager for special treatment.

Handel

Handel refers to contracts between a factory's employees and their private outside customers. We were interested in learning how easy it was for outsiders to gain such access. In factories where we kept an eye on this, we found that the possibilities were unlimited. However, *handel* on a greater scale is achieved only by those categories of employee who have access to materials that are rationed or in short supply.

First of all, it involves drivers and inventory clerks. Apart from the "normal" taking of "saved up" gas from the vehicles' tanks, one may also lift it from the dispatcher's supply within the enterprise itself. Moreover, this may also be done by a driver from outside the dispatchers. Our observer reports: "A driver arrives at the enterprise with five empty barrels. A guard 'counts' them without checking whether they are full or empty. So the driver takes them back filled with oil or gas." (Upon entry he fills in a pass, recording what he carries, and the number of barrels must be the same when he leaves.)

In the clothes factory, we were told how inventory clerks "traded" clothes. In our field experience, however, it was in the industrial construction company where *handel* flourished on the greatest scale. During the 23 days of his study our observer personally witnessed the sale of 10 bags of cement (50 kg each); 3 square meters and, later, 6 square meters of floorboards; a spray gun for paint; buckets; a barrel of paint (50 liters); several liters of varnish; half a barrel of emulsion; and several rolls of tarpaper. Drivers pull up to the enterprise in private vehicles or cargo taxis because these are not inspected by police. Even if the inventory clerk has to split the take with someone else, his income from *handel* still must be very high.

"Side Jobs"

In three factories we observed jobs performed for pay for outside customers during work hours. In the metalworks factory, such jobs were done by welders, one of whom our fieldworker saw taking money from a customer. We also witnessed "side jobs" at the municipal construction company, in two of which our observer himself participated. One involved moving furniture with four other work-ers—for which each was given 400 złoty and a beer. In the other instance, the observer and his colleagues spread soil in a garden, for 500 złoty apiece. In both cases the customers were passers-by who saw workers laying pavement stones in the street and offered them jobs. The observers' reports make it clear that such oppor-tunities occur often and always are taken up willingly—for even when the payment is slight, it is no problem to find time during work hours. At most this entails some increased effort.

Disintegration and Disorganization

It is a general common-sense belief that people steal, "organize," and so on because they earn too little. But our research pointed to other causes.

All the enterprises examined seemed characterized by a relatively high degree of disintegration. Discrepancies of interests among in-dividual team members and deriding gossip about others were re-ported, particularly at the industrial construction company. "Those bastards from the office aren't doing nothing," complains a worker. "They just sit, drink coffee, file their fingernails." Another worker puts down workers in general: "There is no solidarity among work-ers today, they scowl at one another." In the industrial service en-terprise, the observer reports endless worker criticism of the man-agement but always behind its back. There is a huge social distance between the workers and the boss, who in the workers' opinion is a young "big noise" who feels strong because he is a member of the Communist Party. The foreman, an elderly man, "kisses the boss' ass" and likes to drink, "but only with those more important than himself."

In our opinion, the lack of common goals within work groups encourages working for one's own benefit, which, given such a cli-mate, becomes more natural than working for the factory.

Another factor is the organization of time at work. It is only apparently paradoxical that some enterprises go short of labor, while much work time is wasted (from the point of view of the factory's interests). There are two basic causes of this: enterprises need in-creasingly more people because they do not effectively deploy those they have; and the ongoing need for employees, or more accurately warm bodies, is more formal and bureaucratic than actual. This validates the Hungarian economist János Kornai's thesis that the greater the shortage of labor, the greater the "underemployment at the workplace."

As an employee in the clothing factory, one of our observers calculated that his actual assignments took two to three hours daily, as against an official eight-hour workday. The remaining hours were spent in "going shopping, arranging private matters, visiting co-workers on the job to gossip, starting work later, and finishing earlier." Quite typically: "During work hours, two of my acquaintances who worked in the factory's management offices came to the boss in whose office I was just drinking tea and asked me to help them in cleaning the common lounge. As it turned out, they needed me as a third person to empty a bottle of vodka."

In the course of this gathering, which took place in August, our fieldworker learned that, toward the end of October, the factory quite likely would fulfill its yearly production quota. It is worth emphasizing that this factory appears best in every respect, including work discipline, of the enterprises examined. We may presume, however, that the emphasis on "unemployment at the workplace" in this observer's journal follows from the fact that the "unemployed" here had fewer opportunities than in the other factories for privately profitable activity. That discipline was better here than elsewhere probably derived less from motivation, authority, or pride in work, but from the sheer weariness of being idle. "God, why am I doing nothing?" asked one of the observer's colleagues.

"Today was just like yesterday," our observer at the municipal construction company writes in his journal. I came to work at 7:00 and, as it turned out, I was alone for some time. The rest of the employees came about 7:30." On another day he notes: "The job took us no more than three hours, so the rest of the time we were just sitting. However, we did do the job we were assigned." On another day: "At 12:00 they bring the salaries, and at 1:00 the work is over, and we all go to the cloakroom. This time the day ends with two bottles."

Unemployment at work not only encourages private work, it also makes it necessary to "kill time," a function powered by alcohol in all the factories we studied. We can dispense with examples, as all our observers reported drinking during work hours. But to give a better picture of the scale of the phenomenon, let us add that in two companies—the industrial service enterprise and the industrial construction outfit—when given an opportunity to drink every day, the observers did so. Alcohol seems to be the main integrating factor of the worker community in all factories, the lubricant that facilitates friendship.

Drinking in workplaces and during work hours is also linked to private dealing. Alcohol is, as we have already said, a more honorable form of compensation than money (and of much less equivocal value than cash gifts.) Of itself a mode of informality, drinking promotes entering into informal contracts and facilitates informal business dealings at work. We would be inclined, then, to accept as a hypothesis that the development of the informal economy correlates with the growth of alcoholism, at least in our country, in which this phenomenon has historical precedent.

Some forms of private work on public hours—namely theft and lifting—are promoted by wastefulness, which rationalizes and absolves, or simply morally justifies them. Our observer at the industrial construction company records great wastage of materials and tools. In describing a case that shocked him—barrels of motor oil and gas (ethylene 94), the contents of which had been leaking for several hours before they were discovered—he notes that he had seen torn bags of cement, cement allowed to harden, spilled lime, broken plastic windows, usable metal parts scattered around. Cans of glue, solvent, and varnish were left open, and because the next day their contents were naturally unfit for further use, the workers got new ones. Perfectly good tools were "thrown on the scrap heap." It was in this factory that we observed the greatest number of the most drastic examples of theft, lifting, and *handel*. No further comment is necessary!

Employees' private activities have pathological and pathologizing characters whose negative effects are more cultural and moral than economic. One should not view these activities, as do some, as uncontrolled, spontaneous "equalizing" of real or alleged injustice in payment, or simply the fruit of low wages. The level of remuneration has only slight influence on the development of employees' pursuit of personal gain.

Our research not only allowed us to get some idea of the scale of such activities, which merely bore out common knowledge, but also made it possible to establish the important yet hidden social functions played by this half-denied life. "Lifting" is, in our opinion, a pathological activity that can be rationalized either as practical socialization (what is lifted will at least be put to good use) or privatization of state property. Favors play an important role in humanizing interpersonal relations in factories, while other activities such as arranging, *handel*, organizing, and bribes integrate—in varying degrees depending on the circumstances—the groups of workers engaged in them. By "integration" we mean that workers develop common goals and interests that keep them together and ensure cooperation. Enterprises do not fulfill this integrative role, and activities for personal gain supplant the enterprises' official objectives.

In the traditional model of socialist management, now challenged by the reforms, enterprises are treated as if a rigid "technocratic order" could inflexibly endure and exercise authority. Doctrinally speaking, this has a known and defined set of goals authoritatively administered from the top, its internal processes programmed and directed—if not controlled. In practice, however, it is the individual enterprise that functions as a social order: the structure is to some extent fluid, goals are changeable and not always rational, and internal procedures are ad hoc, much less formalized, and not fully controlled.

This discrepancy between the prerogatives of the "technocratic order" and its adaptation to the conditions of the "social order" produces pathological phenomena from the point of view of the enterprise and society and fosters the growth of employees' activity for personal gain.

NOTES

1. The students were participating in a research project organized by Professor Kazimierz Sowa at the Teachers' College in the city of Rzeszów, where the authors are employed. Despite the sensitive nature of the research under the Communist government, the project was financed by the city's "Regional and Local Development and Self-Government" program and the findings published in a state-sponsored small-circulation publication in 1987.

2. János Kornai, *The Economics of Shortage* (Amsterdam: North Holland, 1980).

5

There's the Beef

JOANNA ŚMIGIELSKA

No one remembers unfulfilled promises as well as
the peasant, and few are so driven by straightforward
facts.   —Kazimierz Wyka, 1945

Consumers complain about the high price of meat on the free market; the farmer is considered, if not a millionaire, then at least very
well off. But what surprises me is the high cost to the farmer selling
the meat. It turns out that this king of the marketplace not only
makes no profit on each cut of meat sold, he actually loses.

Is this another kind of philanthropy? I found the idea of farmer
as philanthropist intriguing, and so I began to investigate the profit
structure of the free trade in meat. I interviewed and corresponded
with a variety of farmers and studied the Banach Street market in
Warsaw, a retail meat trading center that supplies more than 40
percent of the total turnover of all Warsaw meat shops. Vendors at
such centers include farmers selling animals raised on their own
farms and private brokers who have bought animals from breeders
to resell on the market.

To raise pigs or cattle, one must have facilities, money, and motivation. The basic resources required are properly equipped buildings and a dependable supply of animal forage.

If these conditions are met, a farmer raises piglets for six or seven
months—depending on the breed—until they weigh 120 kilos, calves
for 15 to 18 months until they reach 500 kilos. The peak of the
breeding season lasts from spring to autumn. The farmer then
chooses among his sales options.

Selling to the State

The farmer can deliver his livestock to the state purchasing centers—which buy at fixed prices and sell at prices equally fixed to consumers. Roundups take place twice a week. Animals delivered to such centers are inspected and graded by appearance, weight, and health: the grade determines the price per kilo of live weight.

Regulations forbid livestock being fed for 24 hours before they are delivered, but very often farmers do so, most commonly with milk, to increase animals' weight.

Inspectors often make deliberately low initial assessments of the animal's grade to try to squeeze material rewards from the farmer. "He glances at the pig, reflects, looks again, but he really glances at me. If I have the brains, I stick 2,000 złoty into his pocket. It's better than trying to appeal later on. You can't win anyway."[1]

The advantage of selling to state procurement centers is the allowance of coal and fodder granted for each pig (270 kilos) or cattle (100 kilos). "It doesn't pay to take them to the centers, for the prices per kilo are too low. But on the other hand it pays—if we deliver a pig, we get coal and forage." "Raising porkers is profitable on the one hand, when you sell them at the centers, for you get an allowance for coal and forage."[2]

Illegal Private Sales

There are two major types of illegal private sales: to a nearby village, and to a dealer.

When a farmer obtains enough private orders through private channels, he usually sells by the cut to people outside the immediate community. He slaughters the selected animal himself or hires a butcher. The animal has to be examined by a veterinary surgeon before slaughter and both vet and butcher are given a "present" of some cuts of meat.

Family, neighbors, and the entire community, which knows who is butchering on a given day, participate in the ritual. This requires the hostess to make a meal of fresh meat, the host to offer vodka, and everyone to partake in the feast. Thereafter, the rest of the meat is sold to acquaintances and acquaintances of acquaintances in nearby villages.

Farmers may also sell live animals to an illegal private broker. The dealer scouts out villages for potential sellers, and since he offers a higher price than that paid in the procurement centers, he has no problems finding sellers. The dealer usually has the animal slaughtered at the farm where he bought it.

If the dealer plans to hire a market stall, either for himself or for a third party, he transports the animal to his own farm or the other party's. Which farm he uses depends on which meets the regulations stipulating that only the owner of a farm of a certain size may hire a stall.

Selling to a dealer, a farmer is likely to get a much higher price than the one offered by the state centers, especially for veal, as slaughtering calves 5 to 6 weeks old is forbidden by law, and the dealer usually has many orders for this kind of meat. "Generally speaking it pays much better to sell live animals to a dealer privately, because you earn more money than in the centers, approximately 5,000 to 6,000 złoty more. For the money you can buy more coal illegally, as when you buy the coal with the allowance from the center you have to pay about 4,000 złoty too, not to mention the bribe. It pays better to buy it from a railroad man [who has access to it because he gets a coal allowance for personal use]." In our village, people sell calves to private dealers, approximately 100 kilos. The dealers from the cities buy them for slaughtered. You get approximately 40,000 to 50,000 złoty for a calf like that. And to sell a calf to the center doesn't pay, because you get less, and you won't get real coal, only on paper."

Legal Private Sales

Under Communist rule it was illegal to sell meat privately until 1988, when a new regulation was issued nationwide (after experimental introduction in 1986 in some areas).

If the farmer decides to sell meat on the legal private market, he must have the animal designated for slaughter examined by a vet, both before and after the slaughtering. After the slaughtering, when the carcass or halved carcass is prepared, the vet certifies it "private slaughter free of trichinosis."

The farmer then transports the carcasses in his own or borrowed vehicle to market at a time booked beforehand with the marketplace management. He has to secure a booth before he can set up shop.

Warsaw markets are open for booking space only on every second Monday of each quarter of the year.

The line of potential sellers starts to form very early in the morning. Many dealers employ front men at a fairly cheap rate instead of showing up in person.

The marketplace is run by the district branch of the state inspection and control office, staff are responsible for setting up the stalls, monitoring hygiene, and verifying that the meat has been passed by a vet. The sellers are furnished with scales, weights, aprons, and axes.

The sellers arrive at 5:00 A.M. The vet on duty collects certificates issued by the local vets and checks the hygiene of the vehicle in which the meat was transported. If these requirements are fulfilled, the meat is stamped "Hyg. and Vet. Control." Meat that is dirty, or covered with blood or bruises, is disqualified. The vet's certificates are handed to the manager about 7:00 A.M. He also collects the sellers' IDs, which are returned when the loaned tools are brought back.

When the vet's check is over, the farmers themselves take the meat to their assigned stalls and start cutting it up—most by themselves, although some hire specialists.

In the Banach Street market, 18 stalls stand outside the main building, all with roofs, counters, wooden chopping blocks, and hot and cold running water.

The marketplace opens at 7:00 A.M. and closes at 6:00 P.M.: about 15,000 people visit it daily. Management estimates that demand reaches its peak before holidays and on paydays. (People tend to shop in the private market especially for holidays, weddings, and family celebrations, and usually buy better meat—sirloin or veal—for their children.)

Stalls rent at about 8,000 złoty a day, but if the farmer finishes selling earlier, he pays less. He must clean the stall, but managerial staff clean the wooden block, disinfect the counters and maintain general order.

The Sellers

Meat salesmen are not a homogeneous group. Among them are specialized farmers who have 100 or more animals in "permanent raising"; farmers who do not specialize in raising animals but keep just a few, a handful of which are slaughtered from time to time; and farmers who raise two or three animals, disposing of them as the need arises. Dealers usually originate from the latter two groups.

Most commonly, those active in the meat trade are married couples. All wear aprons, either medical white or butcher's gray. Practically all men wear hats, no matter what the weather. The men cut and weigh the meat. The women wrap it in paper, not provided by management, and take the customer's money.

Throughout the day the full selection of meat on sale is displayed on the counter, which is wiped off every few minutes. Some sellers praise their meat noisily: "My meat is neat, and I don't cheat!" Others remain silent, and some do not seem interested in business at all.

The sellers are very nice and polite in their relations with the customers. Most patter a lot and try to meet the customers' wishes: "What does the beautiful lady want? Just take a look, such a beautiful piece. Why don't you take another piece, just look how nice it is."

Work can be organized differently. Single women often hire a man to cut the meat while they weigh and wrap it and make change, and I saw one elderly person handling the process with a teenager.

There also may be more than two people at the stall, usually the older members of the family, who supervise sales and take care of the cash. Sometimes they fill in for vendors who have to leave the stall to shop or handle other business.

The money is put away in small handbags. During the day, sellers eat bread from the neighboring shop, dipped in a jar of mayonnaise or jam. The typical drink is tea from a thermos, or some kind of lemonade. Few sellers drink alcohol.

Seldom are there conflicts between vendors. Their contacts are limited to casual conversation about work in the fields, daily life, and plans for the future. But the most common subject is the business of selling meat.

The sellers claim that there are worse and better locations—stalls closest to the entrance are the most prized. Management, however, claims that there are no differences—that profits vary with sellers' abilities: "One has to know how to get the customers."

The vendors believe that certain hours "mustn't be overlooked." About 10:00 A.M. the retired arrive, often shopping for people at work. "Babcia" ("grandmother") buys for the entire family and neighbors as well. About 3:00 to 4:00 P.M. the "working world" arrives and then "you have to cut prices if you want to sell more."

If the entire supply is not sold in one day, it may be offered on the next, provided that the stall has been so booked. Should the meat not be sold on the second day, it is distributed among family and friends. One does not pay friends for services, only for goods.

The sellers think that demand is quite large, although there are definitely bad days, while in state stores demand is larger and steadier, mainly because of lower prices. The sellers say that their meat is always fresh and that their customers are offered a wide selection and don't waste time standing in line. (Queues in state stores are often 150 people long, but at the private market, no queues are longer than 15 people.)

Prices fall in the evenings, on Saturdays, and in cases when the piglet has grown too fast and reached the slaughtering weight at an earlier age. When growth has taken longer, for instance, for pigs up to nine months, the price rises correspondingly.

"I pity some of the customers. You can see that they don't have the money, but they have to eat. But what am I supposed to do? I've got to live on something myself. All I can do is knock the price down, but not when the animal grew for a long time, 'cause I've spent more."

"Sure, it's expensive for those who live on their salaries, but it's not our fault that 'they' [the political elite] rule in such a fucking bad way. I pity most of them old folks. When I see an old lady, I give her an extra pound of meat, but I don't tell her—she'd be offended. They're so self-respecting."

"Don't you think that I don't know that it's expensive, but I've got to get something out of it myself, all I can do is knock the price down in the evening."

It is clear that selling meat in the marketplace entails many problems. The farmer has to slaughter the animal, bring the meat to market (for which he has to obtain scarce gasoline, sometimes illegally) and ensure that the meat is hygienically transported. He must also butcher the carcass himself, unless he wants to hire a professional. And last but not least, while he spends the whole day selling, he has to find someone to take care of his farm.

The sellers say that "the prices for farmers at the state centers should be increased, but the authorities don't care, 'cause they know that the farmer will produce things anyway. There's enough for the authorities, anyway."

Sellers assert that the Communist authorities have brought people to poverty: "Now nobody's gonna have nothin'—workers, intelligentsia, farmers. They've brought socialist equality. Everybody's poor."

"If poverty like this is gonna go on, we won't give them a fuckin' thing. We'll keep everything for ourselves. We'll sow wheat everywhere and we'll end up with the same thing."

"The authorities have let us sell meat at the marketplace, where it's the farmer who sets the price, because it doesn't pay to raise animals [for the state procurement centers]—it's one of the incentives the authorities have come up with."

Whenever farmers talk about whether one can incur a profit from raising animals, they recall the 1970s under First Party Secretary Edward Gierek, when they claim a better relationship obtained between the costs of production and the selling price. "It's tragic now. You just don't want to think about the future. It was best in Gierek's times. Many farmers made it then. Those who didn't, don't stand a chance now."

"If that gang of Communists walked in our shoes and worked like we do and did what we do and got what we get, I wonder if they'd keep the same prices. It was only in Gierek's times when it was better."

"If Gierek came back, I'd kiss his bare balls." "You may complain now, but it was much worse during the war. Then there was nothing to put into your mouth. It's not that bad now."

The Buyers

Members of all social classes buy meat at the private market. Obviously, those doing so least are farmers. But even though they don't buy meat, once they've completed their shopping in other areas of the state-owned shopping complex, they peruse the state meat market to see how high the "free" [non-state-controlled] prices are. They assess if perhaps they themselves should try to sell there.

Customers arriving at the marketplace study the daily updated price list chalked on a blackboard on the wall of the management building. Each seller may quote his own price, higher or lower than the going rate.

Customers check prices and the quality of meat at several stalls before making a selection. They typically try to bargain, both on price and quality. "That's too much, you can't skin people alive.

Knock it down a bit. Be a human being." "Aren't you afraid of God? It's so expensive in the shops, and you want twice as much. You lost your mind, or what?!" "You leave the dog's meat for yourself. I want a nice cut, no fat. I wanna know what I'm paying for."

The sellers tell me that in the old days, in Gierek's time, people did not bargain. Nowadays, bargaining is a fact of life.

There are cases of theft, generally by retired people living on low state pensions. A manager at the Banach Street market described a common method: "A woman stands in the queue, covers the cut of meat with a piece of paper and then carries it off as if it belonged to her, or just pushes it off the counter straight into her bag."

Such customers complain about prices. Some blame the farmers but are at the same time grateful there is a dependable market for meat. "I know it's expensive here, but at least I know what I'm buying, and I'm sure the meat has been inspected by a vet, not like with hawkers or in a bazaar, where you don't know what you're buying."

Hawkers, usually women, are peasants who come to nearby towns to sell meat at makeshift bazaars at prices below the private market. Often they visit government offices, having been by a day earlier to take orders from clerks and bureaucrats.

Profitability

A farmer has several options in selling meat or live animals. A porker qualifying as top grade at the state center brings 336 złoty per kilo of live weight. An average porker weighing approximately 120 kg, will bring the farmer 40,320 złoty.

If he decides to slaughter the animal himself and sell the meat privately by the cut, he can get around 600 złoty per kilo of meat. A 120 kg pig yields about 80 kg on average, returning 48,000 złoty. A private broker will pay 380 złoty per kilo of live weight—45,600 złoty. On the private marketplace, the farmer gets 800 złoty per kilo of meat which brings him a total of 64,000 złoty.

A young married couple who analyzed the economics of pig-keeping in detail for me demonstrated that it costs 61,400 złoty to raise a pig to the slaughtering weight of 120 kg. A farmer selling a rather standard five pigs a day thus gets 13,000 profit złoty per sale. But the stall rent, the veterinary fees, and the cost of transport come to 36,000 złoty. Thus, to sell five pigs is to lose 23,000 złoty, a calculation at first incredible, but confirmed by other farmers. More-over, the calculation fails to include such expenses as straw for bed-ding in the pigsty, coal for the steamer (to prepare potatoes for swill), the cost of maintaining the building, labor, the maintenance of a horse or tractor, and other cumulating indirect expenses. The farmers did, however, admit that one cannot use such a calculation, as they are always seeking ways to cut expenditures.

One way is to feed animals with "leftover fodder." Most farms do not specialize in raising pigs but continually generate resources somehow edible to a pig: farmers put anything lying around—wheat and oat chaff, sugar beet pulp, wheat offal as well as "green" fodder (weeds, clover, and various kinds of silage)—into fodder. They steam potatoes frozen during the winter and season them with kitchen scraps. The waste of local dairies or fruit and vegetable processing plants may be pressed into service.

A farmer concocting this miraculous diet may reduce his costs by 50 or even 75 percent. Contrary to widespread belief, it does not make the animals lose weight—they actually gain on it. Every farmer has his own ways of cheaply providing for his animals: instead of expensive fodder containing hormones imported for hard currency, common sense directs him to reserves close at hand.

This cost-cutting solution is labor intensive and cannot be used on larger farms because of the lack of an appropriate scale of de-pendable supplies. But it may be brought off under some circum-stances: "I 'arrange' the chaff from the mill. I give the guys there the homebrew I make myself."

But the money saved is not proportionate to time spent. "I get, for free, the milk that's gone off, from the dairy, but only the bottled milk, and I have to return clean, washed bottles to the dairy. I take 4,000 liters everyday. My whole family does nothing but wash bot-tles." "We are hardworking. We toil. We neglect our strength and health. We work from early in the morning to late in the evening."

Another man, who found himself by chance at the seaside and saw crowds of sunbathing and swimming tourists exclaimed, hor-rified: "I knew that people go for holidays, but I had no idea that so many people loaf around. I don't understand it. I couldn't survive without working. Isn't it enough for them to rest on Sundays? I'd get them to work with a hoe."

Farmers give differing reasons for raising animals despite the un-profitability of the occupation. Most farmers who raise no more than a few dozen say they decided to farm some years ago and cannot simply switch now. Building and equipping a pigsty with appropriate facilities is a heavy investment, tying up a lot of capital that must be returned by production. To change would be terribly costly. And, given the generally poor state of agriculture, it is unclear what other kind of specialization could be profitable. So farmers report that they keep raising animals anyway, hoping for proper price relations someday.

Some farmers claim that their situation is bad not only because the state has to keep meat prices low, but because other areas of production also are dragging.

The Polish government is continually reformulating farm policy. In February 1988, the price of fertilizers doubled, chemicals tripled, and gasoline went up by 50 percent. The end price of farming products rose 40 percent. In 1987 the price of chemical pesticides rose five separate times.

Other farmers claim that raising animals is not profitable but that they do it anyway out of habit, as the only thing they know. They invoke the ethos of the traditional family farm, in which the farm produces a bit of everything. This model has been handed down from generation to generation, from father to son. The farm grows enough to feed the family, and whatever is left over can always be sold. Farmers say that when they embark on raising a piglet they consider how much they will have to invest, but after six to seven months they cease to count the costs, pleased that they eventually will get some money and can plan what uses to put it to: "When I take the pig to the center, I know they've cheated me, 'cause really it's no profit. But if I take two piglets and get 80,000 złoty, it's a lot of money."

Some other farmers, discouraged by economic problems and the labor intensity of raising animals, switch to less demanding areas of farming.

It is widely believed that farmers do very well for themselves and that their complaints are unjustified. Farmers know this and argue that it stems from city dwellers' ignorance of living conditions in the countryside. Smiling, one farmer counters, "It's always best where others are."

Unlike state farms, private farms have no subsidies to protect them from bankruptcy. On a typical state farm, all means of production, such as fertilizers, gasoline, machines, and spare parts, are distributed by the state, which guarantees a market for the produce. But on a private farm, it is only the farmer's thrift, or sometimes "shrewdness," that determines profit or loss. Hence the farmer has an enormous responsibility if he is to keep the farm profitable with his private means alone. The harvests frequently assessed as "disastrous" even by the state propaganda are above all disastrous for individual farmers. Needless to say, losses from weather conditions and animal epidemics add up to much less than losses from the structure of the agricultural economy.

In the late 1980s uncertainty loomed over the farmers' future, forcing them to choose methods whose only objective is just keeping afloat, investing little or nothing at all. Farmers are not investing in the facilities and pigsties that could make raising porkers more profitable. They buy only the most necessary supplies, minimal quantities of fertilizers, for instance. They do not protect crops with pesticides, nor do they put up new farm buildings, since livestock is no longer profitable and the cost of construction materials, difficult to obtain anyway, has risen.

The farmers I talked with point out that their working day usually lasts 15 to 16 hours, frequently for months on end. They cannot shirk responsibility by getting the signed certificates from a doctor verifying that an employee in a state job is sick, enabling him to stay home. Moreover, on the farm the whole family works and works hard, including children. Farmers envy townsfolk: they work only seven to eight hours a day, and once they finish, "they don't have to worry about anything." The townspeople don't earn much, and farmers believe this is just: "no work, no pay."

Farmers often mentioned livestock raising in the West, with which some had direct experience. They envied their Western counterparts for what they perceived as a widespread respect for farmers, adequate income, security, and mechanisms of contract and insurance that underwrite a project from beginning to end, from quality fodder delivered on time to the pickup of porkers straight from the pigsty.

I heard the following, perhaps apocryphal, story over and over again:

> In a village nearby a farmer took two calves to the state procurement center and received 350,000 złoty. He was pleased and was even more happy when he saw that his son had come home for a few days from his regiment, which was garrisoned in the very town where he had sold the calves. The son was AWOL and the family feast thrown to celebrate his visit was interrupted by a visit from armed and uniformed military police from the son's unit.

But the father was so generous and hospitable that instead of arresting the son, the military police stayed the afternoon. After the feast everyone, including the police, lay down until there was a banging on the door. The hostess, still cleaning up, opened the door and was brutally attacked by two masked men, demanding that she give them the money she had received for the calves.

She agreed to hand it over and said she'd go off to get it. But, unbeknownst to the attackers, she went to wake up the military police. They dashed out, guns in hand, and easily overpowered the attackers. To everyone's great surprise, the hoodlums turned out to be the manager of the local state procurement center and the commander of the local police station.

And so the farmer decided not to take his animals to the state center any more. . . .

NOTES

1. Here the inspector is signaling the farmer that he should pay a bribe if he wants his pig to be accepted in a higher grade. Any appeal to the director of the state purchasing center is almost certain to be ineffective because the inspector and the director cooperate. They have probably worked together for years and maintain a certain "solidarity."

2. The permit the farmer receives at the state procurement centers affords him the right to buy coal and fodder on the official market and hence fairly cheap. But the permit is worthless if coal is not available on the official market.

The Nonmonetary Economy

Introduction

Two elites—one built on Communist Party connections, the other on Solidarity ties—will do much to shape the conduct of business, the privatization of state-owned industries, and even politics in the 1990s.

The Party-connected managers spent the 1980s stepping from political to economic influence in a development that the sociologist Jadwiga Staniszkis has called the "enfranchisement of the *nomenklatura.*"[1] While these "Enfranchised Nomenklatura Men" were switching from political to economic influence, Solidarity activists were moving from risky political activity to economic activity. Upon release from martial-law jails, many jobless Solidarity activists who had honed their business skills by running clandestine publishing houses in earlier years started limited liability companies to trade in computers, electronic equipment and information. These activists have been dubbed the *nomenklatura* of Solidarity.

The *nomenklatura* wheeler-dealers had a headstart on the Solidarity newcomers. Connections in the pervasive state bureaucracy and apparatus protected former Party and police officials who retired early to open firms. Under insider trading, explains Piotr Gliński, sociologist at the Polish Academy of Sciences, members of the former *nomenklatura*—managers whose nominations were approved by the Communist Party as "our boys"—start their own businesses by transferring state property, including entire factories, to themselves or to cronies at cut-rate prices.

In 1991, most—about 80 percent—of Poland's factories remain in the state's hands. Managers continue to operate in a world of nods and winks in which they know not "what" but "who." And, what works in factories, stores, and government agencies continues to derive its effectiveness from the networks and *środowiska* that penetrate and potentiate these institutions.

Stefan Kawalec, General Director of the Ministry of Finance, studied state enterprises in the mid-1980s after his release from martial-law internment. Kawalec tells how a factory manager's personal connections join him to other factories, suppliers, and distributors and to representatives of central authority, less often subverting than making irrelevant "centralized" management and setting the real terms of business transactions: "promotional goods" are incentives not to the customer, as in the West, but to the supplier. Informal transactions have become so common within the state-owned economy as to transform official procedures.

State managers and private businessmen alike now contend with soaring taxes, deregulated prices and costly credit, rent and supplies—all part of the post-Communist economic changes of 1990, which have stabilized inflation but brought deep recession. State-owned shipyards and steel mills have slowed down, as have many farmers and private businessmen: industrial production has fallen by an estimated 30 percent since the last quarter of 1989. Many enterprises are passive—unwilling or unable to respond to free-market incentives. There have yet to be massive layoffs as state-owned factories stretch out employment. Some companies are sharply reducing wages instead of laying off top-heavy administration.

The legal private sector—comprising much of agriculture, construction, small shops, restaurants, and taxis—must still jump through hoops, although it has been the largest in Eastern Europe, generating nearly one-fifth of the national income and employing nearly one-third of the work force through the 1980s. Despite the risks entrepreneurs must assume, the number of businesses increased from 805,879 on January 1, 1990 to 1,028,484 on August 8, 1990.[2]

In 1991 the market is no longer a "seller's market," the index of a shortage economy in which almost everything produced can be sold. Yet, says Stefan Kawalec, as he works with Leszek Balcerowicz, architect of Poland's economic innovations, it is difficult to judge how long even this change can endure. In an economy emerging only at a snail's pace from state ownership, managers still toil in a procedure-bound bureaucracy. The transactional mentality that bridged the fragmentation inherent in the command economy is not simply disappearing with the expansion of market opportunities, but evolving under the stimulus of new circumstances.

NOTES

1. Under the system known as *nomenklatura*, responsible positions in all spheres of government had to be approved by the Party, creating a tangle

of loyalties and favoritisms that precluded broader political and social participation. The *nomenklatura* had the power to accept or veto candidates for any state job, and asserted a final voice over responsible positions in all spheres, from police and army posts to factory management and school principalships on the basis of Party loyalty, not ability.

2. *Studia i Materiały*, Ośrodek Prac Społeczno-Zawodowych Krajowa Komisja NSZZ "Solidarność," Warszawa, 1990.

6

The Dictatorial Supplier

STEFAN KAWALEC

How many ants in offices now nostalgically reminisce
about recent months when there was so much action?
—Kazimierz Wyka, 1945

During Solidarity's first legal period, from 1980 to 1981, the Communist authorities introduced a law granting autonomy to individual state enterprises and proclaimed for them a "three-S" slogan: self-independence, self-financing, and self-management. The law authentically bestowed more independence in decisions about what to produce and how much, how many people to employ, the pay structure, and other crucial matters.[1]

Although the authorities declared martial law in December 1981, the law remained on the books. In 1982, the government stepped up its rhetoric of economic reform, of encouraging "open-market ties" between companies and moving away from the command system, partly to convince a public undergoing political repression and declining economic conditions of the government's commitment to change. Although the authorities did not consent to the elimination of political (i.e., Party) control over the economy, this was the first time they had exhibited so positive an attitude toward market processes.

Authorities in the state economy were divided between authentic supporters of change and those who merely used the slogan "reform" to pacify a society stripped overnight of its revolution of hope.

Few envisioned how "economic reform" would work in practice and such policies as were executed only partially confirmed the rhetoric. Government agencies continued to decide how strategic goods in short supply such as steel would be distributed—to whom, how much, of what quality, and when.

Nevertheless, despite wide-ranging regulation from above of inter-company ties, firms had considerable freedom to choose contracting parties and to enter into direct agreements with them. We set out to learn how they used this freedom, how they developed their market, how they cultivated suppliers, and the informal monitoring mechanisms they developed amid this latitude.

During the period we studied, two basic mechanisms regulated the flow of goods and relations between companies: the official distribution and informal pressure exercised over the companies by authorities; and the real consumer utility of goods—often very far from the official monetary value. In 1985, approximately 80 percent of the raw materials and other goods necessary for production that were purchased by state-owned companies fell into categories subject to nonmarket distribution.

To assess the margin of freedom in relations between companies, we took account both of the absence of officially regulated distribution in certain areas of the economy and of enterprises' ability to sell their products to whomever they wanted, whenever it made most sense and in whatever quantity.

In addition, even in the areas where distribution mechanisms were available through state and other administrative authorities (by way of distribution indexes—an accounting of who and in what amount should receive a company's output), there was a lot of leeway for direct contacts between contracting parties. Parties had to settle what and how much should be produced, the timing, and other conditions of delivery. Moreover, producers reserved the right to dispose freely of whatever goods they produced that exceeded their own production plan or were acquired by working overtime. Between 1982 and 1984, we conducted intensive field research in 39 companies operating in the spheres of production, domestic trade, and services—33 of them state-owned, 6 private. We also interviewed informally managers of 57 enterprises.[2]

The Corduroy Trail

Between 1982 and 1984 the Kudowa cotton mill distributed a certain amount of the corduroy material it produced among its workers. Employees paid 110 złoty for one meter, while the black market price at that time was about 1,000 złoty. Some of the fabric was sold to people outside of the factory or given to "procurement scouts" within it, who obtain scarce supplies for their enterprises by creating incentives for the supplier to do business with them.

The records of how the fabric was distributed came to light during an inspection. Corduroy had solved many of Kudowa's problems: in exchange for material, Kudowa got machinery spare parts from the Świdnica "Iglotech" and the Łódź "Wifama," electrodes and light bulbs from "Róża Luksemburg," 2,000 rolls of toilet paper, car batteries from the Wrocław "Polmozbyt," paint from Tarnowskie Góry, two concrete mixers and 70 meters of bicycle chain from "Romet."

Nor is that all. Other firms also offered valuable goods and services in exchange for material. Many of these requests were written in "bureaucratese."

The government price control agency, responsible for setting prices for this firm and others, petitioned for material and "to arrange your firm's financial matters."

The local branch of "Sanepid" (hygiene controller) applied for material "as a part of cooperation on topics of mutual interest with your company."[3]

There was an application for 10 meters "for citizens of Rzęsisty as a part of our cooperation." Some justifications were more extensive—two times five meters for two maintenance workers from the local telephone and telex system who "with their personal involvement contributed to the fast solution of the telex failure despite difficulties with imported spare parts."[4]

Material was delivered to the Wrocław state-controlled gasoline dealer for an extra ration of gasoline, which in turn went to the mayor "for official use in the material exchange with the town." We know the factory must have gotten something; we don't know what.

The distribution continued: 40 meters of fabric found its way to the local Communist Party committee. Four packages of 2.5 meters each went to the principals of the local schools from which the factory selected its new workers as an incentive to recruit employees for the factory.[5]

This story illustrates the overriding feature of contacts between companies: the dominant, often dictatorial, position of the supplier. It is the customer who seeks a potential supplier and his favors while the supplier picks and chooses among customers and dictates contractual conditions.

Attracting the Supplier

The people we talked with were very careful when discussing their contractual activities because negotiations and agreements between companies typically do not conform to regulations or are downright illegal. Managers were unwilling to enter into details or even to disclose with which companies they had agreements. A procurement scout who described a long search for essential parts refused to name the company from which he eventually managed to buy, or to spell out the final contract. A sales manager said that each day he has to shoo away two or three potential customers who try to tempt him with attractive "side" deals if only he would accept their orders. He named the companies to which he sold his production surplus, but did not explain why he selected them.

Customers must court their suppliers through contacts and paying extra costs, though not usually in money—at least not złoty. The supplier also bears the investment of time and energy. Procurement scouts have to locate scarce goods, existing or potential—no simple feat—and managers have to arrange exchanges, all at the risk of administrative sanction or actual prosecution.

We identified a score of methods that producers and suppliers use in negotiations.

"Promotional Goods"

The common practice of offering goods and various other kinds of bribes to actual and potential suppliers. "Gifts" are much more common than cash. Alcohol and coffee are the most customary presents, but company products and other attractive articles also work.[6] A hardware company sales manager who offered us coffee said that he only began to drink it when it became scarce on the market and so business colleagues give it to him often as a gift.

A supplier's privileges may also extend to his family, which may be offered the chance to buy attractive goods that are in short supply. A procurement scout entices potential suppliers by delivering a requested carpet or washing machine or supplying inside information about how such goods can be obtained. The manager of a state-controlled retail trading company arranged for the manager of a factory producing attractive consumer goods to buy a set of luxury furniture for his son, contracting in return to sell supplies to the trading companies. The manager said that he makes about 5 percent of his yearly purchases by way of such "favors" and, moreover, works at maintaining these contacts as they can bring him future profit.

Compensated Purchase

Typically, one company sells goods to another, receiving in return a favorable chance to purchase other goods. There are several such types of transactions, depending on the kind of goods the supplier finds available to it—say, attractive consumer goods for their employees. We learned that a factory wanted a travel agency to organize a winter holiday trip for its employees' children. The agency replied that the application had come too late, and there were no vacancies. But its representative nevertheless suggested that the holidays still could be "organized" if the factory delivered free as many of the attractive calendars that it produced. Done! The manager told us that with mass production like his factory's, it was always possible to have a certain amount of goods not listed on the books.

A retail trading company we studied annually acquires supplies not listed in the distribution index through its yearly organizing of more than 200 fairs closed to the public in various unrelated factories throughout Poland. These fairs enable factory employees to purchase attractive goods. The managing director claimed that if he offers goods worth 5 million złoty at a fair, he can get 10 to 12 million złoty worth of goods from the producer. Such fairs benefit management by serving as incentives to keep employees from going elsewhere. It is much more difficult for directors to raise pay or offer other benefits.

Companies use the same tactic to acquire scarce supplies. Two types of barter arise here, depending on whether the customer supplies parts or raw materials necessary to fulfill his own order, or whether all the materials supplied to the producer are necessary to do so.

To get supplies of clothing, for example, a trading company furnished the producer with much of the components necessary—desired fabrics, thread, buttons, and zippers, some of which had to be diverted from the retail market where they are in short supply. Otherwise, even if the customer receives the goods, he has to accept the selection and conditions set by the producer.

Or again, the manager of a food processing company turned to a director of another enterprise to help acquire three tons of a manufactured product needed to make a specific product from imported cocoa grains. At first the director replied that he was not able to help but when asked if some exchange might change his mind, professed himself ready to find anything necessary in exchange for rust-proof paint. The manager got the paint—we don't know how—and in return his interlocutor came up with not three, but four tons of the scarce commodity.

In another instance, Company A received an order for a particular good from the government and with it the indispensable scarce raw material needed for production.[7] But the company used some of the material for other purposes, asked the government distribution agency for extra deliveries, and was refused. Company A's manager found out through informal channels that Company B had a surplus of the raw material required and contacted Company B. Fearful lest examiners from the government distribution agency discovered during a routine inspection that the material had not been allocated as ordered, Company B's manager at first refused to sell. But in time Company B sold a sizable amount to Company A, which in exchange passed some of the scarce goods it made to Company B. The whole transaction was disguised on the books.

In a typical transaction a customer sells hard currency, which is difficult to get but necessary to purchase supplies from abroad, to the supplier at the official exchange rate in exchange for an opportunity to purchase some of his scarce products ahead of the game. Reciprocally, the customer may buy materials or parts requested by the supplier abroad and sell them to the supplier at the official rate.

Further ingenuities:

Customers obtain goods by detailing workers to the supplier's company, sometimes to distant cities for long periods. Their original employer covers all extra costs, including accommodation, food allowances, and compensation for separation from family.

A company secures cooperation by purchasing the means of production and leasing them to the producer, receiving in return a long-term contract to deliver products or provide services. We learned of two such cases between publishers and printing plants.

Unfavorable Contracts

Customers agree in advance to conditions that deviate from customary or legal trade regulations. These deviations may be expressly

included in the written contract or unwritten agreement. It is typical
for the customer to make such concessions as these:

- cutting the supplier in on the profits;
- paying partly or wholly for the delivery charge (by regulation,
  it is the supplier's duty to undertake the cost of transportation);
- paying more than the price stipulated;
- conceding a delivery date according to the supplier's conven-
  ience even if the customer has to wait unconscionably long to
  receive goods or gets them much earlier than needed and has
  to pay storage;
- purchasing poorly finished or faulty goods, or goods without
  packaging or in "ersatz" packaging.

For instance, a trading company received an extra delivery of
men's cotton underwear, in short supply, and so decided to send it
straight to the shops and leave the quality check to the shop clerks.
The clerks found the quality of the delivered goods to be exceptionally poor: sleeves of the T-shirts and sides and legs of the thermal
underwear were half-sewn. So the management decided to store the
faulty pieces in the storerooms until the complaint procedure could
be carried out. In the meantime shoppers bought all passable pieces
and started pressuring the shop assistants to sell all remaining pieces
not laid out for sale, accusing them of intent to speculate with the
other pieces.[8] Some customers telephoned the head office, demanding the immediate sale of the disqualified articles and claiming that
such small repairs as stitching seams could be done at home. Under
such pressure, the management told the shop clerks to forego the
complaint procedure and sell at the buyers' risk. The faulty pieces
were sold out immediately.

Avoiding "Difficult" Suppliers

One reason that customers might not demand the strictest interpretation of a contract is the fear that the supplier might, in retal-
iation, boycott a trouble-making customer along with other suppliers
from the same business sector. Often the customer will choose to
incur severe financial losses over losing a supplier. For if a customer
insists too strictly on his rights, he may be subject to a unanimous
boycott by a supplying sector.

A bureaucrat in a huge trading company told us that his company
had practically given up quality checks of durable goods in his sector.

At first it had followed the rigorous instructions issued by the Ministry of Domestic Trade and Services and the local authorities. But when certain manufacturers broke off their contracts as a consequence, the penalties for breach of contract being lower than the costs of warranty claims and poor quality penalties, the company was forced to back down. The producers in this sector actually shunned another company, more persistent in its quality requirements.

We found no cases of suppliers fearing boycotts or being avoided by customers. One supplier admitted outright that his company is always in a privileged position in contracting with customers and always dictates the contractual conditions it enters into. Despite numerous conflicts, there had been no court cases and he said he thought there never could be. Even if a customer were to win a verdict, his position would be pitiful: the supplier's company would fill no more orders from such a troublemaker. The managers of suppliers' firms are in touch with each other and probably would impose a unanimous boycott.

We found plenty of newspaper articles to confirm our experience that suppliers avoid troublesome customers. In one case, five big trading companies tried to organize a boycott of an unreliable supplier during a domestic trade fair and failed. The companies decided not to sign any more contracts with a consumer goods supplier. They thought their boycott would force the supplier to improve the quality of his products, which had been exceptionally poor. It turned out, however, that there were other customers eager to accept the supplier's conditions. After a few days, the boycott organizers were forced to give up and renew their unfavorable contracts.

Avoiding Difficult Orders

Subcontractors providing services (or producers) can—when orders are in surplus—refuse to accept those that might prove troublesome or less profitable. One manager of a publishing house said that Polish printing plants often refuse orders for hardcover books because of the problems in acquiring canvas and other bookbinding materials as well as the demanding and labor-intensive production process. A manager who wanted to publish a hardcover book gave up on the idea after unsuccessful talks with four printing plants and published it in paperback. In another case, when the publisher insisted on hard covers, the book was printed abroad.

Similarly, a manager in a construction company said that his subcontractors refused to take on less convenient jobs. The subcontractor whose assignment included laying cobblestones informed the managers that he was going to accept only those orders that excluded such work. As a result, the manager had to send his own workers to lay the cobblestones.

Influence from the Top

Can local or central authorities effectively pressure unruly suppliers into submission and into more favorable contracts with customers? Often a contracting party requests the authorities to interfere in negotiations, seeking, in most cases, to squeeze the other party into accepting a certain order, fulfilling its earlier obligations, changing the date of delivery, or improving quality. But despite the authority's influence, this is often less successful than direct contacts and offers of barter or other informal deals.

Informal Personal Contacts

This is the most important factor in settling transactions between contracting parties. Often deals are struck because the representatives of the contracting parties are "good acquaintances," the person finalizing the transaction was "recommended" by a mutual friend, or a customer establishes effective personal relations by courting the supplier's representatives. Suppliers' decision-makers are enticed with gifts, personal favors, and money. However, the value of courteous behavior and friendliness in representatives of companies hoping to make deals can hardly be overestimated: a personable, accommodating representative who stands out in the crowd is automatically a more effective dealer.

The manager of a metal hardware company said that if he ordered 30 heaters from the producer, he would wait for them until he retired. Instead, he reported, if he really has to have something, he telephones his friends, who are directors of other factories. In most cases he gets what he needs, finding one colleague with heaters stored away in warehouses. The manager claimed that if such relations among directors did not exist, the production level of his company would be about 30 percent lower. An incident during the interview illustrated this: a colleague of the manager—a director of another factory—showed up unexpectedly. They visited the nearby tool factory together, where the hardware company manager used his influence to have his friend's order accepted by the tool factory's head. Upon return, he reported that his mission had been successful.

The ability to maintain good relations with suppliers is one of the most critical skills of a procurement scout. Company managers are fully aware of this fact and grant scouts bonuses to cover extra expenses for flowers, alcohol, and other gifts. The director of a chemical plant said that, due to great difficulties in acquiring supplies, he often employs attractive young women as procurement scouts (the overwhelming majority in other factories are men).

Company managers themselves usually visit the more important suppliers. Such visits help to preserve good personal relations and facilitate the discussion of informal dealings. For example, a company heard that it might have difficulties getting an essential component in short supply and sent a representative to the central distributor to check the rumor out. After confirming it, the management undertook preventative measures: a group of managers visited five suppliers of the component in question "to renew social relations that would be helpful the next year," as the manager put it.

The Disincentive of Low Prices

There are two main categories of pricing recognized by the state: state-controlled prices and "negotiated"—non-state-controlled prices—such as those established between supplier and customer. Theoretically, the state sets the prices of basic goods such as coal, oil, and flour, and the prices of other goods are negotiated. But this is much more difficult to pin down in practice.

During the period discussed, certain prices were still set by the state, but about 40 to 50 percent of the turnover of enterprises was carried out according to "negotiated prices." In 1984 new regulations restricted the freedom of setting such prices, and some prices were frozen. From 1984 to 1990, companies were not able to set prices freely.

In 1982 and 1983 negotiated prices were legally free prices. However, state-controlled companies did not tend to set the negotiated prices at the highest level allowed by the absorptive power of the market, but instead below the equilibrium level. We observed cases in which state-controlled suppliers, consciously and voluntarily, set prices much lower than their customers were ready to accept. As paradoxical as it may seem, in some cases the customer insisted on setting higher prices, and the supplier resisted. A trading company was offered a shipment of alarm clocks at 500 złoty apiece. The company wanted to pay more than double that price for them and suggested 1,200 złoty. But the supplier decided his profit and taxes would have been much too high. The two companies agreed upon a final price of 750 złoty. State-owned stores immediately sold out the clocks. When they appeared on the black market, their price stabilized at 3,000 złoty.

Price increases implemented by the state-controlled companies were usually not reactions to changes in demand but rather to increased costs or other financial problems. The scale of the increases was determined not by the absorptive power of the market but by the costs of production and the financial needs of the company (for example, to achieve a necessary level of profit).

Sometimes companies in financial difficulty were willing to increase the "negotiated" prices but were unable to do so because of administrative obstacles (frozen prices, for example) or because of informal pressure applied by the authorities.

The behavior of manufacturers who, despite customer encouragement, preferred to keep their prices below the equilibrium level may seem paradoxical. Yet there are several powerful disincentives for companies to sell at higher prices.

First, the steeply progressive tax on profits might absorb up to 90 percent of a company's gains. Greater profit simply brought yet higher taxes. So slight was the increase in return that price rises simply were not worth the extra effort of selling.

Second, the state imposed penalty taxes on wages above a certain level for the job. Extra income would have translated into marginal pay raises. Thus employees, including directors and management (whose salaries were set by the appropriate ministry), had no direct interest in the profit of the enterprise.

Third, mass media propaganda denounced price increases as "unjustified." In this atmosphere a profitable company could have been accused of setting high prices. A director would be open to criticism and potential troubles from the Ministry and the Communist Party.

Fourth, maintaining prices below the equilibrium level made it easy to sell goods. Even products defective from poor workmanship or the lack of proper materials easily found customers.

Finally, all companies operated in a market with a general shortage of goods in which their barter advantage—goods they produced and could swap with other companies—were more valuable than money in satisfying the company's needs. Money alone was not sufficient—even if there was a lot of it. The most pressure a company could bring to bear on a contracting party management's trump card was its ability deliver its scarce product to the chosen customer. The bigger the gap between the demand and available supply, the more pressure could be applied.

A company that under such conditions decided to increase its price to equilibrium level might find itself in a difficult situation. It would increase income, but the product would no longer be in short supply. Its manufacturer would no longer be able to get scarce raw materials, hard currency, attractive goods for the employees and for the managers, their relatives and friends. At the same time the company would actually have to meet quality standards, which, given general shortages and resulting substitutions, was often difficult.

Not only do producers exhibit superficially strange behavior by wanting to keep prices low, so do distributors who insist on buying goods from the producer at higher prices.

Government regulations set a fixed margin of profit on the turnover of many goods. The higher the price the distributer pays, the arithmetically higher its (fixed) margin of profit.

Nonmonetary vs. Monetary Allure

Money and low prices do not entice the supplier; financial means are not enough to acquire desired goods.

In practice, the price in złoty that the customer pays officially to the supplier is secondary to nonmonetary costs. Only in rare cases is a customer discouraged from buying for monetary reasons. The amount of the scarce goods and services that a company can obtain in exchange for an agreement to sell its products to the selected customer depends only on the rate of shortage in the market and the intensity of the customer's needs. Thus the fact that the manufacturer had to pay higher nonmonetary costs to produce his goods does not mean that he will automatically obtain more scarce supplies. Not only is the amount of scarce goods at the company's direct disposal, so is the number of problems soluble through private connections, the time at the management's disposal and of the procurement scout responsible for supplies, and the degree of risk the managers would be ready to take. These factors are by no means inconsequential.

A company's ability to invest in such non-złoty items sets the parameters of its operations, especially its ability to get truly essential goods and services. Potential customers compare the predicted extra costs of a transaction with the expected profit on the goods to be acquired. If they find the costs too high, they back off. A construction company wanted to purchase certain materials from a wholesaler, whose manager demanded in exchange a certain number of apartments[9] for employees. The transaction fell through because the construction company assessed the price as too high.

But sometimes one must go high indeed. A construction company manager reported his company had serious problems getting materials. Practically all were scarce and the shortage of paint was his most difficult problem. The manager decided to bring up this matter at a regional conference of all construction company managers, in the presence of local administrative and political authorities. His strategy was partially effective: all managers were given an emergency paint supply—but only two tons of it. .

Our manager, still desperate to finish a block of apartments, got into his car and, as he put it, "arranged" five tons of paint. He did not explain from whom and under what circumstances he got such a sizable shipment of the paint. We can only assume that the extra costs were very high: the supplier was certainly aware of the value of his product.

Under such circumstances, the direct exchange of goods and services acquires a nonmonetary value. Such a market operates under the command restrictions of turnover, the lack of a universally accepted currency, and the lack of flexible prices. Nonmonetary evaluation is also dependent on shifts in supply and demand. Customers prepared to pay appropriate nonmonetary costs are able to acquire practically everything they want on this market—hard currency, rationed raw materials (especially if imported), and attractive consumer goods.

Barter makes it possible for many companies to survive difficult periods. The sheer effort necessary to obtain scarce goods channeled them to those who needed them most (and could afford the nonmonetary markups).

The lack of a unified currency and the illegal character of many transactions resulted in the market's not being "clear" to its participants. It is difficult to gain basic information on, for example, from whom a given product may be obtained, and the comparative prices of the suppliers.

In capitalist markets, goods are sold by the manufacturers or by specialized trading companies, and sellers advertise publicly. In our market, the most convenient supplier of a product need not be its manufacturer or an official dealer but some other company that uses the product in its production or is capable of obtaining it elsewhere. Companies prepared to sell scarce goods never advertise publicly. A factory with an extensive reserve of a rationed material is unlikely to spread this news around because of the battery of penalties for such "hoarding."[10] Similarly, a company equally obliged to sell its entire production to the state is unlikely to announce publicly that some is available for sale.

In capitalist markets, it is relatively easy to find out what price the supplier wants for its product. The Polish market is more complicated because the product in question is available only in exchange for other scarce goods. Absent a set "exchange rate" for such bargaining, the price expressed in units of one product cannot be automatically converted into a price expressed in units of another product. Therefore, full information about the price of the given product would have to include an aggregated list of prices expressed in units of all the scarce goods for which the supplier was willing to exchange his product.

In no official offer, however, would one be able to find information like this: "The sales manager of Company A likes cognac. For one bottle of it one may receive his signature on a contract for 500 pieces of his product. Or, if you arrange for the director to purchase a set of furniture for his son, you will be able to buy 2,000 pieces. For 500 welding pipes, you will get a chance to buy 5,000; 4,000 for a quick redecoration of the factory holiday center."

Basic information about from whom and for how much the desired product can be obtained is gathered with great effort, through endless trips, talks, and contacts with mutual friends. The high cost of acquiring information means that the participants in this market make decisions and sign contracts on the basis of fragmentary knowledge, without a broad view of the options.

Also participants' chances are unequal. This inequality results from the different degree of scarce-goods liquidity at the disposal of different companies, as well as from that of the freedom of choice among the customers for one's product.

The extent of liquidity determines how easily a scarce product can be exchanged. The more participants interested in a given product, the greater its liquidity. Hard currency counts high, as do attractive consumer goods (especially durables), apartments, and such goods of wide application as paints and varnishes.

Those who have such goods at their disposal can exchange them directly for whatever they need. The less liquid goods are those not directly useful to all participants in the market. Such goods also can be exchanged for practically everything, but this requires further complicated indirect transactions involving more than two contracting parties and mounting costs. The manufacturers of the less liquid scarce goods have smaller chances of obtaining attractive products and services than the manufacturers of highly liquid goods.

A procurement scout at the Kudowa cotton mill summed up business operations: "When 'something' is necessary in the factory, I grab the phone and start making calls. There's no point in writing and sending orders. Once I spot the 'something' I have to get there myself. When I get there, they ask me first, 'What do you make? What do you deal in? What can you fix?' And only then, 'What did you come here for?' "

NOTES

1. When the postwar Communist authorities imposed a Soviet-type command economy, firms were socialized and lost their autonomy to a huge apparatus of control. The important decisions were made not by the enterprises themselves, but through an intricate system of bureaucratic requirements and controls from above.

2. Author's note: The research team was headed by Professor Janusz Beksiak from the Central School of Planning and Statistics (SGPiS).

3. The "topic of mutual interest" was that Sanepid monitors sanitary conditions in the factory, for example, the cafeteria. The cooperative arrangement would presumably be that Saniped would not create any problems for the company in exchange for material.

4. "Personal involvement" is a euphemism for theft of necessary parts.

5. Author's note: This information was gleaned from a report by Marek Henzler, "Jak Welwet Pomagał Zakładowi Przetrwać Kryzys," Polityka 27, July 7, 1984.

6. "Promotional" goods have nothing to do with promotion in capitalist economies, where such goods are used to stimulate demand. Where goods are few, they are incentives to the supplier.

7. Under this system, companies receiving orders from the government

were compelled to fill them under threat of penalty. At the same time, the government was required to supply the necessary raw materials. If the government did not fulfill its obligation, the company had no legal requirement to do so either. However, the possibility of government sanctions for not delivering an order gave companies the incentive to fulfill such orders under practically any circumstances.

8. Speculation means to sell these articles privately at higher prices.

9. Apartments are in short supply and one of the most sought-after goods. Providing apartments for employees can be an employer's selling card.

10. A company is better off looking for exchange partners rather than risking having a surplus of its product.

Acapulco Near Konstancin

PIOTR GLIŃSKI

> If the merchant who came to his calling during the
> Occupation is to continue to do business in the new
> Polish society, he must forget all about the easy life of
> those years.   —Kazimierz Wyka, 1945

The history of the Polish Peoples' Republic is punctuated by periods
of economic liberalization—1947, 1956–1957, 1970–1971, and 1981–
1989—brought on by social and political crises. Liberalization typically energized the legal private sector: entrepreneurs surfaced from
the shadows of the informal economy, and the number of registered
private companies shot up. These "new" entrepreneurs came from
all social backgrounds—intelligentsia, workers, and farmers.

The marked development of the informal economy during the
1970s, partly due to more intensive contact with the West, created
an economic base for development of the legal private sector. Although impoverished, Polish society nevertheless maintained high
aspirations to consume and sought—sometimes dramatically—to better its living conditions. Those people who did not want to fall by
the wayside could choose among emigrating, dealing in the informal
economy, or starting a legal business "for oneself" ["na swoim"].

In the 1970s the state propaganda denounced these activities,
using primitive, populist calls for "egalitarianism," and promoting
odious stereotypes of prosperous growers of flowers, vegetables, and
fruits. Although private entrepreneurs earned their wealth through
activities on the legal, private market, they were dubbed "privateers"
["prywaciarz"] and other such pejorative names.

In the 1980s the legal private sector underwent intense development with a very different outcome. From 1982 to 1984 some

600,000 new employees (5 percent of the work force in the state sector) shifted to the nonagricultural, non-state sector.[1] Income inequality, private ownership, and informal economic activity became more socially acceptable; the prestige of private entrepreneurs rose.

In the early 1980s a body of "free" people—free in that they were not constrained by "steady (state) jobs" emerged. Some had been fired from state jobs for political dissent and found creative outlets for their energies, enthusiasm, and courage in private economic activity, so long taboo in many circles. But their "freedom" was also a lifestyle. Not only were they independent from state work, they were freewheeling, freespirited, and even somewhat bohemian. They also were potentially ready to accept risks and responsibilities, drawing upon inner resources and self-reliance—a new vision under existing conditions. All this fostered a conscious predisposition for work in the private sector.

Most of these "free" people came from the younger generation, unburdened by experience of the ideological stigmatization of private enterprise during the Stalinist years. Moreover, they have had direct contact with Western cultural models and sometimes earn capital from "Saxon work."[2] More than 70 percent of those who started nonagricultural businesses from 1983 to 1986 were under 41 and had at least finished high school.[3] The earlier generation of businessmen was much older and less well educated.

The financial career of a typical member of this "new capitalist class" began in the mid-1970s with regular trips to work in the West. Some members tested their potential for business on Western markets by, for example, selling Swedish paintings door-to-door, a scheme concocted and executed by a well-organized group of Polish "tourists."[4] Confronted by the endemic but unpredictable, the forward-looking capitalist became adept at "organizing" overnight wholesale deliveries of, say, shampoo from West Berlin or coffee from Vienna.

Two contradictory motives prompted people to turn such illegal activity into something at least semi-legal by, for example, registering a private company: the desire to start an honest, lawful, and sensible enterprise "for oneself" and the need to create a legal cover for continuing informal, "second circulation" activities underground. These limited liability companies that required little start-up capital created excellent covers. Of course the legal private, nonagricultural sector remained as tightly linked with the informal economy as it had been for many years.

The real fortunes of the "new capitalist class" were made as economic activity passed from largely informal and outlawed enterprise into open private corporate activity in the form of cooperatives and especially of limited liability companies. The Trade Code of 1934 (never revoked after the war), which made it possible to start such a company with little capital, proved to be the most convenient institutional umbrella for trading. In 1985–86 there were 43 such companies in Warsaw and its suburbs; by the end of 1988, there were several hundred.[5]

The Solidarity-Opposition activists who took part in the "second circulation" (the underground publishing industry of the late 1970s and 1980s) were forced to support themselves as well as clandestine political and cultural activity on resources they earned underground. They established sound economic principles for independent publishing and even introduced an efficient insurance system against confiscation and police repression.[6] The activists developed business skills and became an experienced and qualified managerial cadre, professionally and financially prepared to manage legal private companies. Such activities prepared them for the private economy to come, when a cadre of Solidarity activists released from martial-law prisons was to found limited liability companies. The "Agora" company, for example, evolved from a wing of the Solidarity leadership. It publishes *Gazeta Wyborcza*, Poland's main daily.

Some time during the mid-1980s, Poland came into the electronics era, first with computers. The new entrepreneurs, imaginative and experienced in independent economic activity, conceived and established the market. They spoke foreign languages, had contacts abroad often through working in the West, were bold and willing to take risks, and wise in the ways of the free play of economic forces. These last two characteristics were especially necessary to take advantage of the doctrinal, economic, and legal paradoxes of the real socialist system and to broker effectively between private importers—usually front men—and the state sector.[7]

Many played the Far East card, taking advantage of cheap Aeroflot and LOT (Polish) airline tickets, the system of protective import taxes of some products in, say, India, the excellent and relatively cheap goods available in Singapore, and the much more open borders of Asian countries. Their extraordinary enterprise earned them considerable fortunes from audio and video equipment, watches, and electronics. Experienced in adapting to changing conditions, they steadily perfected their smuggling methods and switched trade routes frequently, opting for the ever more circuitous and secure routes—India-Sri Lanka-Poland or Karachi-Katmandu-Warsaw.[8]

First computer dealers "vacationed" in Singapore and brought computers home with them; later, computers could simply be sent to private addresses for relatively little tax. My aunt delivered one to a firm that had given her the capital, and the firm then sold it either to state companies prevented by law and ideology from buying directly from the source or to the Soviet Union.

For several years, computer companies saturated the domestic market, making Poland a "computer enclave" among East European countries, including the Soviet Union. Because of NATO embargoes on strategic equipment, demand was huge. Now the informal traders have expanded their services to include telefaxes, medical equipment, clothes, kitchen utensils, and all conceivable goods.

It is not surprising that, among all social groups in Poland, entrepreneurs travel abroad most frequently. Some 35 percent took trips at least once from 1984 to 1986,[9] and this was a luxury or at least a special opportunity for material benefit.

Lifestyles of the Rich and Nouveau Riche

In the 1970s there was one type of private businessman and one ethos, characterized by the "cult" of entrepreneurial spirit, energy and ability to cut deals, "flexible" ethics with respect to customers and end-users, and membership in one's tight-knit *środowisko* and distance to those outside it. These qualities remain important to doing business successfully in Poland, but in the 1980s several new types of entrepreneurs have emerged from completely different backgrounds and experiences. All types are united principally by their common role in helping to usher the nation into the postcommunist era.

The *"kombinator"*—schemer, and sometimes even swindler engaging in clever speculation—is regarded as somewhat unscrupulous. Oriented toward fast and easy profit, he makes dishonesty come naturally with state bureaucrats as well as with state and private contract partners and clients. Entrepreneurs of this type prey on the rule-bound social and economic system by resorting to their repertoire of cliques, contacts, and bureaucratic "ins," holes in the legal system, gray areas of the law, and the elementary absence of competition. It is a seller's market, where practically everything produced can be sold. In 1987 more than 70 percent of private businessmen said they did not fear competition.[10]

Practically speaking, a *kombinator* does not seek to help change or reform the system. Rather, his work serves to reinforce it. Most often he is active in areas of the private sector that offer opportunities for large if illegal profits.[11]

In contrast to the street-alley image of the *kombinator*, the "Capitalists" are modern, Western-styled managers active mostly in foreign firms, joint ventures, limited liability companies, cooperatives such as computer companies, and large craft workshops such as cable, car parts and sewing machine factories. A Capitalist is not perceived as seeking shady deals; he tries to avoid clearly illegal activities if at all possible. He takes advantage of employees' connections with former state administration and state factory managers, but as much as possible in accordance with the law. He aims at bold investment and development of his business; he is educated and employs professionals.

The Capitalist strives for a Western and managerial lifestyle. He and his family live well at the company's expense, frequenting luxury hotels, fashionable bars and restaurants—the dozen or so recently opened places such as "Santana" in the wealthy Warsaw district of Saska Kępa and "Acapulco" near Konstancin where places must be reserved in advance, and prices are too steep for ordinary citizens.

A Capitalist shops at the state-run Pewex stores that sell mostly luxury imported goods for dollars only, and the well-stocked "Różycki" or "Polna Street" bazaars where private traders peddle expensive foods, quality clothes, and stereo equipment, largely obtained on frequent trend-watching trips to the West. The Capitalist loves—as does any nouveau riche—to be served by eager servants, whom he engages for personal affairs. This raises his prestige, at least in his own eyes. His company-paid drivers double as gardeners, and his suppliers furnish—without distinction of billing—his corporate and family necessities. His many obedient secretaries, in addition to fulfilling their office duties, bring him lunch from a restaurant or chilled champagne while he sits in a wicker chair giving orders over his portable telephone or entertaining guests in his company's garden, thoughtfully set amidst the splendor of a prestigious Warsaw district.

The Capitalist receives a constant stream of clients and "guest-partners," work cronies from his *środowisko*. Friends and acquaintances roll up to the company pad in their latest model Mercedes and BMWs. He spends his weekends with them and his family windsurfing on Lake Zegrzyńskie 20 kilometers from Warsaw, and takes his winter holidays in Egypt or at Austrian ski resorts. He works hard, earns a handsome income, and knows how to spend.

Unlike the Capitalist, the "Committed Craftsman" engages in business mostly for self-actualization. He looks to find meaning in life and through work "for himself" and to secure a niche affording independence and dignity. He is not a pawn in someone else's game but the agent of his own decisions and activities. He may publicly advocate capitalism and economic liberalism, as a form of political protest, but he is no Capitalist.

He believes that work is intrinsically worthwhile, viewing it as a kind of creativity through which enterprise, initiative, and organization constitute their own reward, even if calling for more effort, requiring more devotion and leaving less free time than work in the state-owned sector. He is solid and honest in his work and contacts with clients. He invokes the prewar tradition of craftsmanship, and the culture of solidarity. Often he refers to the prewar code of craftsmanlike conduct based on the confidence of those it served. He takes pride in his company and in its products. He is also proud of the active, consciously and independently chosen route he has taken, and looks down on "worthless," passive state employees, who complain about their lot, their meaningless work, and everything else they can think of.

The Committed Craftsman adopts a defensive attitude toward the state administration, seeing it as an opponent, rather than a partner. He puts down the "cronyism" and "fixing" that pervade the bureaucracy, an attitude that justifies in his own eyes his engaging in slightly unethical actions, reluctantly of course, in the name of providing his family with a decent living.

In all other spheres, economic profit is subordinated to higher values, such as the company's good name, the social utility of the activity, his own and his clients' satisfaction, independence, "being a decent man," or simply doing the work he likes. The Committed Craftsman is often a creative type with a deeply personal attitude towards his work, even if only a blacksmith shop, and his product, be it a simple bolt. Each machine in his shop, with its own history and brass name plate, is unique and behaves individually, but reliably. As a good craftsman, he understands it man-to-machine, knows its "humor," what is best for it and what it hates, and the best spot for it in the shop.

The Committed Craftsman often has a profound sense of social responsibility and social service. He may be active in one or more independent grass-roots associations or clubs that have sprung up to improve the quality of state-provided housing, education, and environmental control, and to lobby the government to free restrictions on private enterprise.[12]

An "Enfranchised Nomenklatura Man" is a representative of the *nomenklatura* who became an "agent"—by creating a limited liability company through purchase of shares from state-owned companies. This is called "personal privatization" [*"uwłaszczenie"*]—making state property one's own. Either he owns only part of a state company, or he treats the company as his own property. From his workplace he takes anything that can be used as capital to help launch a private enterprise: raw materials, machines, cars, and so on. Former employees of transportation companies, for example, hung onto their permits to buy cars at a discount, which came in handy for those who wanted to become private taxi drivers.

Contacts in *nomenklatura* circles are precious for "arranging matters" within the bureaucracy. The Enfranchised Nomenklatura Man often takes advantage of influence, position, and legally ambiguous areas or even breaks the law. His main capital is not money but rather his privileged position of "access" to policymakers and bureaucrats. This enables him to secure deliveries of hard-to-get raw materials, to impose obligatory selling or buying upon his contract partners, and to obtain tax relief for "his" company.

The economic conduct of this type of businessman consists mainly in using the mechanisms of state intervention for his own economic gain. This is a typical "negative enterprise" that obstructs the working of the natural laws of economics based on money and markets, competition, supply and demand. The Enfranchised *Nomenklatura* Man favors the creation of monopolies and practices an unethical model of management. His lifestyle resembles those of prominent people from the Gierek era of the 1970s. He is proud of his achievements—even if they are monuments of economic stupidity. He flies a company plane, has his own sports club, and hunts with colleagues, retiring at night to the luxurious lodges built for high-level officials in the 1970s.

There is much dispute about how Polish businessmen will adapt to the new political circumstances of the 1990s: Will the *kombinator*, Capitalist, Committed Craftsman, or the Enfranchised *Nomenklatura* Man model prevail? Some argue that Poles cannot become real businessmen because they learned how to do business in a nonmarket economy without competition. They learned only to "arrange" and exploit informal contacts to overcome bureaucratic barriers. They learned only how to make profits over the short run in an economy in which nearly everything, no matter how poor the quality, was sold. Their perspective is anything but long-term.

Others stress the stamina and modern characteristics of the "new" private-sector elite, as evidenced by their work, lifestyle, and social involvements. They founded the numerous *środowisko*-based economic clubs and societies that inspire educational centers, which spread a doctrine of classical liberalism and "economic freedom."[13] Through the contacts, Western methods, and technology they are introducing, as well as changes in property law, the new set will eventually stoke the state sector and help to impose modern economic principles upon it.

The success of economic reforms depends not only on the measures themselves, but on which type of entrepreneur emerges as a major player in Poland's slowly changing economy.

NOTES

1. Author's note: Zdzisław Zagórski, "Pozarolnicze Klasy Prywatno-własnościowe we Wspołczesnej Polsce" (The nonagricultural, self-employed class in contemporary Poland), in Edmund Wnuk-Lipiński, ed., *The Fifth Poland-Wide Sociology Conference* (Warsaw, 1987).

2. Many young adults, such as university students, earn hard currency by going to the West, especially to western Germany. There they can make in a summer vacation many times what an entire year's work brings them in Poland.

3. Author's note: Małgorzata Czarzasty and Cezary Sowiński, " 'Prywaciarze'—A Kto to Taki?" (Private businessmen—who are they?), *Biuletyn CBOS*, no. 2, 1987; Paweł Ruszkowski, "Opinie Wybranych Grup Pracowników Przemysłu o Formach Organizacji Własności w Gospodarce" (The opinions of selected industrial workers on forms of ownership in the economy), *Biuletyn CBOS*, no. 2, 1987; Edmund Wnuk-Lipiński, "Spectrum Polskie" (The Polish spectrum), *Więź*, no. 1, 1988; see also results of research conducted by Władysław Adamski, Edmund Wnuk-Lipiński, Lena Kolarska,

and Andrzej Rychard under the auspices of Polacy '88, Institute of Philosophy and Sociology, Polish Academy of Sciences.

4. These people traveled on tourist passports but in fact went abroad to earn money, not to see the sights.

5. Author's note: Iwona Bartczak, "W Pół Drogi: Warunki do Działań Przedsiębiorczych" (Halfway there: The preconditions for entrepreneurial activity), *Więź*, nos. 2–3, 1987.

6. For example, if a car transporting illegal books was searched and confiscated, an "insured" underground publishing house could claim indemnity.

7. It was much easier for a state enterprise to buy computers from private importers than directly from foreign companies, dealing with which they faced much higher taxes and a lack of hard currency. State firms generally did not have dollars or could not make such purchases for dollars without traversing a lot of bureaucratic restriction and red tape. But they had a lot of złoty. State firms were reluctant to buy directly from private people, but could buy from private middleman companies that had purchased from private individuals and added a level of guarantee and sometimes software packages for a suitable markup.

8. An Oppositionist acquaintance recalls running into three acquaintances from Warsaw on a 1988 trip to Singapore. None knew that the others were there; all were engaged in computer trading.

9. Author's note: Czarzasty and Sowiński, "'Prywaciarze.'"

10. Author's note: Ibid.

11. Currently many *kombinators* work the legalized "black market," where the rate often changes from one day to the next by several tenths of a percent.

12. In the late 1980s a worsening economy and weakening government opened the door for hundreds of grass-roots organizations and private enterprises. Many Solidarity activists redirected their efforts from the political to the economic, putting part of their proceeds back into foundations to lobby for better policies in many areas that were the prerogative of the socialist state.

13. The most influential economic societies—the Cracow Industrial Society and the Warsaw Economic Association—provided a "middle ground" between the Communist government and the Opposition during the late 1980s when Polish politics were polarized. After Solidarity's landslide of 1989 and takeover of the government in 1990, these associations exerted considerable influence on politics, the economy, and society. Both served as political bases for their founding members. Aleksander Paszyński, founder of the Economic Association, and Tadeusz Syryczyk, co-founder of the Cracow Industrial Society, were appointed ministers of Housing and Industry, respectively, in the first post-Communist government.

PART IV

Reclaiming Responsibility

Introduction

Years before Solidarity formed the first non-Communist government in Eastern Europe, Poles had learned the art of organizing—and not only underground. In the latter 1980s, hundreds of people founded voluntary associations—even in areas for which the socialist state claimed exclusive responsibility, including housing, precollegiate education and the environment. Organizers sought, and many received, government registration enabling them to operate openly—to raise money, hold public meetings, and publish independently of the state.[1] Before the political revolutions of 1989, starting an organization or business had become a ticket to success in Poland.

In a slightly tongue-in-cheek article extolling the virtues of both nudism and Buddhism, Jacek Kurczewski, director of Warsaw University's Institute of Applied Social Sciences, attributes the efflorescence of voluntary associations to the need to reassert responsibility for oneself and others, a backlash against the personal irresponsibility the communist system abetted. As contributors Pawlik and Firlit and Chłopecki have explained, irresponsibility was built into the system; theoretically everyone was responsible, but in practice no one was. The Solidarity movement of 1980–81 also was a statement against passivity and a shared search for self-realization, not only for freedom.

This search was cut short by martial law. Youth who joined "Oasis," a Christian movement under the wing of the Polish Catholic Church, during those depressing days were looking more for self-realization than salvation, according to the sociologists Barbara Lewenstein and Małgorzata Melchior of Warsaw University's Institute of Applied Social Sciences.

Kurczewski contends that such movements of the 1980s—many alien to a society both Catholic and communist—were catalytic to the creation of new *środowiska*, bringing together representatives of different social groups.

Several other contributors, however, point to the limited capacity of voluntary associations to expand beyond their originating circles. They observe that organizations tend to arise from a single *środowisko*, and so far have not proven able to go beyond it. Father Andrzej Kłoczowski suggests that organizing itself is more important than the groups' stated purpose and reduces the groups to "a form of psychotherapy." The very act of bringing together like-minded colleagues and drafting a manifesto is often the most essential activity of a group's entire history.

This sets limits to the creation of more extensive, embracing entities such as political parties: political movements form themselves around new leaders, issues, and interests, rather than around longstanding relationships. Today there is little apparent coalition-building among *środowiska* and especially not around the creation of movements with national policies in mind.

There is much antagonism: the divisions within Solidarity-Opposition[2] are especially visible following the deep social conflicts among *środowiska* that surfaced during the presidential campaign of late 1990. The Warsaw-Cracow Opposition *środowisko* from which was largely drawn the government of former Prime Minister Tadeusz Mazowiecki, and Solidarity leader Lech Wałęsa and his followers, waged a bitter *social* conflict with one another which smolders on after the election. Surprise candidate Stanisław Tymiński mobilized a longstanding *środowisko* of apparatchiks and secret policemen and galvanized *środowiska* and voluntary associations will do much to shape Poland's electoral and political arena and the structure of its civil society.

The Solidarity movement of 1980–81 remains the ultimate example of Poles' ability to act collectively and mobilize people of different social backgrounds around shared interests—if only in opposition. At that moment, an unprecedented union of intellectuals, workers, and farmers sought to transcend the traditional barriers of Poland's *środowisko*-bound society. In the 1990s volatile issues, such as abortion, may again gather together many groups which up to this moment did not know how much they had in common.

NOTES

1. In post-Communist Poland, laws on association have been liberalized; a group is required only to register its name and statute with the court.

2. Solidarity-Opposition is composed of two somewhat connected groups: the long-standing Opposition—the close-knit circles of dissenting political discussion and activity mostly evolved between 1968 and 1979 (above all in intelligentsia *środowiska*), and the great body of Solidarity activists who forced their way to the forefront of the workers' resistance when Solidarity was born in 1980.

8

Shared Privacy

JACEK KURCZEWSKI

> Experience soon showed clearly enough that it was
> better to sit off in a corner than to show initiative.
> —Kazimierz Wyka, 1945

A gray residential block in the suburbs of Warsaw. I take the elevator. The guide knocks and introduces me. The faces are rather distrustful. All sit barefoot in a room, conventional except for a portrait of Hari Krishna. I join them. I listen to the creed and taste "prasad," a Polish version of the ritual Vedic vegetarian dish. It's not bad. Youths with shorn heads enter and genuflect before the altar. . . .

On a summer's evening, from beyond the Vistula I can hear the rumble of a crowd of many thousands, gathered at the stadium. When I pass the entrance, I see guards on duty. Well-dressed people are everywhere; families with children. All the parking places near the stadium are taken. A cross built for the tenth anniversary of People's Poland hangs over the stadium. This is the first authorized public assembly in Poland of the Jehovah's Witness movement, possibly the third largest religious denomination (in terms of active following). Although the gathering itself is legal, the movement still is unregistered—that is, technically illegal. . . .

Beyond the big city the road twists and turns into the countryside. We walk to a palace on which a banner of the Socialist Organization of Polish Youth is draped. Then across the stream to a cottage. Actors pour in from other cottages. They feed us pies and tea. In the main room they briefly explain their principles and then coax the spectators to dance with them. After sunset we walk over the fields to the show. Then, for the spectators, a nighttime return to the city, but the actors remain in the country where they live and work. . . .

Alcoholics Anonymous gets together to exchange experiences of personal success and failure. Intellectuals and workers go on a pilgrimage to Jasna Góra, a national Catholic shrine of the Black Madonna. A group of street demonstrators demand that a court decision concerning the storage of radioactive waste be reversed. The residents of a seaside resort town organize against the nudists who annually gather on the local dunes. Trade unions are appearing, along with unauthorized political parties, alternative artistic movements, and religious sects. All this began as martial law drew to its close in the mid-1980s.

In recent years such groups have aggregated into a momentous movement. They have matured in contrast with and yet in the context of the stagnation of officially created and supported entities. Do these groups have anything in common, and how should we look at them? One popular conception is that they emerged only in reaction to political repression—that they serve as the channels through which the spring flood of opposition, contained by the might of the militarized Communist regime, disperses to fertilize the fields. Another is that they simply are the Polish version of the worldwide differentiation of culture.

Neither explanation sufficiently accounts for the groups' growth or what they represent in the Polish context. To be sure, neither geographical nor political boundaries are able to hold back global cultural processes. American models of conspicuous consumption in the form of bell bottoms reigned with forgotten antecedents in Russia—even during the early 1920s—the time of Stalin; the Mao hangman's suit rode the tides of cultural revolution into the wardrobes of Western intellectuals. Of course tempo and intensity vary with the distance in terms of politics and abundance as well as of kilometers from the iron triangle of culture, which runs from Paris to London to San Francisco. Quarantine cordons cannot protect against an epidemic: Poland also suffered from the Beatles and the Rolling Stones, long hair, the freedom of sexual encounter, pacifism, "the just-relax-attitude," and narcotics.

However, the Polish experiences deriving from and mediating these phenomena—cast against a background of Communist social order and economic backwardness—had their own special qualities, as did the reactions to them. Most importantly, these phenomena were more superficial in Poland than in the West, as the cultural elements were replicated without the social climate that gave rise to them in the West. The best evidence of this is that the adoption of counterculture fashions in Poland of the 1960s never had a politically confrontationist character here. It was merely an attempt to catch up to world culture.

The Polish version of *Hair* was not a protest against the establishment but, at most, partook of the muddled pacifism of Czesł aw Niemen's songs, a religious musical of Katharine Gaertner or a spectacle in honor of the Polish People's Army with such top popular entertainers as singer Maryla Rodowicz and actor Daniel Olbrychski. In contrast to Western protests against the Vietnam War, against nuclear armaments and capitalism as such, the Polish countercultural milieu was *apolitical*, admittedly a kind of willy-nilly ideological self-determination in the Polish People's Republic, since official Communist doctrine held that everyone ought to be politically "engaged" in support, of course, of the Party-State line. Furthermore, the nonconformist milieu was not large and, given its elitist and cosmopolitan character, not well rooted in mass culture.

However, in the last decade, the simplest way to characterize Polish alternative movements and milieus was "political," for they took on a more or less conscious opposition to the Communist system. Rock musicians of the early 1980s expressed contempt for the regime and its supporters; their music developed in the general spirit of contesting the regime. Whenever I talked with them, I detected their guilt at what they themselves considered "collaboration" with authority: they felt forced to participate in politically exploited performances. In one notorious case, an internationally renowned rock band applying for a leave permit was told one was available if the band would perform its aggressive, independent songs at some occasion staged to endorse the martial law regime. The issue was heatedly argued in the rock community. Some urged that musicians should not betray their art and ought to concern themselves only with music. But this was not a common view.

Rock music was no more politically "engaged" than other movements. In the 1980s Poland was thoroughly politicized to a degree unknown in its post-World War II history. The rock musicians who howled contempt of the "Reds" and cheered their frustrated young audience with the chorus "Moscow is on fire!" were simply voicing the national mood expressed by thousands with only less artistry.

Collective Action under Communism

The entire structure of the Polish People's Republic rested on arbitrary and discretionary administrative power. No collective action was legal unless officially registered and approved. People could not congregate freely without approval of the given association as such and of its charter, and until 1989, there was no legal recourse should an application be denied. The grounds for acceptance according to the law in force were "social utility of the association."

Assemblies also were subject to the law: meetings in private homes had to be registered with the local government except for weddings, social occasions, and religious services in designated buildings. This did not mean that people informed the authorities of meetings they held with neighbors about going in together on buying a water pipe; but nevertheless, it did mean that any meeting at home, let alone one held in public, could be deemed illegal and broken up by the police.

Not surprisingly, in such an unfriendly environment the natural goal of even the smallest gathering—be it a psychotherapeutic practice, a consumer protection group, or an amateur theater troupe—was to obtain authorization. After all, Poles lived in a country where a citizen was expected to have a personal identification card on him any time he left his home. And, although it might seem part of a Polish drama of the absurd, it came out in the regime's dying days that at some state offices even the identity card itself had to be supplemented by a notary's confirmation.

From its beginning in 1972, the history of the Polish nudist movement abounds in examples of various maneuvers toward legalization that were troublesome for the government as well as the private citizens involved. Nudist activist Sylwester Marczak explains: "We have those who advocate a spontaneous, informal movement; and we also have those who want the official seal of authorization, initiation fees, and the devil knows what else. We have debates as to whether nudism should be elite or egalitarian, plebian or snobbish, and meanwhile, everyone wants to be a leader."[1] Marczak himself was reprimanded by fellow nudists and warned not to use the title "chairman." Marczak retorted that it was hard to be the chairman of an organization that did not exist and that there was no harm in competition among organizers. "After all, I don't have a monopoly on taking off underwear!"

It is difficult not to agree with him. But the very checklist of steps needed to carry out elections and plan nudist rallies (not the least of which is securing accommodation and food) to represent the interests of a crowd of anonymous (though one cannot say faceless) nudists to the local authorities, shows the need to organize.

As early as 1977 a nudist activist attempted to legalize the movement as the "Society for the Propagation of Physical Culture." This attempt failed, but authorities became more lenient as a result. Notably, the police stopped levying fines for nude sunbathing on the beach.

Although the usual forms of joint action have continued to develop, such as rallies gathering people from all over the country, there has been no greater progress toward legalization. "We think," a nudist leader explained, "that it is better to meet as a friendly group of nudists on the beach in the summer than as the legally nonexistent Polish Naturalist Association in interrogations with the civic militia."

Further events at home pushed the nudist scandal into the background but also gave the nudists an unexpected opportunity: instead of urging political freedom, pressing for freedom to become nudists. In October 1980, the prominent journalist Józef Kuśmierek asked the First Secretary of the Central Committee of the Polish United Workers' Party, "Comrade, do you really want our youth leaders to be content with forming unions for nudists, body-builders, and hippies, which you so kindly permit, by reason of their apoliticality?"

Truly favorable winds began to blow only toward the end of 1982 when the first regional branches of the Polish Naturalist Association appeared. During the seventh congress of nudists, the Provisional Central Administration of the Polish Naturalist Association was founded. After drawing up the bylaws, application to register was submitted to the proper government department, and refused on the grounds that the proposal "did not speak to the common good" and that the nudists' activities could be carried out in many other already existing organizations. In the city of Wrocław in 1983, the authorities denied registration but had to admit that the activities of the Wrocław nudists were legal; only the fact of forming an organization was not. When it later turned out that it did not fall under the structure of the Society for the Propagation of Physical Culture, a neighborhood sports and recreation center agreed to the creation of a nudist club under its auspices.

Thus far I have been discussing the relatively recent past. I often argue with my fellow sociologists, who assume there is *one* System in postwar Poland, not subject to any change. I contend that, if there is such a thing as "the System," it has changed, and this in turn has pushed people toward further change. Both sides, it seems, have contradicted themselves. A System designed to control all activity has lowered its threshold of repression enough to allow social movements that undermine the System's basic assumptions even if ostensibly engaged in such nonpolitical and diverse activities as sun-worshiping, transcendental meditation, rock music, or the independent monitoring of industrial safety. But spontaneity, that is, the uncontrolled emergence of non-state independent initiative itself is the negation of the System. On the other hand, if people assume that an immutable System is above them, sooner or later, more or less consciously, they engage in one or another form of social movement that implicitly denies and thus undermines this immutability.

The best way to look at the post-World War II history of Poland is as a *process*. The vicissitudes of Stalinism at its peak in 1949–50 are incomparable in terms of human suffering even with the repressions of martial law declared on December 13, 1981. The more oppressed society was also on the surface more obedient even though repeated outbursts in 1956, 1957, 1966, 1968, 1970, 1976, 1980, and the mid-1980s manifested the System's only immutable element: the normative structure of society that focuses on basic freedoms and civic rights.

In the 1970s the flaws of the old Stalinist model of social organization became obvious as people became less and less willing to participate in organized activities, and new social needs could not find protection and expression within its confines. In this model, organization was a conveyor belt, carrying ideas from the avant-garde center to the masses, who repaid this with mobilization and support. It is difficult to part with such a legacy, especially since it provides such a deceptive feeling of security. It is not surprising that even purely local social initiatives, such as that of local history lovers, experienced endless difficulties even after the death of Stalin in 1953. Even though these initiatives were supposedly useful and at least not harmful, they were inconvenient for centralization.

In December 1970 strikers already had enough of the top-down official trade unions and expressed dissatisfaction with their leadership. What can one do with needs and concerns that don't fit the model of real socialist culture? Should we create a Nationwide Society of Nudists, with a centralized activist cadre condemned to leadership? Or keep quiet about the bothersomeness of organizations such as these, doomed to spontaneity and transience, thereby evading the rigors of planning?

Let us consider another aspect of these organizational problems with the help of the somewhat more serious example of consumerism. Under Communist rule there was no room for a consumers' movement; consumers could seek restitution only through the state's commerce organizations and the Party-controlled Women's League. News about anything like consumer protection in the West was censored.

The first academic paper dealing with the Western consumer movement and proposing the creation of corresponding structures in Poland was published in a professional journal in 1958, but silence followed. We know nothing of any citizens' initiatives in this area: probably there weren't any, due to general apathy and to lack of information. The government didn't attempt to create such initiatives either.

Then suddenly in 1972 the Ministry of Domestic Trade suggested establishing a "Nationwide Council on Consumer Affairs" to which representatives of various officially acknowledged organizations were invited to represent the "enlightened" interest of consumers. But the matter interested neither the government nor the official trade unions. For lack of support, the council became a powerless agency affiliated with the state-sponsored market research bureau "Opinia," established so that an ambitious wife of one typically male Communist Party Politbureau member could have a visible post. As was common with such official creations, both the Council and "Opinia" mimicked Western institutions and thereby offered fictitious remedies to a population, which nevertheless had to crowd in queues for basic goods. The attempt to emulate Western institutions on paper continued, however, and in 1974 the Minister of Domestic Trade created a Consultative Council of Consumers Affairs consisting of 27 representatives of mass organizations, science and industry.

In 1976, the chairman of the council proposed its dissolution on the grounds that it had become a dead institution and that none of the measures that it had proposed—the creation of consumers' associations, systematic examination of the marketplace, founding of periodicals—had been accepted by the authorities.

Useless attempts at organizing a consumer movement from above began in 1972. In September 1980, in accordance with legal statutes on domestic commerce, consumption and the marketplace, some consumer activists prepared a consumer protection statute, according to which the Sejm or the State Council was to create the "Union of Polish Consumers." But the times had already changed. Andrzej Nałecz-Jawecki, organizer of both consumer and nudist movements, hit the nail on the head when he urged the creation of a grass-roots Federation of Consumers in 1981, which found a wide public response in the face of deteriorating economic conditions. Earlier there had been no lack of need or desire, only of the possibility of taking action. But the example of consumerism shows that when a hospitable climate for social activity manifests, even if only temporarily, entrepreneurs, prudent organizers, and those eager for concrete daily work will appear as well.

Responsibility and Recounterculture

People complain that everyone else is sinning, writes Wojciech Pawlik, in "Intimate Commerce." This means, in fact, that everyone sins. People also feel no guilt, thanks to the mechanism of "they-ism"—the displacement of responsibility. "They" are the guilty ones. Traditionally, two attitudes surround this transfer of responsibility. One accepts the "they-ist" thesis in a more or less subtle form; the other points out the ease with which most of society rids itself of responsibility for its own behavior.

The essence of Polish anomie derives not so much from a persistent inability to satisfy continuously rising aspirations or on the rapidity of changes, but rather from precisely this permanent social structure that enables individuals not to answer for their behavior, and that rids groups and communities of responsibility for the state of affairs that touches them directly. The absence of responsibility is an inherent feature of this social structure. Nowhere else does this feature express itself so well as in the domain of socialist property, for which theoretically everyone is responsible but in practice no one is. Thus, the reconstruction of civil society requires a return to responsibility.

From this point of view, every new movement is an experiment in reclaiming responsibility for oneself and others. These movements are diverse in contents and stated goals, and can diversify even further.

What I am trying to say is that even in their rough manifestations, they deserve our respect insofar as they aim to reclaim lost responsibility for one's own fate and that of others. The liberating civil society needs to enable each of its members to accept personal moral responsibility in order to reclaim for each the status of free human agent.

Each of the movements described here—from Buddhist to nudist to consumer—is centered around self-expression. Traditional cultural elements are adapted to this expressionist ethos; each movement proposes a particular way for the individual to put down roots in the universe. In this way these new movements do not become merely attempts at an impossible return to that which has already passed. For this reason, I describe the new philosophy with the term "recounterculture."

Recountercultural movements often take conflicting directions. It rarely happens that the same people will demonstrate against permissive standards of behavior in schools and also for the right to go nude, although I see the two as having a lot in common. I am interested less in the differences among the various movements and more in what is shared by them and in what earns them the label "recounterculture."

First of all, there is a certain degree of discipline in the groups, a consequence of the very need to organize. Even where this need is made necessary by an unfriendly environment, it has a disciplinary impact. Administration, commission, registration, spokesman, declaration, motion, charter member, president, business hours, renting of halls, official service, candidates' apprenticeship—this terminology carries vague needs from within into a believable form in the world outside one's head.

Another unavoidable point is that certain rules, even if unspoken, are always necessary. The Marquis de Sade observed that even in an orgy, some rules are necessary.

There is, finally, a certain positive vision that accompanies even the nudist movement. This vision varies in cohesiveness and quality, vacillating from a vision of the entire society to that of a regenerated individual in a certain role. However, the common trait is a positive judgment of what is healthy and proper, and the recognition that attaining this standard demands a certain individual or collective practice. As a result, the old language of counterculture has survived with its characteristic emphasis on spontaneity and freedom, but this time accompanied by the knowledge that freedom must be regulated and spontaneity rightly encouraged if they are to serve to realize the group's objectives. If it were really a question of impulsive and complete self-expression, wouldn't it be enough to content ourselves with the experiences of any alcoholic or drug addict?

Perhaps I have upset someone by lumping together so many varied phenomena as religious activism, therapeutic exercises, and the nudist movement. But all are part of the general social and political landscape; all, to varying degrees, help to form that landscape. Moreover, they cannot remain indifferent with regard to each other, but must take a stand.

Furthermore, they must take a stand on the political situation—even the naive organizational charter of the nudists: "in today's socialist society, we should not and there is no need to express social differences through dress" (Declaration of the Polish Nudist Society, "What Are We Fighting For?" 1979) or, later, that "the Supreme Being created man naked!" (Declaration of the Polish Nudist Society, 1982).

Not only the local administrators, militia, and church authorities, but even the highest government authorities refusing registration must take a position on the Polish Nudist Society. Through Cardinal Józef Glemp, the Catholic Church noted that "the authorities' tolerance of the illegal nudist movement is strange." He added: "It would perhaps be possible to understand a desire to bathe or to sunbathe with a group of people, who gather and throw off their clothes in some designated corner. On the other hand, dedicating a television program to such a movement is embarrassing. The program was meant to amuse, but in fact had nothing to do either with the beauty of the human body, the liberation of man, or the preservation of nature."[2]

All this was provoked by television coverage of a nudist event: in April 1991 the press reports that the Polish Naturalist Association was trying to get an audience with Cardinal Józef Glemp to explain the movement's character. Indeed, can the authorities' tolerance of nudist propaganda be accidental, given the limitations on more basic social activities? For the government, a nudist's naked rear end is less threatening than a clothed arm raised in Solidarity's two-finger victory sign. One senses a desire to concentrate public opinion on that rear end, rather than on Lech Wałęsa's moustache.

I have already mentioned ideological declarations, which promise expression of individual rights through orderly and legal means. The right question might differ from case to case. Nudism, for example, offers not only nudity (for it is certainly possible to do this more easily by simply undressing), but nudity as an expression of the autonomy of the individual—as a right that one fights for while walking to one's spot on the beach. This disrobing is regulated by legal statutes and local custom. Self-expression is of course assured not only by actually unclothing the body, but by *striving toward the goal* of unclothing the body.

It is worthwhile to consider whether the recounterculture character of such a movement can be gleaned from the motivations and experiences of ordinary members. It is certain that the further we are from the central leadership of the movement, the more confused and less clear the motivations for participating. "I came with a friend because she wanted company." "I thought it would be something different, but I stayed, because it's hard to leave in the middle." "We all just signed up." Such almost contentless reasons are not infrequently given for joining one or another social movement.

The appearance of the mass social and political Solidarity movement of 10 million in 1980 was related to "recounterculture." At least during the first, legal period of its history in 1980–81, the most obvious reason for participation was self-expression, both political and religious. The dominant feeling was one of freedom, recovered at last. There was, of course, a lot of expectation that the union would help to better life in Poland, but this instrumental element became overshadowed by people's rejoicing at first victories: the first strike, the first public parade, the first Holy Mass held in a state-owned company, the first uncensored newspaper, the first non-Communist leader appearing on the news, the first collective bargaining with management, the first negotiations with government representatives.

Beyond a doubt, 1980–81 offered thousands of people directly and millions indirectly the experience of expressing their true selves in public. Of course, this true self was largely a social construct. The sentiment of the nation was that the falsehood of the artificial propaganda image of public and private Poland had at last been abolished and that the truth of the individual as well as of the nation stood revealed. The opinion that, until then, nobody had dared to speak out in public suddenly appeared if not in the Party-State controlled television then at least in Solidarity's bulletins and newspapers. People felt free to say in public that they were Catholics, that they were not Communists, that life was ugly and the system absurd. Even in the state-controlled schools, the history textbooks underwent change to come closer to historical truths known to some and intuitively felt by most others.

The revolutionary character of Solidarity did not, however, prevent it from having a positive vision of new order. I cannot escape thinking that the revolution took form as a trade union movement only because of some external restrictions. Even if no one thought of Solidarity as only a trade union—it was also a national liberation movement as well as a social revolution—the trade union form compelled some tribute to be paid to it. Solidarity union leaders engaged simultaneously in negotiations concerning the political structures of the country and safety rules in the factory. Participants in the movement needed organizational order and direction because of the shocking novelty of the situation in which they found themselves— and which they had helped to create. In the summer of 1981, the local union chapters and regional assemblies discussed the union's draft program and finally settled a lengthy document accepted at the Gdańsk Congress in fall 1981. The self-governing Poland there envisioned encompassed all aspects of social life from kindergarten and elementary education to ecology and tolerance of minorities. The religious quality of the vision was not only a metaphor. The vision was conceptually consistent without being elaborated, not known to the average follower who still felt secure precisely because Solidarity had some positive vision for the future different from endlessly doomed programs of the Communist Party.

First and foremost, Solidarity incorporated traditional Polish and Catholic traditions, in contrast with the discredited official ideology. However the participants in this movement might act in private, publicly they appeared under the sign of the cross and the crowned eagle of the Polish nation. Unsurprisingly, the social activists from the Independent and Self-Governing Trade Union Solidarity did not meet with the avant-garde of world culture without conflict and misunderstanding. The complicated cultural structure that came into view can best be symbolized by a triangle: (1) higher culture, represented by those artists participating in world civilization; (2) official culture—a conglomeration of various products prepared by the propagandists and bureaucrats in accordance with the working program of "real socialist" culture;[3] and (3) mass culture, that is, the traditional Polish and Catholic heritage, with all its faults and virtues. The legal Solidarity period from 1980 to 1981 provided the opportunity to grant this last cultural layer equal status with the others. And so some people, both in the government and in the avant-garde intelligentsia, heard Solidarity's voice as that of the past. But this return to inheritance was achieved on a new level, with emphasis on self-expression, human dignity, and autonomy.

Some interpretations of human autonomy impute to the individual only rights and claims in regard to others and disregard the individual's duties and obligations. But such claims entail no obligation with regard to autonomy itself, with regard to others, or with regard to God. The popularity of such a vision of human autonomy is not surprising in a country where, for decades, the official theory has been that a citizen has certain rights only after having dutifully fulfilled all obligations to the government. The political prerequisites for the propagation of the counterculture doctrine of autonomy, and particularly that concept of the individual's unrestricted independence from others, are if anything overdetermined. But when I asked the Warsaw residents whom I interviewed, "Does the individual have an obligation to society?" the most common response was that there is no debt at all, neither of the individual to society, nor vice versa (39 percent), and even of those remaining, advocates of the primacy of society (36 percent) outnumbered supporters of unconditional primacy of the individual (27 percent). The conceptions of autonomy popular in Polish society seem closer to the more rigid version in which the various human rights are accompanied by various obligations. After all, only in the more rigid version can the concept of human autonomy really be connected to that of human dignity.

In its desire to organize, Solidarity shared another essential characteristic of recounterculture movements: their socially heterogeneous character. Solidarity leaders came not only from the working class and from the Gdańsk shipyards. Apart from electrician Lech Wałęsa, one could find university professors, bus drivers, engineers and designers, professional opposition politicians, and physicians among the leaders. Since 1980, I have maintained that Communist society produced its own new middle class composed of educated and skilled people, whose aspirations were cut short by the *nomenklatura* barrier, making it impossible for a non-Party member, and to a degree for a rank-and-file Party member, to influence his conditions of work and neighborhood and to participate in political life. This new middle class encompassed skilled electricians as well as university professors, and Solidarity's leadership reflected this occupational and professional heterogeneity.

The phenomenon is not restricted to the grand case of Solidarity. A study of the leaders of the then beginning consumer movement that emerged in the early 1980s found 14 workers, 11 economists, 4 teachers, 3 journalists, 1 lawyer, 13 other white-collar workers, 2 army officers, and 2 farmers.[4]

This heterogeneity is important as it implies that the social gaps in such an internally diversified movement were nevertheless somehow bridged. Within a socially homogeneous movement, the already existing networks reproduce themselves. When a factory goes on strike, new leaders may emerge but the channels of communication are basically the same as those used by the workers in their daily work. When the society goes on strike, as in fact has been the case since 1980, new channels of communication must be created to integrate factories with universities. Until 1980, these workplaces drew on *środowiska* isolated from one another, with few mutual contacts indeed. Because Polish recountercultural movements are heterogeneous and the *środowisko* is homogeneous, there is even more need to create daily channels of interaction between various *środowiska* as the prerequisite for a movement.

The 1980s revealed a surprising variety of interests and attitudes behind the mask of a society that on the one hand was held to be Communist and, on the other, to be Catholic. Although more than 90 percent baptized Catholic, Polish society displayed curiosity about a variety of cultural aspects alien to its Catholic tradition, ranging from Buddhism and charismatic movements to transcendental meditation and bioenergy therapy.

Although anti-Communist and displaying a strong entrepreneurial spirit, Poles also have brought, paradoxically, trade unionism to a culmination unparalleled in any other capitalist or communist country. The currents that surfaced with the help of selective repression applied by the last Communist administration in the 1980s may have been momentarily superseded by the victorious Solidarity in 1989, but the real heterogeneity of attitudes soon came forward.

The current debate on abortion, with only a minority supporting absolute prohibition—and a slightly larger minority supporting unlimited freedom of abortion—is a good example. Those movements and currents like Solidarity, which will remain the paramount example of Polish ability to act collectively in order to promote individual freedom, are the areas where people with different social backgrounds are attracted by shared interests and create a new *śro-*

dowisko. The difficulties of creating authentic political parties in the new, democratic Poland relate to the fact that political *movements* do not arise out of already existing *środowiska* but, rather, form themselves around new leaders, new issues, and new identities.

NOTES

1. Author's note: Sylwester Marczak, *Gazeta Młodych*, February 2, 1988.
2. Author's note: *Przegląd Katolicki* 36, 1985.
3. Author's note: Official term coined by Soviet First Party Secretary Leonid Brezhnev in the 1970s, applied to the real practice of the communist state in contrast to the theory of socialism.
4. Author's note: Unpublished study carried out by my student, Zbigniew Lasocik, 1988.

9

Escape to the Community

BARBARA LEWENSTEIN AND MAŁGORZATA MELCHIOR

We were like a child who has vodka poured into its
mouth and thus can claim that it has to swallow.
—Kazimierz Wyka, 1945

"Anomie" has been a popular instrument among Polish sociologists for describing our society and particularly Polish youth throughout the 1980s. Sociologists point to the breakdown of the sense of social ties, the blurring of values, the loss of any sense of authority, and the lack of leaders through the martial law years and beyond. This, they say, has produced anomie.

At the same time, however, there has been a dramatic increase in spontaneous culture, including the revival of rock music, and the appearance of various youth movements such as Buddhists, punks, heavy metal, and skinheads. We have studied "Oasis," also called "Light-life," a religious movement that also experienced a great surge in membership during martial law. Although Oasis, unlike these other movements, actually was born and cultivated in Poland, its leaders had similar Western Christian movements in mind.

Oasis bears a similarity to various Western church movements and organizations, especially Notre Dame Teams—a married couples' movement in France, the Italian "oasi" movement, and the charismatic renewal movement created on the wave of Western youth rebellion. But "Light-Life" incorporates many elements of Polish tradition, such as "scouting," which has been important in youth training, education, and activity.

Through participation and interviews in Warsaw parishes carried out mainly between 1986 and 1987, we set out to describe one religious youth movement. Many of our observations pertain to the movement's relation to the outside world and the social conditions under which it flourished. We interpret the abrupt increase in the number of those who joined and its prominence among young people as a particular reaction to the imposition of martial law and the general social situation that followed.

Oasis is a religious movement housed inside parishes of the Polish Catholic Church. Father F. Błachnicki, the movement's main founder in Poland, began his activities in the southern town of Krościenko in the early 1950s. It is important to remember that the movement was born under Stalinism—the most repressive period in Polish and East European history. The communist government's strong anti-church policies banned any pastoral work, except for large-scale masses, including organizational meetings and ministering to believers.

It was in this difficult context that Father Błachnicki began to work with youth, first specifically with small groups of altar boys. In response, the local authorities waged a campaign against religious gatherings and against the right to assemble. Yet the movement continued to attract new members. The local authorities responded by pronouncing the movement "dangerous" and limiting its leaders' activities. Eventually Błachnicki was imprisoned and Oasis suspended. However, after his release and the Second Vatican Council emphasizing the role of youth in church life, Oasis, still under Błachnicki's direction, spread throughout Poland. It was at this point that Błachnicki perfected the present form of the movement with an eye on Western religious movements of the time.

Błachnicki modeled his groups after the prewar scouting tradition of youth service, which carries a very positive connotation in Polish culture. Scouting had become a tool of communist education, and Błachnicki's "Oasis" was conceived as a kind of counterpoint to the officialized version. Of course this contributed to Błachnicki's political problems.

Oasis incorporates elements of scout tradition such as campfires, hiking, earning stages of religious as opposed to natural "knowledge" taken from physical training of higher-ranking scouts.[1] In the early Oasis a group head was called "unit leader," after the scouting tradition. Only later was this changed to "animator"—after someone who animates, or encourages others to participate in special activities.

In addition to purely religious aspects, the movement's main goal is to prepare youth in parish communities to realize Catholic principles in church and public life in practical terms. The instruction program propagates the slogan "new man," "new community," and "new culture." According to the program, the movement wishes to create a new person—someone whose life is filled with faith and who acts according to its principles. As a member of a "new community," the "new man" should help to build Christian communities, which in turn should radiate a new evangelical culture into all spheres of human life.

The Polish Church reportedly has a "center" that plans and coordinates all the nationwide movement's programs and important activities. But it is difficult to pin down specific information about who comprises the center, how, and where indeed the center is. It is said that Father Wojciech Danielski currently leads the movement. Operating through a hierarchy of information, knowledge, and influence, all decisions about the program to be carried out on a weekly basis flow from the top. People at each level know only what they need to know to carry out the predetermined program.

Movement activities usually take place in groups or "communities" numbering a dozen or so members, led by priests called "moderators." Within the communities, the next level of hierarchy is the "animators"—those members who have at least three to four years' experience in participating and leading Oasis community groups and are directly responsible for the communities. Religious training takes place in stages: achieving a given level qualifies one to try to attain the next level. This process implements a sequence of programs keyed for age group, achievement level, and involvement of participants. Either while on excursions or at weekly parish meetings, members of the movement are taught the principles of Catholic ethics and truths of the faith. There are lectures on the basics of faith and detailed exegesis of individual biblical texts. Members are urged to implement these truths and values in the life of their community. Oasis attempts to train its participants in Catholic teachings to influence wider social circles—to fight against alcoholism, social indifference to the misery of others, and the "moral corruption" of the individual.

Martial Law: Community vs. Anomie

What inclines members of the movement to participate in Oasis, and why did they sign up in the first place? We found that joining the movement was not motivated by a religious search, but above all by a search for a protective community.

Youth who joined Oasis instead of a rock or other counterculture group tended to be persuaded by the popular conviction of the positive character of the Church and things associated with it. As one participant put it: "What attracted me was a wish to meet new people, because it is a movement of the Church and there everybody tries to live according to the principles of the faith. I knew they were decent people, not just anybody."

The second main reason for joining Oasis was that it better served the needs of many youths who were disoriented by martial law and were searching for a place in society. Many people described the shock of martial law in terms of a sense of helplessness, of being lost and disoriented. Young people were perhaps more vulnerable than adults to the effects of the sociopolitical crisis. They were less rooted in the long-established pre-December reality of affiliation formed for political activity and resistance. Oasis guaranteed protective and communal relations, and the youth found that it met their essential interpersonal needs.

The daily experience of martial law intensified the fear caused by the real menace of the sociopolitical crisis, but also an underlying sense of anxiety. This heightened the need for affiliation and a search for warm, safe interpersonal relations that could buffer the tension.

Sometimes people joined the movement to meet new people, to change their peer group, because they failed to be accepted elsewhere. As one participant put it: "I had been rejected by my circles many times and really this is why I joined Oasis."

The Oasis community lessened the sense of anxiety by guaranteeing protection, a sense of security, endowing individuals with a feeling of their own worth and accepting them. One participant thus distilled the atmosphere of those years: "Hostility is everywhere, some cannot live with it. Young people do not know what awaits them, what to do in life. They do not see a place for themselves." And another adds: "Martial law was a shock for everybody. Pessimistic moods started to overwhelm the young who were looking for something."

Since the founding of Oasis, the Church estimates that 200,000 to 300,000 people have been involved in the movement. Membership doubled under martial law. When trying to explain why membership in Oasis rose so considerably from 1982 to 1984, the movement's participants, especially the experienced animators, described the state of youth consciousness in terms of the absence of life prospects, a disordered sense of the future, and inability to find a place in the world—an anomic state indeed. "Ordinary" members of the movement, younger as a rule and less experienced, talked more about their individual ways of "experiencing" the community. We asked youths why they joined, their motives for staying on, and also what they gained from their participation.

To many of the young, the religious aspects of Oasis were incidental. At least at first, young people usually cited the warm atmosphere, mutual help, and understanding that they find there. As one girl put it, "I was fascinated by those people. They were so wonderful. Everybody offered their help. I could tell them everything. I felt good. That was at the beginning. God came later."

Religious motives such as the wish to deepen one's faith, contact with the so-called Living Church, tended to become important only in the latter phases of participation. While addressing why they stayed in the movement, some interviewees cited specifically religious reasons; but when discussing the reasons for becoming interested in and going on to join the movement, hardly anybody referred to matters directly connected with religion. The most frequently mentioned motive was a willingness to be involved in "something," belonging to "something." As one interviewee put it, "I joined Oasis because I wanted to meet new people, to have a *środowisko*, I did not care for any idea." Another participant told us, "It was a period when people did not know what to do with themselves. I simply wanted to be engaged in something."

Oasis vs. Rock Music

The martial law period created the conditions for Oasis to become a nationwide movement in which tens of thousands of people could engage in mass escape. The legal Solidarity period energized and expanded a new youth culture overall. New groups were founded, many of which were imported from the West—such as punks, skinheads, and satanists. Also, the youth could join underground organizations such as Freedom and Peace (WiP) (a pacifist group) and "self-education circles" organized by the underground structure— an alternative form of high school one could get into if one had the right contacts and was trusted. Small circles of Buddhists also cropped up among the intelligentsia.

Why did the young choose Oasis over other alternatives to the state, such as youth counterculture movements? First, not just anyone could join the underground and Buddhist groups. They were more elitist than Oasis and had more of an intellectual character. Second, the popularity of Oasis arises from its community emphasis and status as one of the very few alternative orthodox religious movements on the youth market.

Many of the youth we talked with at the beginning stages of their participation (up to two years) did not know the basic goals and principles as advanced by the ideological leaders of the movement, even though meetings are held at least weekly. They may speak of experiences connected with deeper interpretation of faith, with the first "real" contact with God (such as speaking in tongues), but otherwise do not register other elements in the movement other than those that directly satisfy these needs.

Interviews with novices, who are in what we called the stage of "getting," are characterized by an exalted state of euphoria arising as much from the exploration of communal life as from first religious experiences. Oasis interviewees pointed to what they gained from their participation: a better frame of mind and mood, joy in life, self-confidence, ability to cope with the problems of everyday life—all protective functions of the community.

A mutual ethos seems to appear only among the participants who stay in the movement for longer than two years. Veteran Oasis members express common outlooks and beliefs. Their answers to a number of questions bear striking similarity. Earlier, that is, at the beginning stage of participation, answers to questions on broader social phenomena regarding outlook on life are chaotic, and judgments often are made out of contradictory criteria.

Membership in an Oasis "new community" involves almost total subordination of an individual to the group's requirements. Community participation is placed above one's own individuality and distinctiveness. Thus, for instance, in any given Oasis group, we observe a surprising similarity of professed opinions or expressed attitudes. The movement has a *total*, cult-like character. The "new community" especially becomes a "perfect tool" for influencing young people's minds, of making them conform to the requirements and aims of the movement, of unifying their views and attitudes.

Finally, let the statements of some participants of the "new community" illustrate a problem that attracted our attention in the course of the survey. One of the movement animators admits that "it is worth resigning from many important things in order to found a community that has the same ideals and that aims at the same objective." Another participant states openly that "in Oasis one cannot be too big an individual. One should develop in the community. I have been totally renewed," he adds with pride. "I do not remember anymore what I used to be like, and I do not want to remember."

Oasis and Civil Society

During the 1960s and 1970s, church activities for youth were more an attempt to renew internal parish life than to broaden the influence of the Church in the wider society. In light of this limited activity, Oasis was naturally more suited to preparing its members for parish work than for proselytizing and social outreach. As the Church hierarchy itself confirms, the proof of Oasis' effectiveness during these years is in the increasing number of recruits to the priesthood.

The movement's popularity after the imposition of martial law gave the Church an opportunity to expand its outreach. Alongside Oasis, the church introduced a variety of social initiatives in which Oasis members participated. Some members even organized these other activities, which included the "Crusade for Self-Liberation" in which young people abstained from drinking alcohol to set an example. Priests initiated the charismatic movement, a Catholic renewal movement of the Holy Ghost [Duch Święty] and "home church" movements in which circles of married couples met regularly. As such members of Oasis as Zbigniew Nosowski confirm, the intention of all these efforts was "a spiritual deepening of people engaged in the country's sociopolitical changes—to provide them with an evangelical prism through which they could assess their own social activities. Altogether it was a huge attempt to evangelize the nation."[2] Within this framework, the Church counted on active youth participation.

Recently, the attraction of the Oasis movement has weakened, and once again, as in the 1960s and 1970s, Oasis has become a normal parish activity. Even its organizers say it has become "routinized."

However, the experience of the 1980s demonstrated to the Church hierarchy that such a movement can be a vehicle to widen the

Church's influence. The current political changes in Poland, as well as the worldwide crisis of the Roman Catholic Church, have awakened the perception among Church leaders that the Polish institution's hitherto leading position is endangered. One way to strengthen its position may be to step up activities such as Oasis. Other attempts may be the introduction of compulsory Catholic religious instruction in public schools, for which the Church is now fighting. Although it is difficult to imagine the reemergence of such ideal conditions for Oasis as martial law, the Church may attempt to initiate similar movements to assure its continued leadership.

NOTES

1. This is similar to "levels of advancement" or "stages on the Eagle trail" in American scouting.
2. Authors' note: "Drzemiący Olbrzym," *Więź*, April 1989.

PART V

Pontiffs, Reds, and Rebels

Introduction

The political landscape of Poland has shifted at the top since I set out to compile this book in the late 1980s: the Church has lost its status as the only independent political organization and is under threat. The Communist Party formally has gone into oblivion, but *środowiska* founded on Party connections are reasserting themselves in economics and politics. Groups within the former Opposition and the Church are making their influence felt: a few people from a few *środowiska* have their fingers in a multiplicity of pies—in policy, government, business, parliament, and foundations, and are adept at cultivating international contacts. Poles talk of such elite groups as "parlors" ("*salon*"). Members of the same parlor share social connections and background, and mix socializing with politicking.

Our contributors at once tell the stories of their lives and the influence of their *środowiska* on society as a whole. Contributor Adam Szostkiewicz, identified with the influential Catholic weekly *Tygodnik Powszechny*,[1] from which former Prime Minister Tadeusz Mazowiecki also drew his identity, was chosen to be press spokesman in Mazowiecki's fall 1990 presidential campaign. Many of Mazowiecki's cabinet members, including, for example, Krzysztof Kozłowski, Minister of Internal Affairs, were drawn from Warsaw and Cracow elite. Contributing former Oppositionists Piotr Szwajcer and Wojciech Arkuszewski also are affiliated with this *środowisko* and are furthering its priorities through publishing and trade union leadership. Szwajcer directs the huge, formerly underground NOWA publishing house; Arkuszewski is vice-president of the Mazowsze chapter of the Solidarity trade union.

In "The Elitist Opposition," Arkuszewski points out that many rank-and-file, as well as local Solidarity leaders, distrusted and resented the closed character of the elite intellectual Opposition during the Solidarity movement of 1980–81. Presidential candidate Stanisław Tymiński tapped this anti-elite sentiment in the 1990 campaign: his supporters (one-fourth of all voters) were anti-Solidarity, anti-Opposition, and anti-Church, according to public opinion polls.

NOTES

1. Those associated with this paper form a liberal, intellectual circle traditionally opposed to the conservative wing of the Church hierarchy and often at odds with the Episkopat.

The Church

I found it much more difficult to obtain material on the actual life and organization of the Church than on any other subject in this book. Because of the Church's standing as the most enduring voice against foreign rule under more than century of partition, and more specifically as the only institution capable of challenging the Communist state, public criticism of the Church has been almost taboo. As one acquaintance explained in 1988: "You have to champion the Opposition and to criticize the Party, but the Church is a sacrament."

All contributors discussing the Church are deeply committed to its fundamental calling and mission: two are priests, two lay activists. Two pieces, both distinctly critical, appeared in Catholic journals, one under a pseudonym. The others are edited interviews I conducted in June 1989, before the first champagne thrill of Solidarity's landslide went flat.

Adam Szostkiewicz, a young Catholic layman, addressed an open manifesto to his fellow believers in the underground, but officially tolerated, journal *Bez Dekretu* (*Without Authority to Censor*) in June 1989. Both his high standing in religious intelligentsia circles (and the Opposition entities interlocking with them) and his position as a contributing editor of *Tygodnik Powszechny*, lend special authority to his words. Szostkiewicz bemoans "impotent parish councils" and that views divergent from those of the hierarchy go unaired. He and many others active in the Church take their criticisms much further: Poland has not yet experienced Vatican II.

The Dominican Father Andrzej Kłoczowski, a friend of Szostkiewicz, provides a counterexample. A philosopher of religion who heads a seminary and has served his order for 30 years, Kłoczowski places the accent of his mission on human relations and on the individual dimension of religious experience—not unlike the self-realization that Poles have been searching for, as contributors Kurczewski, Lewenstein and Melchior have shown. Kłoczowski complains that "religion in Poland is too much a form of social existence and not enough a form of existing in silence and loneliness. . . . [I]n Poland religion is what man does when there are many of us."

I interviewed Kłoczowski the day after Solidarity's landslide in June 1989. "Now we'll find out how Catholic Poles really are," he reflected. "The most dangerous moment in a man's life is victory." Kłoczowski foresaw the Church threatened and also predicted the impossibility of a victorious Solidarity being able to preserve the mystic unity of opposition: "Things won't be so simple anymore." Kłoczowski warns that "the great triumph can become triumphalism." In 1991 these words prove to be prophetic.

All contributors point out that the Church, which no longer can claim standing as the only legitimate institutional alternative to state authority, is under threat; not of persecution but of being deemed irrelevant and losing parishioners. Lewenstein and Melchior's prediction that the Church might attempt to step up its activities in order not to lose influence has already been borne out: the Church has pressured the government into restricting abortion and divorce. Directives from the Ministry of Education (under pressure from the Church) have established school prayer and religious instruction in what was previously a completely secular school system and stipulated that only priests (and those approved by their bishops) are suitable to teach religion above the eighth grade.

So at a time when the privatization of socialized property lags disappointingly, the socialization of religious teaching appears to be a model of success. In "What Goes on in Catechism Class," Teresa Hołówka, a writer, professor of logic, and devout Catholic, laments the Church's formalism—notably the bureaucratized, rote religious instruction that serves administrative objectives. The Church no longer permits Hołówka—for three years a catechism teacher in a high-rise suburban parish—or others like her, to teach children. Her frustration with the "expansiveness" of the Church, "its penetration and sense of being present everywhere as a right," emboldened her to publish her article here under her own name instead of under a pseudonym, as in Poland.

Since the end of the Gierek era in the late 1970s, Kazimierz Jancarz has been a parish priest in the town of Nowa Huta, one of Solidarity's first and greatest industrial bases. Deeply involved in the Christian University of Workers, he was close to many Solidarity activists. His is a story of the Church triumphant, of how an active infrastructure of the laity helps to build a vibrant church by coopting and outflanking obstructive authorities. Individually, officials are coopted, and even become enthusiastic participants. Nothing seems to stop Father Jancarz in his mission, and despite his claims to the contrary, not much stopped him from telling me about it in the interview. He was recently transferred to an outlying parish.

Although many of the Polish Church's problems have a familiar ring to Westerners, they are compounded in a country where the political influence of the Church goes deep and has been further encouraged by the demise of communism. The end of 1990 saw an anti-Church backlash: its popularity fell from 95–98 percent to 75 percent from the beginning of 1990 until the spring of that year.[1] Seventy-one percent of presidential candidate Stanisław Tymiński's supporters opposed the Church's involvement in politics.[2]

NOTES

1. "The 1990 Election," *Życie Warszawy*, December 5, 1990.
2. Ibid.

10

A Church Without Laity

ADAM SZOSTKIEWICZ

Journalism should call a spade a spade.
—Kazimierz Wyka, 1945

The laity's place in the Church—the topic has been run into the ground but to no avail. Everything has probably been said about it: during Vatican II, in numerous books, papers, statements, and private conversation. And the laity is still absent from the Polish Church.

Impotent parish councils—where they have been established at all—relieve parish priests of their most taxing administrative duties—overseeing construction of the hundreds of churches built in Poland each year. But the council's work does not change the priest's exclusive control over finances!

This has deep roots dating back to the Stalinist era of the 1950s when the Church withheld, on a nationwide basis, crucial data concerning the everyday functioning of its parishes, especially finances. Then it was risky to discuss such matters openly. The state could use the Church's financial affairs as a pretext to ruin the Church, or at least to impose fines or other restrictions. Although many things have changed since Stalinism, day-to-day management of church affairs has not. This causes alienation. People do not believe they can influence the church's conduct of its affairs in any substantial way.

So the laity has settled down on the fringes of church involvement. Committed members are active in various movements, aimed at community and mutual help, a deepening of spiritual life, and practical application of the gospel to daily living. The church hierarchy treats these movements with reservation since, after all, they

are transplants from the West. Some of them—like the Oasis movement—had to struggle for years to be recognized and accepted by
hierarchy. Obviously there are some bishops who support such
grass-roots initiatives of the faithful. Individual priests responsible
for pastoral work among specific social and professional groups—
farmers, workers, intellectuals, artists, teachers, university and secondary school students, and the sick and handicapped—lead organized ministries among them. If incorporated into the Church's formal structure, these ministries do not arouse greater objections from
the Church; the bishops tolerate and even encourage them. But
decisions concerning the shape of the Polish Church and its everyday life are made without any substantial lay involvement. Lay
members who wish for change usually find that the spirit of the last
Vatican Council has yet to take hold in Poland.

What are the reasons for this? The two that priests mention most
often are reflexes left over from fear of infiltration by security agents
or hostile state-controlled elements and the inability of the Polish
laity to take responsibility for its Church.

Infiltration by security agents is not mere fiction, but reiterating
this threat is no solution for the "besieged stronghold" syndrome
that pervaded the Polish Church. On the other hand, if we examine
whether lay members really are "immature," everyday observation
will show they are. Their religious knowledge is not profound, they
lack a sense of responsibility for the Church, and their identification
with it as a community of the faithful is weak.

But how can you feel responsible for something you perceive as
a bureaucratic entity that provides routinized religious services? How
is it possible to identify with an institution in which you feel like
an atom in an anonymous crowd? You hear constantly from the
priest that you are practically nothing. Priests often lecture you that
you are cowardly, degenerate, sinful, and "nothing" in front of God.
In fact, you do not feel spiritually welcome in the church, more often
like the petitioner of a spiritual bureaucracy, even an intruder. In
such an atmosphere you prefer to withdraw from active participation
in parish life.

The Church's shortcomings are easily apparent if you compare
Sunday mass in a church that serves residents of a typical "socialist,"
depersonalized block high-rise apartment complex with a mass cel-
ebrated within a circle of friends and acquaintances by a priest who
is a friend of the participants. Why is the second eucharist experi-

enced more deeply, and why do you leave such a service stronger in spirit? Because you regain your individuality.

The homily in particular sounds different—it is addressed to specific people, as opposed to an anonymous crowd. Theologically speaking, there is no difference—nor can there be any—between these two masses. But the atmosphere of the latter makes a huge difference to the participants.

What picture of life emerges from sermons, conferences, church documents, conversations with priests, seminary students, and active lay members?

Poland—that nation of turbulent history and troubled present and future—is the culprit. What may not be surprising in the wealthy countries of the West—although it is disturbing even there—is downright distressing in a country lagging behind at the very tail-end of the world's civilization. The main claim to national pride is of course the Polish Pope. So, besides John Paul II, almost no other pastor of the Roman Church is quoted in homilies anymore. The Pope's authority in religious and spiritual matters is exempt from any discussion. His sagacious ethical analyses, his catechesis, are worthy of attention and reflection, but his authority sometimes is used to block the sound exchange of views and arguments. This attitude is contrary to the spirit of pluralism in contemporary society.

In Polish churches, so-called Catholic social teaching is presented as if it was not an object of numerous heated and intellectually rich disputes outside the borders of our country. In homilies, cliches about "practical materialism," "preoccupation with consumption," "cult of money," and other public sins are common. Not only is the Western world scourged for such faults, but also we, the paupers of Europe. Although these accusations are also present in Catholic liturgy around the world, in Poland they are the result of anti-materialist church efforts against the increased consumption encouraged by the policies of First Party Secretary Edward Gierek during the 1970s. During the mass, the crowd is silent. It is only after people leave church, talking among themselves, that they start to compare the priest's words with the reality of their own poverty, not to mention the luxurious cars (by Polish standards) of some parish priests.

Tirades against the materialistic and atheistic West will not change the fact that the West continues to be not only the object of dreams but, more and more, a significant source of supplies through relatives and jobs which enable Poles to settle down quite well along the Vistula (i.e., Poland).

I know that one's own problems are more important and that every national church is occupied first of all with local matters, particularly if they are so painful and difficult as Poland's. Sometimes, however, it seems to me and to many in Catholic intellectual circles that Church teachings are narrow and simplistic. It is as if catholicity did not mean universality but ethnocentricity.

But let us return to the laity. There is one more reason—maybe the most important one—for its absence from our church. For years the clergy has borne the sole responsibility, and masses of the lay faithful have been passive. This has resulted in their subconscious consent to being the passive subject of pastoral and any other church activity. Thus, the vicious circle closes. The threefold function of the People of God remains an empty formula, and the laity yields to the native tradition of overwhelming, omnipresent clericalism.

Without opening up to the laity, without putting into motion the great energy potentially inherent in it, without creating outlets for this energy, our Church cannot cope with the challenge of the times to come. Many believe that the laity should take partial responsibility for the course of Church events. We might start small but usefully with enlivening parish councils and founding a truly lay Catholic press which scarcely exists here.

At present the Catholic press is first and foremost an outlet for the teachings and views of the hierarchy and those lay people who are closely affiliated with it. As a rule, it does not print anything that could stir serious debate among Catholics; it does not reflect the actual pluralism of Catholic opinion. Yet there is plenty of diversity. The ongoing debate over abortion is one example. Whether a Christian Democratic Party should emerge as the political representative of Polish Catholics is another. People affiliated with the influential independent Catholic weekly *Tygodnik Powszechny* are adamantly opposed to such an idea. Some high-ranking bishops support it, and those allied with Catholic papers such as *Ład*, an arm of the Church hierarchy, are strongly in favor. But these differences in views are not reflected in what gets published.

Looking into the more distant future, one might think (and why not?) about such luxuries as Catholic radio and television stations. Truly Catholic mass media should, however, be the articulators of Catholic public opinion which, unfortunately, hardly exists here. Otherwise there will be only television broadcasts of the holy mass and small-talk lecturing by priests.

In a pluralistic, sovereign Poland, the Church will cease—I hope—
to be an ersatz for political society. All those politically engaged
laymen who joined it mainly because there were no other outlets
will leave it for political activity. Many writers, artists, intellectuals,
private entrepreneurs, and youth activists will pull out.

Some Catholics believe it is time to initiate an ecumenical movement that would beneficially challenge the Church. Lay people
might start to organize spontaneously and on their own around
matters important to them. It would be welcome if a Catholic civil
disobedience movement, protesting abortion or the death penalty
would emerge from the bottom. We could organize a nationwide
meeting of active lay Catholics preceded by similar local and regional
meetings.

I want to emphasize here that I do not have in mind any crypto-
or open political activity or laying the ground for some future political party. I am concerned with creating a spontaneous organization of lay Catholics to bring about change within our Church
without disrupting its hierarchic and formal structure. I propose that
we put aside the passively malcontent attitude and take note of the
crisis of spirit and moral leadership in our Church. Perhaps it is not
too late. I am afraid, however, that if nothing changes, if Polish lay
Catholics do not advance to openness and self-government, and if
they do not become co-hosts of their own parishes, the situation
here may develop analogously to that in, for instance, Spain, where
the coming of parliamentary democracy was accompanied by an
avalanche of secularization.

11

What Goes on in Catechism Class

TERESA HOŁÓWKA

The very exclusion of the most important processes of collective life from responsibility and active participation necessarily provoked a profound moral corruption, a corruption generally not intentional, but resulting from the very necessity of surviving within a system based on falsehoods that served those in power, on injustice as a principle.

—Kazimierz Wyka, 1945

I teach religion in a parish on the outskirts of a large city, in a high-rise bedroom suburb of several thousand people. Parish life is concentrated around an old church building, not so much packed to the utmost, as simply inaccessible to most of the faithful. There are faithful who have never seen the church's interior because it is so small. Moreover, at Holy Mass everyone, except a handful of old women, stands under the open sky. At other times the church is closed for fear of thievery. Luckily, however, the hurriedly constructed but spacious parish house has room for a library, religion classes for all grades, meetings of altar boys, the "rosary" women's club, and other prayer groups. But not much more happens there. The Covenant of Families has been in existence for two years, but its activity is limited to a monthly bulletin posted on a blackboard. An artist makes decorations from cardboard and foamed polystyrene, which hurt your eyes. The choir died of natural causes, and few people come to meetings with authors who, I must admit, are rather unknown.

But who could do more? Priests on duty until late at night? Nuns absorbed in teaching ten hours a day? The librarian who always confuses the weekly *Tygodnik Powszechny* with the daily *Słowo Pow-szechne*?[1] The more ambitious faithful have "opened their eyes" in recent years: afternoons they travel by car to one of the fashionable downtown churches to take part, as they say, "in absolutely fasci-nating performances." The rest have had enough, having returned from work in overcrowded buses, queued up in the high-rise sub-urban supermarkets, and then checked their children's homework. They have only one wish: to gulp down just anything and fall into bed. On Sundays after Mass they hurry home to spend time with their families—at last.

This parish is an "ideal social mixture": the reasonably well-off workers from the factory nearby who overdress their daughters in first-communion creations from "Komis" shops;[2] and the poorer nurses, teachers, and office workers who rummage through rental shops in search of white communion gowns for girls and suits for boys, or frantically call their acquaintances for a loan.

"Couldn't the Church do something about this vanity fair?," asks one of the intelligentsia grandmothers sadly. "When I was young, children were dressed in identical, linen smocks that the Parish Committee sewed for everyone."

In my high-rise suburb, lower ranking soldiers and policemen live next door to people living on nobody knows what: sometimes escapades to Turkey, sometimes on endless queuing up in shops for goods that will be resold for profit, sometimes by renting rooms to Arabs and their merry misses (prostitutes). Well-to-do peasant-work-ers from run-down suburban dwellings reside next to members of the new financial aristocracy: owners of suburban businesses and small factories, around which kitschy villas are mushrooming. "Lo-cals," residents of little houses demolished by bulldozers, who now occupy apartments owned and allocated by the state, live next to "newcomers" from the entire area and newcomers from the old, prestigious districts coming here to escape air pollution. Thus fam-ilies standing side by side at Holy Mass usually have nothing in common beyond the same faith.

Ours is a parish like hundreds of others, a parish in which the religion of an average Pole is shaped, that average Pole who rarely sees or hears what goes on in the Catholic "parlors" and bishops' palaces.[3] He is influenced above all by what he hears or sees at mass and catechism. The average Pole goes to religion classes for 12 years. What does he get out of it?

First, an impression that it does not differ much from the secular "school obligation." Here are some common explanations for attending catechism:

- Otherwise I can't go to First Communion.
- I won't get a certificate, without which I can't have a church wedding.
- If I don't attend class, the priest will be very cross with my parents. (The priest visits parishioners during the Christmas season, checks children's notebooks, and takes notes in a thick parish book, or he asks parents at confession whether they send their children to catechism and refuses to grant the "delinquent" parents absolution.)
- My mother would cry that she's ashamed before others: everyone attends class but me. It's enough that she's divorced.
- My old man gave me a whack, saying that I'll grow up to be no good, that I might start taking drugs. But he himself doesn't believe in anything. I'm not interested in catechism, 'cause it's nothing but wishy-washy talk, like sermons. Don't do this, don't do that. I don't know myself yet whether I believe in anything. I'm reading about Buddhism—a friend lent me a book. I attend classes only for the sake of peace at home.
- When I didn't go to catechism last year, 'cause Mother worked the afternoon shift and I had to babysit my brothers and sisters, the parish priest didn't give my mother the Certificate of Faith so that she could be a godmother. And so she couldn't be godmother to Auntie Halina's little Sebastian.[4] Auntie Halina was awfully cross at us because she had been helping us for many years, and we seemed ungrateful by not returning the favor. Now my grandmother doesn't leave bed and tells me to attend religion classes or they won't sprinkle her coffin with Holy Water. Without sacraments you go to Hell, don't you?

The catechism room is more crowded than the school classroom. There are forty, even fifty students. The religion teacher has to shout to be heard over the uproar and jostling. A religion lesson often consists of a prayer, roll call, questions on the subject discussed during the previous session, and a new subject. One has to sit still in a stuffy room and do nothing but listen. So pupils prod their neighbors, play "sea-war" (a popular game), do math homework, or write notes to fellow pupils. When they can't stand it any longer, they crack jokes that rouse the back benchers and anger the teacher. At last something is happening!

"I think I'll resign," threatens a lay religion teacher like myself from another parish. "I don't have enough strength to go on. I'm incapable of pacifying a frolicking herd. Last year I didn't want to give certificates to six of the worst pupils, who almost never attended classes. Even when they did come, they did nothing but interrupt."

There are always some bad apples, just like at public school. My superiors told me: "We have to draw people to Church, not discourage them!" But most pupils are not really unruly. The anonymous crowd is to blame. Once there was a blizzard, and only one-third of the class showed up. Not the same kids. Sensitive. Thinking. They relaxed, asked questions, and expressed ideas of their own. Normally when I ask about anything, they repeat crammed formulas or make silly faces. One must understand it, though. It is not easy to risk saying something unique in the presence of 50 randomly gathered people. Teenagers are emotionally caught up in working out the meaning of life, good and evil, and the order of the world—intimate matters naturally better discussed in private.

It is not possible to divide pupils into small groups, since there is a shortage of religion teachers, although no one says this out loud. There are few volunteers despite the fact that the intelligentsia has become more involved in Church life. I know several people who enrolled in theology and enrichment courses. It is more effective, however, to be active in the Catholic Intelligentsia Club (KIK),[5] write for the Catholic press, or compose poems about the Virgin Mother, than to struggle with someone else's children in a shabby parish. I wonder if those who organize such activities under Church auspices, who applaud the attendance and zeal of the converts, who take great pleasure in reading out well-known names, give a single thought to where this enthusiasm is more needed. Ah, what pleasure it would be to gather them to give their testimony here, on the outskirts, where there is neither the great Father X, nor Mrs. X, the charming editor.

My acquaintance, a retired teacher, thought to herself five years ago: "Why should my granddaughter and her peers learn the most important things in an overcrowded classroom?" First she put up a coat rack in the catechism room since no one else had seen to it; children had been sitting in their coats. Then she decided to help the Sister teacher. My acquaintance had been a math teacher for many years, but does one really need anything more than faith, good contact with children, and catechism knowledge to prepare the little ones for their First Communion? But it turned out that without a certificate showing one has passed the evening course for religion instructors, it is impossible to start—just like in the school superintendent's office, just like everywhere. As if human good will and impeccable qualifications did not matter at all.

Psychology and pedagogy are in the course syllabus for religion teachers.

"I explain," says the retired teacher, "that I already know it."

"Yes," I hear, "but that was not Christian psychology."

I always thought that there is only one psychology. I know the children's psyche, I say, I taught for over 30 years. At last I came across a parish priest who was looking for religion teachers who liked children. Unfortunately, he is not alive anymore. His successor checks up on me, monitoring whether I verify that the children have pasted circles in their notebooks in the color of the chasuble (a special priest's garment worn at the Eucharist) to designate their attendance at special children's masses. This is one of the many modes of "evangelizing" parents. Meanwhile, I myself heard mothers discussing which one of them would go to identify the confounded chasuble on Sunday and report to the others what color it was. "It isn't suitable to criticize the Church, particularly given the present political situation," one hears. Meanwhile, the halls outside the catechism room buzz with murmur.

The atmosphere in the rectories is strangely familiar. Plump, meddlesome ladies play first fiddle. The unwitting audience nods, sighs with effort, and sometimes shrugs its shoulders in a gesture of helplessness. Everyone quiets down when a cassock (priest in clerical garb) flashes past. I hear these comments:

- The vicar demanded that fathers of those children going to First Communion sign sobriety vows. There are no drunkards in our family, and I consider this approach to the matter blackmail!
- In our group the religion teacher said that parents should go to confession together with their children. Most likely I would have gone anyway, but after that, I didn't feel like it. I don't like being forced to do anything. There's too much compulsion everywhere. At least the Church could do it differently.
- The harder life is, the more obligatory pieties are imposed. Children have to come to early morning mass during Advent, be present as their satchels are ceremonially blessed by a priest

sprinkling holy water over them at the beginning of each school year, and learn litanies. Older children can go by themselves, but you can't let the younger ones go alone. It's not like in the old days. Now there are cars and drunkards everywhere. And it is the youngest who are told to do most. "They" (priests and clergy) do not queue up, cook, or wash, so they don't know what it's like to dash every second day to church with a child, they don't know how a woman feels then.

- What will I do when the "white week" (of the First Communion) comes? I think I'll have to take sick leave from my job 'cause I work the afternoon shift. Will my little one become more pious because of it?

- Because of these religion classes, we don't even have one day a week when we can all simply sit down to a family dinner, or at least be together. The three little ones each have religion class twice a week at different times. When I was a child, we used to go only once. Religion is not physics, what could have been added to it? I went to the religion teacher and asked whether the class couldn't meet once a week, even if for two hours because I can't manage any longer. He thundered: "Are you a Catholic mother or not?"

- It used to be that at least they didn't drag the youngest children into it. Now not only first-grade pupils, but also preschool and kindergarten children are urged to attend religion class. Isn't prayer enough at this age? And on top of it all, additional teachings before Confirmation, a lot of retreats and supplementary masses. It used to be that religious instruction for engaged couples, parents, and godparents was enough. Before long, we retired people will have to attend some sort of pre-funeral instruction. Just look around. In our times there was less of this stuff, yet the people were better.

- My mother prepared me for First Communion. Once it was sufficient just to pass the exam. We studied from a small gray catechism and I know it by heart even today. The book from which my kid is learning makes my hair stand on end—it is a thick volume, scribbled by some theologian who probably has never talked to a six-year-old.

What remains in people's hearts and minds? After eight or nine years of instruction, teenagers have difficulties answering simple questions. Unless something rings a bell and an appropriate formula comes up, they are completely lost. Which commandment is the most important? Maybe "Thou shalt not commit adultery." What is idolatry? "When you worship pagan idols." What are pagan idols? "I don't remember, that was in ancient times." Have you ever come across idolatry? "Oh, no, we are a Catholic country, aren't we?"

Why do we say "in my thoughts and in my words, in what I have done and in what I have failed to do?" "Because those are the teachings of the Holy Church and Our Mother." How can one sin by one's words? "When one uses dirty words." And how can one sin in what one has failed to do? "When one doesn't go to Holy Mass." What are dogmas? "They are the code that is given to worshipers to believe in." Do you remember any? "Fast and abstain on the days appointed." Would you be able to say how piety differs from bigotry? "A bigot is more pious, prays more." And where does the phrase "Satanic pride" come from? " 'Cause all sins are instigated by Satan." Can suffering have a positive side? "Yes, because it resembles the Atonement." You're right, but could you give an example of when suffering brought about any good? "Well, no. Suffering is punishment for sins, after all."

The average knowledge of the Gospel, not to mention the Old Testament, is next to nil. I am sorry to have to admit that. The only teenagers I know who are competent in this matter are children of a Protestant family. The girl was introduced to Polish "culture and tradition" by her mother, an atheist. The students I meet as a professor of philosophy do not know the meaning of terms such as Holy Ghost and Trinity. The names of Mary and Martha are empty of association. Students cannot summarize the main message of the Sermon on the Mount. They do not remember who said "No one can serve two masters," and in what context. They confuse Pilate with Judas and the Transfiguration with the Ascension. Is this a second illiteracy?

After one year of teaching religion, Iliya Ehrenburg's[6] mockery of the Church comes home to me: "To you God is neither Bread, nor Life, but a jar of ointment, once prescribed by someone to someone. The jar stands on the shelf in the bathroom. No one throws it away simply because no one notices it any longer."

"To listen does not mean to hear," says an elderly acquaintance, a Catholic deeply engaged in the Church.

"This is word inflation," he continues. "Look how long the Liturgy of the Word and the Homily last together. It is interesting that the less a given cleric has to say, the longer he preaches. The present

Mass is overtalked, as is our entire era. Before Vatican II deprived us of our Latin Mass, perhaps some believers would fall asleep in benches. But others could concentrate at least once a week, withdraw from everyday hubbub, think a bit about God and about themselves, pray in their own way from the bottom of their hearts, not at the word of general command. Church music also has been butchered, for what is now being crammed between collective recitations is not music at all. Now with the organ playing softly in the background, people have to recite long memorized responses. And the second problem is this pseudo-progressive theological jargon. I know the religion textbooks and what children write in their notebooks."

Materials for religion instructors are seldom helpful because what prevails in them is pure rhetoric, or some naive attempt to adapt to "trends" prevail in them. They cite "academic authorities" spouting theories that undermine Darwinism, and a standard list of scientists and thinkers for whom Heaven was not a fictitious place. "And I can give an equally long list of thinkers who didn't believe in God," a smart 16-year-old once shouted.

On the other hand, there are some reports of strange happenings, probably from the annals of the Psychotronic Society, that were intended to prove the existence of an immortal soul, but which obviously do not prove anything. There are lyrical arguments about the "miracle" of life (love, devotion, and so on), which rises above all scientific calculations. They slam Freud and Malthus without even summarizing their ideas. From time to time, edifying anecdotes are offered, at which the teenagers, already familiar to some extent with the intrigues of secular life, secretly giggle. If we consider that these teaching aids are hardly available anyway, it is clear that most teachers are left to their own inventiveness. Luckily, no superiors come to monitor religion lessons, and teachers do not have to account for how they have "followed the syllabus!" But one nice vicar was really embarrassed to tell me:

"You see . . . it reached me . . . er, that you said once during class that a family can be a nest of greed and selfishness and that Jesus Christ himself taught that sometimes there are matters more important than a family."

"Am I to censor the Gospel *ad usum delphini*," I replied. "If anyone comes to me and does not hate his father and mother . . . And how many sins are committed in the name of the family? How often is the family the cause of something one does against one's conscience—in order not to disappoint Daddy's hope or not to harm the children. In the sense that I had in mind, there is no 'crisis of family life,' about which we hear so much from the Church. On the contrary, family life flourishes. To break away from others, to grab what one can and go triumphantly home, slamming the door behind the whole world. I think, Father, that we cannot close our eyes to the present situation!"

Father continued: "Yes, yes, an up-to-date approach is very welcome, but not so arbitrarily though. . . . You must consult, ask for advice. See what other colleagues are doing."

Other colleagues highlight "hot topics" that also are taken up from the pulpit, in pamphlets, and in the press: respect for the life of the unborn, the indissolubility of marriage, happiness (as if automatic) of families with many children, alcoholism, pornography on television, drugs, contraception as the effect of mistakenly understood sexual life. The trouble is that these topics are discussed obsessively, without any restraint or understanding. And from the darkness surrounding the rectory, one hears trembling, whispers:

- It's the fourth week now that we've been discussing nothing but the problem of alcoholism. I have a headache. Father'd better go to the workers' hostel. That's where they do the boozing.
- During the Tuesday meeting, when Arek said that Christ himself changed water to wine, Father threw him out.
- I think that people drink 'cause though they go to Church, they don't actually believe in anything. They don't see any sense in life. In Church they are told over and over again that this or that is a sin.
- In our group, on the other hand, the religion teacher says that AIDS is God's punishment of sexual perverts.

I will never forget how astonished I was when my own children, then eight and nine years old, started to kiss my hand and my husband's after they came back from religion class once. Why? "We'd like to thank you for not killing us before we were born."

The moralizing results in a well-known effect: adolescent teenagers have the impression that Catholic ethics refer exclusively to the sphere "from the waist down." They find it difficult to understand that one may "treat someone else as an object" not only in sexual intercourse, but also in a queue or on the street. They stare with astonishment when they learn that a cook's lifting food from the kindergarten through a back door or a clerk's flaunting his authority from behind the post office counter also are objects of moral judgment.

A family therapist I knew once told me of other consequences: "I have often wondered why people married in such a hurry, to just anyone, the sooner the better: particularly the younger generation. I came to the conclusion that in most cases it is the fear of being single."

I have a grievance against the Church here: instead of restoring the right proportions to those fears, it amplifies them. If all emphasis is on the family and the family appears in every context, there is no place for friendship. Have you ever heard a sermon about friendship? There is no place for single people, although not everyone should establish a family. There is no place for childless women and men, who may feel left out when they continuously hear that they should have children.

Moreover, there is the question of women. They have gone to work, and it is probably impossible to change that. People prefer to be financially independent; being maintained by someone else often breeds bitterness. But the Church's model is still that of Supporter and Home Priestess, and it is presented in such a way as if deviations from it are almost sinful. In fact, they usually result from economic necessity. How many couples have I met whose conflicts were not caused by any "excessive" professional aspirations at the cost of the husband and children, but by women overworked to the limits of endurance? Husbands think I am joking when I tell them one shouldn't mistreat one's neighbor. "What neighbor? It's my wife! What's all this about? I give her money. I'm not unfaithful. I don't drink."

So I teach my youth that everyone, particularly those within one's reach, is a neighbor. I discuss with them C. S. Lewis' beautiful essay on friendship. I explain in the best way I know that we are never truly alone and that God's unique plan, which is within each of us, does not necessarily correspond to what the world expects from us. I try to interpret Christianity as a challenge rather than as a collection of prohibitions. I try to rehabilitate old notions of "restraint," "virtue," "godly fear," and "fortitude." In vain. After one more year of teaching, I can feel that it is like talking with the blind about colors or chatting about roses in a burning forest. This is not an isolated impression. I hear from many other religion teachers that people needed for this sort of work must be of some extraordinary type— with charisma, or simply with a whip.

One handles the younger children somehow but one is helpless when facing teenagers. Perhaps the Church really has to thunder its message, especially in the case of the most elementary, biological matters. Perhaps it has to emphasize the family and kin because other relations have ceased to exist. Perhaps there is no other way out but discipline, certificates, coercion to attend because otherwise those young people would not come at all. Of course, there are some bright faces in the catechism room, and one notices that these children pray not only on Sunday. They are those who enter Oasis and go on pilgrimages. But as in the rest of our lives, it is not they who take the lead. It is the back benchers, growing more numerous year by year, that take the lead. Lolling about, cynical, dressed in expensive boutique clothes, a generation is growing up. One does not know how to talk with them or how to manage them. They are experts in "real life," and they come to show off this knowledge. Or to put the religion teacher "in her place."

"Ha! Ha! If one were to worry about his own conscience, he would end up in the nut house. Ha! Ha!" The kids look pityingly upon some poor sucker who plays by the rules and doesn't even own a car.

I console myself that this comes simply from these teenagers having eyes too. They see which principles work in reality. Are they going to reject these principles themselves? After all, they live in a society where virtue is not so much unrewarded as simply persecuted, and systematically at that. They live in a terminally ill society, which considers itself Catholic, but where it is difficult to find a real Christian. And let no one pull out the statistics on pilgrimages, the number of churches being erected, attendance at Sunday Mass, and so on. Western journalists put it well: It is a nation of churchgoers but nonbelievers. Perhaps it is true that in the West only 10 percent go to church, but these 10 percent differ considerably from the rest in their lifestyle and in their attitude. Here, being a Catholic does not mean anything. It is not even the normal human hypocrisy, or the usual discrepancy between declarations and deeds. It is almost a schizophrenia.

A shop assistant mistreats an almost blind senior citizen, although the picture of the Virgin Mary hangs above the cash register. Just try telling her something. Or try to take up a collection in your high-rise apartment block for the funeral of a neighbor, or persuade someone to help a sick mother look after her five children. The state-run Polish Committee for Social Aid or the parish should see to it, he will say. One should let them know. And if someone has produced a bunch of children, he should look after them himself. An acquaintance once asked the guy repairing his washing machine: "You carry a banner in processions. Don't you feel awkward to charge half the customer's monthly salary for two hours of work?" "What's one got to do with the other?" answered the good Christian craftsman.

I am starting my third year of teaching catechism. I ask the older ones to write down or suggest orally problems of interest to them. Silence in every class. Later they put scraps of paper on my desk. In all classes, on every scrap, is the word "Satanism."

NOTES

1. *Tygodnik Powszechny* is a legal opposition weekly, an intellectual paper dealing with social issues associated with the Catholic Church. *Słowo Powszechne*, on the other hand, is a nationalistic, authoritarian daily and the mouthpiece of the Catholic PAX organization that cooperated closely with the Communist government.

2. A komis is a state-run shop where one buys used items, often luxury goods that have been purchased by private individuals on trips to the West and sold to the komis at higher prices.

3. The parlor (salon) refers here to a Catholic elite that socializes and politicks together and is especially influential in public and political life.

4. Everyone who wants to be a godparent—a spiritual sponsor of a confirmed child—has to have a letter from his parish attesting that he is a good Catholic.

5. The Catholic Intelligentsia Club (KIK), in operation since the de-Stalinization of 1956, was known for strong opposition to the communist government.

6. A Russian writer, popular in Poland, who was critical of European culture and the Roman Catholic Church.

Triumphant Religion

An Interview with Father Kazimierz Jarcarz in Nowa Huta
(Following Solidarity's June 1989 landslide victory)

> This is no idealistic morality, but one deriving from
> pragmatic goals drawn from direct experience.
> —Kazimierz Wyka, 1945

In 1970, the year of the uprising,[1] new apartment complexes were
built. Father Józef Kurzeja put up a makeshift building to be used
as a church. There were problems—the regime persecuted him for
this. He used the construction of this building as a rallying cause to
organize people.[2] He taught children religion and the need to build
a church. Moreover, the apartment complexes were growing. The
first one had some 10,000 inhabitants. Others followed. Now the
parish numbers 45,000 people, and a new apartment complex that
will house 15,000 people is being built. The parish will reach 60,000
people. It already has split into two parishes.

But the beginnings were difficult. First, the priest had to go among
people; they had to get to know him. He started by teaching children.
Later he organized committees to advocate building a church. It took
four years and cost a lot of sacrifice and effort. In the end, in 1974
when Cardinal Karol Wojtyła[3] got involved, we received political
permission. Most likely this approval had to come from the Soviet
embassy. It was the result of social pressure, numerous delegations
and petitions, and the fight put up by the citizens and Father Kurzeja.

Finally, building got underway. There was an architectural competition. The priests who worked here at the time established a plan
or a list of needs. Mr. Budkiewicz won the competition. He had been
an architect on the Wawel,[4] in charge of reconstruction.

The construction began. All costs were paid out of donations.

People pledged how much they would donate and brought their money. The money paid for the plot. Later we bought construction materials, both officially (we had a permit) and unofficially.

It is impossible to describe—and frankly, one should not describe—how we bought those materials. It is sad that it was impossible just to go to the store and buy things, but everything was rationed. And that is why we had to use names of different people to buy different things. It is not my goal to teach you "Red" arrangements.[5] Officially we could have material allocated, but these allocations were only enough to build one column! And besides, for a church there was no opportunity to buy cement, but an individual citizen could buy 1.5 tons of cement, so people brought their IDs and through connections (our parishioners worked everywhere), we were able to buy the necessary cement.

We had to buy 3,000 tons. Such was the system, and it took a great deal of creativity to work it. Donations paid for everything. Father Kurzeja drove around other parishes and "came up with" collections. He went to the mountains to get timber. He gave sermons, and people donated one or two trees. Then he sent a truck and brought the lumber back. The costs were much higher. One donor, Mr. Ciechanowski from London, contributed a larger sum of money. And that's how the church was built.

We used two types of contacts to get our materials. We said: "Listen, we are building a church." The Church is everywhere. Even in the local bricks, wire, and steel warehouses, employees feel they should help the Church. We traveled all over; we visited half of Poland and said: "Listen, we are building a church." The response was, "O.K. we will help you somehow." Faith unites people. They know there are problems, even now. People know I want to renovate but do not have the materials. So they try to do everything they can to help. They call friends and say, "Listen, the priest needs this and that, because he is building," and the friends help. For official purchases, there are bills and receipts, etc. But one also "arranges." It is sad. This is the system—arranging things and giving bribes.

Arranging embraces everything. An outsider cannot understand it. People go and ask their friends. "Listen, I need this." We had to pay people because they couldn't cover the cost of trips out of their own pockets. Not everyone was from our parish. People from other parishes also knew that a church was being built here. Everywhere where churches are built, people have to travel and lose one or two days "discussing deals."

You asked me to tell you what deals. I won't tell you because you are not a secret policeman, though you ask the same questions they ask. It is impossible to describe; I will not tell you. Truthfully, I won't tell because I don't know myself. I go to a woman and say, "Please, arrange this for me." I don't know how she does it. I know she spends a lot of time helping me out, she uses her friends and, by some miracle, says "Father, I managed to arrange it. Here is a receipt."

There is a system: I pay her for her time and effort. Some materials can be bought officially; those in short supply have to be "arranged." There are receipts for everything. I buy something in a store and get a receipt. But if I need something that is not available, I'll say to you: I need this or that. You have your contacts, whom I do not know, and you arrange this for me. Then you say: "I had to go here and there and it cost me 1,000 złoty." So I give you 1,500 złoty, because you had to travel, you lost time, you had to give someone coffee, and so on. These are "contacts." But when churches are built, bribes usually aren't necessary, because people say, "No, I also am a Catholic, I also want that church to be built, so I will donate the time and the cost of my travel."

If someone builds a private house, then it's obvious: "I'll 'arrange' cement for you, but you have to pay me a cut." Churches—it's a different matter.

Without these "contacts" and "arrangements" we would have built 100 churches at the most, instead of 800. Of course among the parishioners, among those who come to church, are bureaucrats, policemen, and the like. A captain in the secret service who had persecuted Father Kurzeja made the first large donation. Some months earlier he had put a gun to the father's head and said: "If you don't destroy this church, I'll shoot you." And later on Father Kurzeja, who suffered from a serious heart problem, went to a sanatorium where he happened to share a room with his persecutor. They got to know each other and became friends. Then the captain got married in our church because he had never had a church wedding,[6] and he donated some 50,000 złoty, which amounted to $500 then—a substantial sum.

Most of these people—policemen, administrators, and so on—are believers. They know that a church is needed, that it is ours, and that it will stay after we are gone. So they help. There are some bad people too, but both priests and parishioners know who they should and who they shouldn't approach for help.

People felt the need for a church. Obviously, there were diffi-culties. Nothing could happen officially. When a state-owned en-terprise was built, the state provided materials, but for churches there were no materials. And that is why we did what we did.

Now the parish comprises the second and third generation of Nowa Huta residents.[7] Forty to fifty percent of them work in the steel mill or in Cracow in various enterprises. They come from around Cracow, from the Tarnów, Rzeszów, Przemyśl, Kielce, and Sandomierz *voivodships*. These are good people. They have been uprooted. They come from various circles. The parish consists of 50,000 people—that is insane. A parish should have no more than 7,000. Then I could deal with everyone individually. But the parish is diversified.

There also are those who used to farm but abandoned their land, their home, and came to settle here. These are children of those who built Nowa Huta and now work in Cracow. Some of them grew up in old run-down apartment buildings in Cracow and have moved to new apartment complexes. The young workers often were not allocated apartments (by the state) but managed to arrange them somehow.

Mostly we have young people. We have very few funerals here, approximately 100 per year. By contrast, there are a lot of christen-ings, around 1,000 to 1,300. We have many weddings—these chil-dren grow up fast. This is not a traditional parish where there is an equal distribution of elderly, young adults and children. Here every-thing happens in waves.

The Church has been hierarchical for 2,000 years. We do ac-knowledge that the bishops are above us, and they govern. A Cath-olic, a believer, who rejects this notion ceases to be Catholic. This is very simple for me. There is a wide margin of freedom within this hierarchical structure. I feel very free. I can do whatever my conscience and my need to serve people tell me, even though my superiors may not like it. It has happened to me that my superiors have disliked some of my actions, but they have never punished me. Maybe the hierarchy wanted to resolve certain problems dif-ferently, but I have always thought that I should be with my people, so I was with them. Time has shown I was right.

I am obedient. I vowed obedience as a priest, and I do obey where faith and morality are concerned. Otherwise I wouldn't be a Cath-olic.

When there was a strike in the steel mill, some priests went to the Cardinal and asked whether they could go to the mill. I didn't inquire, I just went. It was last year, on May 1. Priests came and asked the management to let them enter the mill, but they were not allowed.

I was invited to go, so I thought it was my duty to be there. I went in, said Mass, and cheered up people a bit. Everything was all right. Father Zalewski also went. But my superiors were not very happy about it. They asked why I had gone, and so on. I said it was my duty. They respected that and nothing happened to me. Of course one can conclude that the bishop prefers not to interfere. Yet I think I have a wide range of possibilities and freedom. If I look at state and Party structures, I see that discipline is more visible there. The top decides and those lower down have to follow orders. The general rules of parish functioning are determined upon by the Conference of Bishops, but I decide about details. If I do something wrong, I will be reprimanded or transferred; I will not be punished.

There is a wide margin of freedom and possibilities, but control from the bottom is a different matter. Unfortunately, the system is very clerical. A month ago I was in the United States and observed that lay people are a lot more involved in church matters. Here, when lay people got involved in parish life, they were persecuted for it, even fired from their jobs, so the clergy had to take a lot upon itself. If anyone is to be punished or harmed, let it be priests, and leave lay people alone. Now parish councils have been established and so lay people have more influence. However, we all still have to be careful, because there are many state regulations restricting church life. We still have to take care of a lot of matters secretly.

What kind of matters? I will not tell, period. The Church is strong because priests can keep their mouths shut. It is different in the States. Everything is done openly; everything can be done. Here if one takes up a collection to build a church and says how much people donated, the state soaks us with 60 percent tax. If I make public how much I collect and pay 60 percent of everything I collect, what can I build then? A chicken coop?

In a sense, my hands are as dirty as everyone else's. We all live in mud since we have to manipulate the "Reds." On paper everything is fine.

Along with the authority come some painful decisions. Lay people contribute a lot to parish decision making, but not about liturgy or the Mass. I decide about these things. I get to know people—some participate in the council—but how much we can decide depends on how much the state interferes with parish matters. There are two types of interference. The Church in Russia was destroyed because communists infiltrated parish councils and the councils demanded that the priest be removed. I have to say, however, that people appreciate that priests live to serve them. On the other hand, the relationship between the clergy and parishioners resembles that of a father and his children. I was supposed to be transferred under bishop's orders to another parish but was not, due to social pressure from the parishioners.

Priests enjoy a higher standard of living, but this is because they are single and do not have families. I have a car, a color TV, and an apartment. There are priests who would give up their own clothes and shoes, but there also are priests who hide everything for themselves, just like others.[8]

I, for example, received a lot of aid from the West, but it all went to the people. Others distributed it; as a rule I did not get involved. I built a church retreat camp in Jasna Polana; now I will build a sanatorium for children—all due to American aid and Mrs. Barbara Johnson[9] who offered financial support. It all depends on the individual. Of course, there were people who took advantage of the aid.

I have to admit that the aid helped me very much. There were hundreds of people here every day; I would not have been able to afford to offer them coffee or tea. I got tea and coffee in aid packages, so I told everyone—please, help yourself. A lot of people slept here during the strikes.[10]

If I had a family, a wife, children, I would live in poverty. Unfortunately, because we are not paid, we do not have insurance. Many priests have families; they go abroad and they have friends. Most of our income comes from these sources, I suppose. Honestly, in the parish it took years to buy a car, a Fiat [a small car manufactured in Poland under Italian license]. I had to save for a year or two or three. I didn't buy anything else, not even books.

I brought some money back from abroad, but I invested it in the parish. We were building a new rectory because the old one was in ruins. It was 200 years old but had not been renovated for 100 years. Everything had to be done.

In Edward Gierek's era I was able to buy $100 a month [on the black market]. I lived reasonably well and could still afford to buy $100. My salary was 10,000 złoty. One dollar cost 80 złoty. I used to leave 2,000 złoty for myself to buy books. I didn't have a car and I didn't buy alcohol. Nowadays, a priest gets on average between $15 and $30 a month. People think that priests live high on the hog, but this is a myth. I see it when I have to provide for my brother priests, give them food and take care of the parish.

There is too much boot-licking [on the part of the priests lower down in the hierarchy] and too little openness. But it all depends on the individual priest. I, for instance, respect my bishop, and I talk to him the same way I talk to you now. There are priests who are very authoritarian—from the top down. I try to be in the middle. If I have to say something to my superiors, I tell this to their faces, not behind their backs. I also can communicate with those below me.

Undoubtedly, the prestige of clergy in Polish society depends on the fact that priests sacrifice a lot for their people. Priests teach religion, and nobody pays them for it. If I hire a religion teacher, I have to pay her. But I don't have to pay a priest. Generally speaking, most priests (about 80 percent) are very intelligent, well-read, and knowledgeable about different things. The more a priest is involved in people's affairs, lives for and with them, and helps them, the higher his prestige. And there is the religious element. We are a nation of believers. A priest is always a priest, as my mother taught me, no matter what he does.

A priest's authority is considerable and rests on his religious authority. There also is human authority, which results from the sacrifice that I mentioned. A friend of mine built a church; but later he married and nobody said a bad word because the church had been built because of him. I liked the parishioners' attitude. They said: "He was unlucky, we didn't pray hard enough for him, we didn't help him here. He had problems so he had to find someone he could confide in."

On the other hand, there are threats to a priest's authority. It is threatened by certain myths, some of which are created by priests themselves because they live in isolation and are deprived of social contact. My home is open to everyone. This is the hardest punishment, harder than being sentenced to life in prison.

The Church was unprepared to distribute relief aid in the 1980s. A large family with many children was theoretically needy. But what if the parents came in a Mercedes to pick up the goods? Were they really needy; should I have given it to them?

Some things I will tell, but some things I will never tell.

NOTES

1. In 1970 in Gdańsk, Szczecin, and other cities, strikes and street riots culminated in soldiers shooting at least 50 people to death and wounding about 1,000.

2. It was explicitly illegal and punishable to build anything without governmental permission. Thus Father Kurzeja's activities had much broader implications and their very execution was a contest to the authorities, whether or not he intended this.

3. The cardinal working in the Cracow area who became pope in 1979.

4. The Wawel is the late-fourteenth-century castle in the city of Cracow.

5. An informal term for the deal-making necessary to arrange things in the "Red" (Communist) bureaucracy.

6. Most Poles have two wedding ceremonies—civil and Church. Communist Party apparatchiks and security functionaries were prohibited from church involvement and thus could not be formally or visibly involved in church activities, including weddings.

7. Nowa Huta is a workers' town not far from Cracow known for its huge steelworks. The town was built during the Stalinist years as a model socialist industrialized town, one in which the Church had no place.

8. Relief food, medicines, and equipment poured into Poland from Western governments and private organizations in the early 1980s. Some of the goods were designated for delivery through Polish state organizations; others through the Church.

9. Barbara Johnson is an American millionaire of Polish origin.

10. Strikes in Nowa Huta before the founding of Solidarity and during martial law drew nationwide attention.

13

Onward Exultation:
The Church's Afterglow in
Communism's Collapse

An Interview with Father Andrzej Kłoczowski
(Following Solidarity's June 1989 landslide victory)

> If . . . the psychology of the Occupation is not to weigh
> heavily on the moral health of the nation, it must be
> examined most carefully.   —Kazimierz Wyka, 1945

I won't talk about parishes because I don't know parishes. I never worked in one. In youth or other ministries we try to adopt a different style. Look at the Catholic Intelligentsia Clubs that fomented the Citizens' Committees[1] and helped during the election. The Citizens' Committees are the motor of Solidarity and the motor of democracy in this country. Where were the Citizens' Committees? In the Catholic Intelligentsia Clubs.

These people are intelligentsia brought up in the youth ministry. To understand the influence of social life on the democratization of this country, you have to understand all these dynamics. The style we use in the ministry has inspired many people to participate in Citizens' Committees. It does have influence.

In the Church there are certain tendencies and groups that are searching for this new style. They want to find themselves.

I will tell you a story on this subject, from the prehistory of Solidarity. Twelve years ago, there was a group of students from Cracow who cooperated with KOR—the Committee for the Defense of Workers.[2] It was a very interesting group. Half of the group's members were people connected with the youth ministry, and half were anarchists whom we laughed at. It was a countercultural group.

Among them was a young student, Adam Szostkiewicz [a contributor to this book]. Another of these students was killed under mysterious circumstances by the police. There was a demonstration here, a mass was said, and that's how a student committee of Solidarity was created. That was 1977. The word "solidarity" had already appeared here, and it came out of this pluralistic circle consisting of believers, Christians, and atheists. These people were united by solidarity and a common cause: educational reform. Later, these people from the Student Solidarity Committee were elected in a democratic vote to Solidarity's regional council, because they were ready to work on behalf of a social cause and to take on this responsibility. They had a feeling of moral obligation.

I think that relations between Solidarity and the Church do not stem from the fact that the bishop orders others to work. It is ethical inspiration. In the West, to be against totalitarianism one has only to read Alexander Solzhenitsyn. But here it is a problem of ethical courage, a feeling of responsibility for something bigger than one's own life.

I think it would be very bad if a Christian Democratic Party were established in Poland. I definitely would oppose it. I think that a Christian can be a socialist in the Polish Socialist Party,[3] he can participate in such a party, but I am afraid that the creation of a Christian Democratic Party would mean that bishops would get involved in politics. I'm definitely against that. I speak out about my conviction. I'm against it because the temptation to strengthen one's power would be great.

The Church is here to serve. Jesus Christ said, "You are to serve." Serve mankind; serve humanity. But this service has to be very specific. We should not strive for privileges, and for a privileged situation. We only need good working conditions to serve people. There are many priests and lay Catholics who believe as I do. Undoubtedly, there is a certain tension here. Others may envision the institutional frame of how the Church should operate differently. This is what we debate—how we are to shape the Church as an institution. It means that we have to respect our fellow parishioners. It is very important because people here are more and more sophisticated, and they know democracy. Ten years ago, we had to teach professors how to organize elections. In the end they learned. But undoubtedly there is tension here, and the Church is not homogeneous.

It seems to me that real prestige is when I say, for example, that a priest possesses authority that stems from the fact that he lives according to the Gospel. It is obvious. When he deviates from the Gospel, he loses his authority.

It is not enough to wear a cassock to possess authority. One has to earn it. People are very critical. Taking things for granted or ordering people about does not work. Maybe in a little village, but not in a big city. Most clergy still come from the countryside. You have to remember that the paradox is that the power structure, both in the Party and in the Church, is of peasant origin. Both Party members and bishops are sons of peasants.

They share a cultural background and are influential in their communities by virtue of the careers they chose. There is a certain psychological relationship between them—they understand each other. There is a common mentality.

To understand how it came about that most of the Party and Church activists are drawn from the same structure, one should note that the social group most destroyed during the war in Poland was the intelligentsia. There was Katyń, Auschwitz, and the Warsaw Uprising.[4] Then a people's government, a Communist government, was being established and needed an apparatus. Where were the reserves of future elites? The village. A large, overpopulated village.

There was no working class. A working class needed to be built. So there was enormous migration, not only to Nowa Huta, but also to the Party and state administration. This migration was sucked into the Party apparatus. For example, most of the Party members come from around Rzeszów. In Władysław Gomułka or Edward Gierek's times, there were lots of villages that had their secretaries.

There was a similar situation with the sons of peasants who went to become priests. They thought differently, had a different value system, but were still peasants' sons. This meant a certain type of mentality. New things are happening now in Poland because children of these peasants moved to cities where there is a completely different culture, different outlook on the world, different sensitivity, different system of values, and a much more pluralistic and mobile society. The priests are not satisfied with the traditional, village-based religiosity. They are looking for a different style.

Now the situation is different. For instance, there are fewer students from villages enrolled in seminaries. More and more of them come from cities. These are different people. They have a different sensitivity. But where it will lead, I don't know. The influence of the village resulted in the nonintellectual character of the Church. Nowadays, deacons want a higher level of education in seminaries, they are not happy with their professors. This is a good example. They simply have deeper, more intellectual needs. I see this because I lecture myself.

During the election, a number of Party members had their pictures taken in front of the church. I saw a Party member who showed a picture that had been taken in Rome during an audience with the Pope. One Party member said: "I am both a Communist and a practicing Catholic." This is dangerous because it's an attempt to manipulate.

For us as members of the Church, it's also dangerous because it may mean that we are so important that it goes to our heads. Simone Weil said that the most dangerous moment in a man's life is victory. Not defeat, but victory. It is the most dangerous moment. Because when we win, we make the biggest mistakes. And I think that's where the Polish Church is right now—at this dangerous juncture. The great triumph can become triumphalism. This is a grave sin of the Church. The Church is a religious structure, and its power stems from religion, not from the political power structure and other things. We are here to serve. If one forgets about it, everything becomes a facade. Such a facade will fall, and that will be the end. I think it is extremely important to realize it and say it aloud. We in the Church, we the clergy.

Religion in Poland is too much a form of social existence, and not enough a form of existing in silence and loneliness. Teilhard de Chardin[5] said that religion is what man does by himself. But in Poland religion is what man does when there are many of us. I am afraid of this. Despite what Tischner[6] and a few others say, I think, and I do it, that we should proclaim a healthy individualism. We need this healthy Protestant element, in the sense of Søren Kierkegaard's loneliness in front of God. From the standpoint of religion, this dimension is extremely important. The gospel is not to praise people, but to demand from them. And demands are what man has to go through individually, in his conscience, which is a free conscience. In my opinion, it is the most fundamental matter now.

I even organized a conference on solidarity and loneliness. There has to be an equilibrium. If there is only solidarity, then we have a group. Man is overdirected. And this is against the gospel, in my opinion. However, what is great in this tradition, in regard to the experiences of Western Europe, is that Poles know that God and man are not antinomic values. We are entering theory, but it is important for our understanding. The very sense of modern atheism and laicization is not a problem of scientific ideology, Darwin and so on, but more one of Sartre and Nietzsche, who hold that one cannot be fully human if one believes. Yet, in our experience, these are not antinomic values. A Pole does not think that if he is Catholic he is not free.

That is why I think that this individual dimension is necessary. It is the most important thing now. Because everyone understood they had to be *against*, they believed in Solidarity. It was good then, but now the individual is important, because unity is disappearing.

You asked me about the influence of youth ministries not only on Solidarity, but also on what is happening now. We organized lectures and other activities at a workers' university in Nowa Huta. There was a workers' university in Nowa Huta all the time, and all those who now are active in Solidarity went through three years of lectures on the economy, sociology, history, and so on. The lectures were not only on religion and some were even given by nonbelievers.

Among the students, these activities had more of a uniting character. However, as far as workers are concerned, those who attended the lectures were delegated by underground structures of Solidarity. That unity was already present. I am talking about martial law. I remember the first class. I entered, and there were 70 young men, each with a mustache a la Wałęsa. Seventy "Wałęsas" sat there in Nowa Huta.

The workers were more aware than the students of what they wanted. They were more mature. In my opinion, students are rather immature and a little spoiled. Their working-class peers are a lot more mature and know what they want. Anyway, being a student is somewhat of a pretend life. In addition, students don't know what they are going to do afterwards. In Poland, the worst thing for your career is to graduate from a university. There is no work, and one earns very little anyway. An engineer who graduated from a university earns three times less than a worker. This is one of the reasons for this crisis. Young people are frustrated.

I see the ministry as the preparation of certain elites. I understand an "elite" as a group of people who wants to serve, who is not passive, and wants to be active. It is educating a certain group of intelligentsia, because youth ministry means educating intelligentsia. As you know, both in Russia and in Poland, the intelligentsia has a great social importance. It is the mechanism of change. In Poland we have a great opportunity because we have developed an understanding with workers and now have this exchange. We organize lectures for them, and they strike for us. This is power together. This is the great power of Solidarity. This is preparation of future elites.

In Cracow Solidarity began with youth ministries and the Student Solidarity Committee. The illegal materials delivered to the steelworks during the September strike of 1980 amounted to several tons. Who produced it? Students from Cracow. It widened these people's horizons, that this work bore fruit. I think that the Solidarity movement would not have happened if it wasn't for the intelligentsia who were searching for accommodation with workers.

These meetings in the church, lectures and so on, weren't an explosion, but a form of survival. To a great extent Solidarity survived at churches where it found refuge and where this consciousness-raising work happened. In this sense, it was very important. A moment of survival. Where else could people gather?

Out of necessity the activities of the ministry overlapped with union work. This overlap was somewhat unnatural since a union should be active in a factory, not in a parish. Now things are more normal—everything has returned where it belongs.

In my opinion, nowadays the most important question is how to go from the present economic model to free enterprise. This is a problem. How to do it? Solidarity wants economic reform and social justice. The reform has to be either that of Thatcher or Reagan, and here, because we have social-democratic values, there will be tension. I predict tension within Solidarity, between the social-democratic and liberal[7] factors. This is a real tension that will increase. And all of these political clubs and so on are nothing more than a game played by older gentlemen or younger ones. This is simply a form of psychotherapy.

Solidarity as a trade union will have to defend the workers and have a social-democratic appeal on the workers' behalf. Those who are now members of the Parliament will have to choose what coalitions to build with those in the Communist Party. These are important problems and, in my opinion, the Church has no idea how to solve them. Our social science is a mixture of populism and social democracy. The Church cannot understand this anymore than it can in the Third World. I visited Brazil. There are two methods: to save people from starvation by producing more or by dividing more fairly. In my opinion, one has to think how to produce more. Then there will be something to divide. The Church has always stressed that things have to be divided fairly, because it stands for social justice. This is an element of intellectual backwardness in the Church.

I am both a liberal and a conservative. One has to see reality as it is at the moment—to see that it is antagonistic. Solidarity is one big banner behind which many different things are hidden. Everybody loves one another as long as they are in church. But when they start solving real life problems, things won't be so simple anymore.

NOTES

1. Solidarity Citizens' Committees were founded in local communities across the country to organize the June 1989 election for Solidarity, which won in a landslide.

2. KOR (*Komitet Obrony Robotników*) was formed by a group of intellectuals in September 1976 to supply legal and financial assistance to imprisoned workers and their families in the aftermath of the political unrest of the previous June. In the late 1970s KOR was the principal group responsible for underground organizing and publishing.

3. The Polish Socialist Party (PPS), a long-standing informal group in opposition to the Communist government, was registered in 1989, thus enabling it to operate openly and legally.

4. During the war up to 12,000 Polish officers were executed at Katyń in the Russian forests; one and half million people perished at the Nazi concentration camp Auschwitz; and 150,000 Polish civilians and 16,000–18,000 soldiers died in the Warsaw Uprising.

5. Pierre Teilhard de Chardin, a Jesuit and one of the most important Catholic philosophers of the twentieth century, is an intellectual and moral authority for Polish liberal Catholics.

6. Jozef Tischner is a well-known philosopher-priest aligned with the Polish Opposition under Communism.

7. "Liberal" in the nineteenth-century free-enterprise sense.

The Opposition

Throughout the uneven course of postwar Poland, the anti-Communist Opposition, though always seen by the Communist Party as an enemy, was persecuted with notably varying intensity, sometimes even tolerated. The lives of all three authors here have been intimately and irrevocably intertwined with opposition *środowiska*, whose closed nature the authors emphasize.

Piotr Szwajcer, now director of the formerly underground NOWA and president of the Independent Publishing Association, argues that the category "opposition" is abused. One cannot understand the entire web of the multifunctional *środowisko* in terms of only one manifest thread of its "activities"—public deeds. Opposition is not just a life choice but a lifestyle.

Wojciech Arkuszewski is well placed to show us the essential characteristics of an Opposition *środowisko*—an exclusive "physical nest." Since he was in junior high school, his circle of friends, activities and life possibilities have been guided by this *środowisko*—from editing underground journals by way of eluding the authorities during martial law, to helping build the movement that went beyond opposing the regime to succeeding it. Arkuszewski is vice-president of the National Solidarity Committee "NSZZ" and a close aide to former Prime Minister Tadeusz Mazowiecki, his elder by 20 years and his mentor for more than two decades. Specially known in opposition circles as a fount of information on the movement's personalities and activities, and an unshaken believer in the cause, Arkuszewski nevertheless shows, in an article specifically written for this book, how a lifelong commitment has also led him to be its critic from within.

In a clandestine situation impelled by danger from without, the distinction between "personal" and "professional" activities becomes almost nonexistent. Accordingly, private and job-related finances become mingled. "Tadeusz Wróblewski's" article on "Opposition and Money" (the pseudonym conceals a known activist) asks fundamental questions about the financing of the Opposition elite, pointing out that this has come overwhelmingly from outside Poland and mostly from the West. How many prominent Oppositionists could not answer that simplest of questions—"What do you live on?"

Many clandestine recipients of Western money now find themselves in government or Parliament. Some have formed foundations that seek Western aid, now legal. Long-standing *środowiska* influence how this aid is distributed, even if it flows through government and Parliamentary organizations. In a society with surging social inequalities, the question of who gets Western funding is a growing source of antagonism among *środowiska*.

Piotr Szwajcer contends that the Opposition has been sealed against the outside world, perceiving itself as a chosen few and separating itself from the rest of society after the manner of a purist sect, not a revolutionary call. Psychological separation and absolutism take precedence over political goals. All this has been a source of alienation to many people outside this *środowisko*, whose anti-Opposition, anti-Solidarity stance candidate Stanisław Tymiński effectively galvanized through his strong showing in the 1990 presidential election.

14

Opposition Against Society: In Pursuit of a "Normal" Life

PIOTR SZWAJCER

> We must scrutinize our mortgaged independence care-
> fully. . . . We should not conceal it behind pretty
> speeches.   —Kazimierz Wyka, 1945

We have been studying those who chose unconventional, yet socially significant, life paths through the 1980s.[1] One group thus examined was "the Opposition" and we had to confront the fundamental problem of criteria for membership in this group. Categories generally applied in the social sciences, including that of social movements, are clearly inadequate to explain the Opposition; such categories are imprecise, or derived from theories evolved to analyze completely different conditions.

We also found that dictionary definitions of opposition are useless: political groups that oppose the political group or government in power, or people who entertain political opinions that conflict with those of ruling parties. To employ the criterion of "opinions" (in the sociological sense of attitudes and values) could lead us to believe that from 79.5 percent to 96 percent of Polish society belong to the Opposition—at the very least, the somewhat more than 70 percent of respondents consistently answering "no" to the question: "Would you want the world to evolve in the direction of that form of socialism that exists in Poland?," asked in many surveys in our country over recent years.

Abuse of the terms "opposition" and "oppositionism" raises many problems. These are criteria imposed from outside, which the people we interviewed feel to be forced upon them by the "abnormal" quality of reality. It is analytically incorrect to describe all the components embraced in the entire web of civil interaction in terms only of one single component. Transferring this entire web to the political plane creates yet further misunderstandings. As Tadeusz Szawieł writes: "It is not possible to properly conceptualize democratic opposition in Poland under the categories of political objectives and programs, or in terms of activities leading to their realization."[2]

Given this realization, we decided to employ the concept of Opposition as a community—informally structured and bonded together—uniting a spectrum of individuals engaged in specific acts of resistance. Perhaps it is more correct to speak about communities and groups living partially outside of and partially in conjunction with the world of real socialism. When attitudes are not centrally significant, only activities can serve as criteria. Independently of how we define "opposition," it will always encompass those people whose "noncriminal crimes" brought upon them harassment, internment, arrest, or dismissal from jobs or upon whom other repressions were brought to bear. Thus, participants in our research form a distinguishable community.

These criteria of "opposition" have certain consequences, notably that of excluding those active only during the legal and quite different period of Solidarity. It suffices to recall that particular preoccupation with the experience of freedom—that emphasis on openness, legality and formalization of activities that characterized those shining Solidarity days.

Our participants are therefore activists in "illegal" Solidarity undertakings—editors, publishers, printers, distributors, and journalists in the "second circulation" (the unlicensed and underground publishing circle), organizers and participants in many of the unregistered organizations and social initiatives that emerged during the past few years. Many were actively involved in activities outside the law throughout the 1980s; many as well have at different times and to differing degrees decided to withdraw from such activities. This text draws on 28 recorded and transcribed interviews lasting 2 to 4 hours each. All respondents were male, most of them living in Warsaw. The youngest was 29; the oldest 41.

Opposition as Lifestyle

We glean a profile of the Oppositionists' social identity from how they employ the category "we," how they assess their own role in society, and what they say about the meaning and goals of their activities. For example, the editor of an underground newspaper who had identified the underground with the Opposition thus observes: "I think that the underground is different mainly in lifestyle. I do, however, limit this underground to my newspaper circle (of editors, writers, and publishers). All in all there are a few front lines of activity and up to 20 activists who do *something* (engage in some illegal tasks, even if only nominally), and that's the whole underground."

On the other hand, a Freedom and Peace activist[3] reflects on the divisions in Polish society: "Many of those who live well benefit from the way the system works—basically the *nomenklatura*, army, and police. But the Opposition establishment—a kind of economic underground—benefits too. This is what we mean when we talk about large underground publishing firms that are fully commercial enterprises operating through surreptitious and systematic illegal dealing and acting on gangster-type principles."

A trade union activist, co-founder of a political party, states: "The opinions expressed in *Res Publica*, an officially published though not proSystem monthly, or those of *Tygodnik Mazowsze*, an underground newspaper of the Mazowsze Solidarity chapter, and often those of *Polityka*, a weekly official—though not hard-line—newspaper, resemble one another—illegal or legal. But I remain 'on the other side' [of this uniform establishment]. I am interested in what people are talking about in their workplaces and factories. We are on the other side of the barricade. The division between the second [illegal] or first [official] publishing circle is unimportant."

These typical examples permit us to challenge the widespread opinion that the Opposition constitutes a *single* community or cohesive group. Opposition activists by no means identify themselves with the entire category of those whom outside observers lump together as one community. Our interviewees used the expression "we" in a very constricted sense, confining it to fellow members of such narrow categories as a publishing firm, journal, or "structure," referring to themselves and the circle with whom they cooperate closely and continuously. Sometimes "we" also embraces those engaged in similar activities such as other journals or other trade union publishing houses. However, not even once did the "we" category extend over the range typically assumed by outside observers such as American journalists and political scientists.

The emphasis on one's own special qualities and mission, often to belittle the status of others, serves to build one's own standing. Not only are there fundamental differences in the kinds of opposition activities that various opposition circles engage in, but also in their underlying identity and goals. Such a statement argues that, for example, the phenomenon being studied does not fall into the category "social movement." All definitions of social movements with which I am familiar assume a common sense of identity or goals or both as a condition for a given community's existence. The participants in our research do not make such generalizations possible.

Let us now turn to the widespread belief that the goal of the Opposition's activity is to attain power, or—in its weaker version—to struggle to change the political system. Our interview material persuades us that these assertions are, to say the least, misleading. Most of the interviewees have much more complicated attitudes toward the political system. They do not see ideological believers, or what they call "real communism," as a threat in their practical world. This judgment has manifold implications.

First, in carrying out their activities the greatest obstacle they encounter, and one that also determines their goals and the theater of their activities, is neither the System nor the raw facts of power. That frequently discussed dimension of "us" and "them" (where "they" are the authorities or even more, the system and all who go along with it) is practically absent from the interviews. The scheme is: "we"—the society and the system (which includes all entities that have comprised and accommodated with it)—determine the sphere of activity. But the third component is much less significant. One of the individuals we interviewed said, for example: "Communism ceased to be a problem years ago. The system can be changed—that's the smallest problem." Another one asked: "How can an opponent like the Communist Party be taken seriously? So-called communists, who, thank God, aren't communists? You can't regard them as political opponents. It's a sort of grotesque sludge that actually has died but lies there by grace of inertia and geopolitics."

These statements illustrate a theme that runs through nearly all the interviews. "Society"—what has happened to it and what continues to happen—is the reference point. What has happened to "society" is variously described, although the terms "Bolshevism" and "Sovietism" have made special careers. Within this framework informants describe the people—"society"—as passive, apathetic, decaying, and "demoralized bedlam." One interviewee bemoaned society's passivity: "Not having an opinion on any matter whatsoever, lack of attitudes and judgment, a 'nothing,' a blemish on the system. That's the worst. I detest it."

Opposing "Sovietization" through "being" and through activity impelled by conscience lies at the essence of "the Opposition." This does not mean of course that people are indifferent to the system. Oppositionists appeal to ideas of democracy, political pluralism, and sovereignty, and ultimately to life in a "normal country," but on a much more distant plane. Yet Oppositionists realize that these appeals have little potential for fruition. For as one of our interviewees put it: "We'll be able to handle the problem that for 40 years people lived under Communism. But unfortunately and naturally, they learned something from it."

It is no accident that when our interviewees look to Poland's future, they are reluctant to contemplate the chilling social costs that sudden eruption might entail. Almost all assume that such a convulsion could be much more devastating than anything from the Solidarity period. It would only serve to obstruct their activities, and above all, it would not change much. Yet they attribute the obvious changes in the public climate over recent years to this resistance and to a general intransigence.

The Opposition did not pit itself against the abstraction of Communist rule. Our interviewees did not envision Communism as an ideological problem and certainly not as an intellectual one. For our participants, the fact that the authorities lied and that communism was morally wrong and in all other respects simply revolting is self-evident. The ideological aspect barely exists; it sought only to maintain the power structure, of which ideology was the merest facade. The notion that representatives or defenders of the Party-state system might act out of higher motives practically never appeared. They had been hammered into Communism, and had become "stupefied," "weak," or finally and most often, cynics and careerists.

Communism, real communism or socialism, in our interviewees' eyes, as immoral as it is, is also abnormal, and this is very significant. Almost everyone resorts to the word "absurdity" to describe everyday reality—one juxtaposed with the other or rather to supplement "Sovietization" and "demoralized bedlam." "Normality" as contrasted with what is going on here and now also manifests itself much more widely than the sphere of everyday activity. The following statements articulate this: "All the faults of capitalist coun-

tries, or I would prefer to say 'normal countries' are more natural,"
or: "There is this world where societies have managed to arrange
their life in one way or the other and then there is this gigantic,
terrible historical and global mistake, which is called Communism,
or 'real socialism' as they refer to it lately. That's the Soviet bloc—
a mad web, a terrible net of circumstances. It's of no use, right? One
shouldn't live here. One shouldn't have to live like this!"

The specific attitude toward the authorities which sets out, successfully enough, to deny them any moral standing ministered to
Oppositionists' psychological comfort and, most of all, helped to
justify their life's choice. Given the potential and actual costs of such
a choice, this required constant justification indeed. It is not accidental that, however prominently ethical and moral explanations
figure in the interviews, they were offered only hesitantly. The interviewees were reluctant to use grand words or truisms. As one
put it: "I decided that it is right to do such things, and I started
doing them. That's it. Why is it right? You could use grand and high-
sounding words, but what for? It's so clear-cut that it's easy to understand. The whole point of this activity is lost when you use
elaborate and scientific definitions."

When discussing why people do what they do, one almost gets
the impression that they believe any other choice of conduct would
have been *unnatural*. Their track was self-evident. "It all started in
the '70s when Mirek Chojecki invited me to travel with him to
Radom and then to Ursus.[4] I think that I've walked down the same
kind of road as most people from my generation I know," or: "Everyone was doing something: It was natural." An impulse best described
as duty lurks in the background of the interviews, and might even
be stressed as the following instance does admirably: "Every Pole
over 30 is well aware of what country he lives in because he sees
it every day. I was able to find out on my own, because after all I
went to a TKN lecture[5] by myself and started reading such books
by myself. And it just seems to be the individual's duty."

Explicitly moral justifications are therefore usually hidden or
veiled. What does appear in the forefront is the need to do something—present in almost everyone's experience and most emphasized by those for whom the declaration of martial law on December
13, 1981, was a moral challenge. "When I looked outside my window that 13th of December, it was like—I can't just do nothing, I
must do something. . . . It was such a moment, that martial law, an
absolute nightmare. People were terrified. Me too. And that's de-

grading—a grown-up guy walking around frightened. This is the kind of moment when a person has to stand up straight and do something. He must, or else he won't be able to live with himself."

So the very act of taking part and taking sides becomes the highest value. The particular knowledge of how society has been Sovietized and the nature of those in power reassures the people who have so chosen that the other side has no trump card of righteousness; "they" are passive hacks or at most careerists. At the same time, such a sense of what is fitting radically polarizes differences of doctrine and policy to a plane in which all moral and ethical considerations fight on "our side," all differences in the camp of the good cause are insignificant. The others engaged in the system are conceded no ethic, no ideology, and, in practice, simply no moral values whatsoever.

Therefore, we can conclude that to define the Opposition as anti-Communist is about as meaningless as saying that it is anti-racist or anti-Nazi. The time when one had to have some opinion about Communism seems to have gone forever. Also, Opposition activists did not perceive the System itself as a problem, since they discarded the policies its doctrines dictate without discussion.

Opposition activists were consumed by the passion of entering public life on their own terms and in entering upon and creating activities in the public sphere. The terms "activity," "participation," and "public sphere" act as guideposts, without which it is impossible to comprehend Polish Opposition. When we look at "the Opposition" solely in light of its members' considered actions, it appears to be a constellation of independently functioning groups, small circles and individuals with little in common apart from a common repudiation of communism and a commitment to activities that the communist regime illegalized.

Still, a careful reading of the interviews allows us to state that above all these differences, it is possible to find a common sphere embracing all those thus involved, a sphere determined by the activity itself, by having convictions and acting upon them.

The first emotion is not the will to victory: it is self-respect. This will contrasts with passivity and helplessness, which are regarded as the "normal" (in the sense of being widespread) model of life in our country. "I will never be a 'wimp,'" as one interviewee put it. This "normal" life model (and here our interviewees employ two words: "Sovietization" and "demoralized bedlam") is entwined with dependence and subordination, especially in systems such as ours.

Another interviewee explains: "It forces us to lie, to do things we don't agree with, to be with people with whom we don't want to be. Opposition activism is an exit from that world. It gives people the opportunity to create their own world, to undertake activities that they consider right and to do it with those that they themselves chose."

For our respondents, it is only this created world, decidedly different from their surroundings, that comes to constitute a "normal" world—the world as it should be. Moreover, it is a reality beyond which they do not seek to go. This willed ignorance and isolation from the surrounding world is usually quite conscious and is regarded as the price that must be paid to realize one's own lifestyle and participate in history. As one respondent expressed, "It's unthinkable to have a guy like that telling me what I can or can't read. Or telling me that he knows better whether I can travel, stay at home, or go outside. I think that a person has the right to make his own decisions."

Oppositionists speak of a widely shared feeling of duty, the sense of mission to transform Poland into a country in which it is possible to live "normally." Moreover, this affords considerable psychological comfort. Such a "mission" to act, even if it does not bring victory, proves one undefeated. And so it became an enduring way of life in the Poland of the 1980s. For in the words of one Oppositionist, "To lose means to give in."

NOTES

1. This article is based on research conducted jointly by Anna Kobiałka, Piotr Pacewicz, Zbigniew Rykowski, and Piotr Szwajcer.

2. Author's note: Tadeusz Szawieł, "Social Structure, Attitudes and Ethos Groups (On the Possibilities of Social Evolution)," *Sociological Studies* 1–2:84–85, 1982.

3. Freedom and Peace (WIP) is a pacifist organization launched by Oppositionists in 1985 originally to win elective alternative service for conscripts. That goal eventually achieved, the organization has taken up ecological and other issues.

4. Mirosław "Mirek" Chojecki founded NOWA (*Niezależna Oficyna Wydawnicza*), the largest underground publishing house in Poland, and served as its director from 1976 to 1980. Radom and Ursus were the scene of workers' food riots in 1976. NOWA's publications, then just founded, helped to keep workers and others informed about police repression and efforts to

assist the victims' families. Piotr Szwajcer is the first director of the legalized NOWA.

5. TKN (*Towarzystwo Kursów Naukowych*) was the "flying university" gatherings of intelligentsia from 1977 to 1981 which sponsored conspiratorial seminars and lectures for youth.

15

The Elitist Opposition

WOJCIECH ARKUSZEWSKI

Success always leaves behind a residue of yearning for
what used to be and an aversion to the forces that did
away with it.   —Kazimierz Wyka, 1945

Opposition in Poland has passed through several phases since the
1950s: the stage of adamant intellectual defiance of the Communist
authorities; that of dissidents in demonstrable resistance; that of
union organization, embracing both intelligentsia and workers; that
of underground conspiracy. Now the Opposition must assume the
choices and responsibility of government.

Each period has required and attracted people with different tem-
peraments, talents, and skills. All periods have one factor in common: the need to organize and to act, all in the face of some greater
or lesser degree of obstacles and danger.

After the war came the long process of creating social and political
organizations independent of the state. From 1953 to 1956 journalists and editors purged from the independent Catholic weekly,
Tygodnik Powszechny, often met privately. They called their gatherings the "Catholic Discussion Club."

Such groups were isolated indeed. That renowned opposition
figure Jan Józef Lipski, still widely respected as an Opposition authority, regularly met with an informal circle of university colleagues, thinking it the only such group. He discovered other such
circles only several years later. Perhaps still others remain known
only to their participants.

In the 1950s the disaffected felt isolated, lonely, and without
recourse. It was risky just to bring like-minded people together.
Participants felt endangered although they were being punished

only for thinking together—just a few people talking socially in private apartments. This was political opposition under Stalin.

After the unrest and partial de-Stalinization of 1956, the authorities conceded the publication of several opposition-oriented, but state-controlled, newspapers of very limited circulation. A network of discussion clubs sprang up. Upheaval within the Communist Party shook to the surface some groups of reformists with access to the mass media—which they lost during the next few years. Elite circles of distinctly opposition character began to take shape, composed of social scientists, humanists, and young people from Warsaw University. Protest became articulate within the state-sponsored writers' organizations.

The possibilities for action were limited; society was dispersed. But only quite selectively did the authorities resort to repression. Eminent intellectuals and the elite critics of the system were allowed much more leeway than unknown persons of completely alien, namely anti-Marxist, ideology. Communists could get away with more far-reaching criticism of the communist system than anti-communists. Because this view is not held by most of my own *środowisko*, I will back it up with court verdicts.

A group of boys at a Gdańsk school who let out the word that they wanted to create an underground group—but never in fact did so—received ten-year jail sentences, the strictest penalty passed in the closed trials of the 1960s. Adults who remained on the margins of the Communist Party but at the same time partook in opposition activity, received sentences a third as severe if any at all, especially if they confined themselves to intellectual dissent. An eminent opposition writer, forced out of the Party, showed up at the office of First Party Secretary Władysław Gomułka, raised hell with Gomułka's right-hand man and was thrown out, not in the slightest fearing that the authorities might confiscate his passport. He left that same day without interference to assume a scholarship abroad.

The Communists' easy treatment of their own people combined with the slow evolution of a large body of experienced activists—from communist reformism toward open resistance—to give the Opposition a large membership of the disillusioned as well as of born opponents.

Of course there were Oppositionists who did not begin as Communists. Catholic activists from the *Znak* [Sign] movement exercised some influence, acting as they did with the tacit consent of state authorities who felt the weight of the Church's influence. For more than ten years, a small group of *Znak* leaders served as the Parliamentary opposition. Other Catholic opposition groups centered on Warsaw's Catholic Intelligentsia Club (KIK) and Cracow's independent Catholic newspaper, *Tygodnik Powszechny*.

An Alternative Life

In the earlier 1970s, the Opposition's main activity was talk, usually at parties among family and friends. Another form of political opposition emerged in the 1970s: an alternative way of living, isolated from official or public modes, regarded as illegal by the authorities. People who had served out the prison sentences inflicted by the political trials of the 1960s formed its core. Others, deprived of jobs and passports for their activities in earlier groups, joined them. Younger enthusiasts poured in and began to set the pace. I have observed that people rarely become political activists on their own. There always is some circle from which they learn how to act and what to do. At social gatherings, one met students who had begun their political careers during the 1968 student demonstrations. One was introduced to writers and critics, lawyers defending the objects of political prosecution, and some elderly people who had been politically active before 1947—the year the Communists finally took power. The elderly included conspirators from wartime, a few peasant activists, old Christian Democrats, and sometimes disillusioned Communist retirees.

Some groups grew out of Catholic student ministries. But in our communist country, many groups that cultivated opposition were communist in origin: young people affiliated with the Warsaw Catholic Intelligentsia Club, Warsaw University students active in the official Students' Union, several (communist) Red Scout teams in which it was the fashion to criticize the government. In the 1950s and 1960s, the most well-known Red Scout team found its leader in Jacek Kuroń, who many years later became one of Poland's most important political opposition leaders and served as the country's first post-Communist Minister of Labor. Kuroń was still a Communist at the time he headed the Red Scouts, and thus began to reeducate as an Oppositionist the young Communists he had supervised as a Red Scout master.

The Red Scouts sought to indoctrinate children in Marxism. Pupils complained of "totalitarian upbringing." Fortunately, the instructors themselves underwent a deep and rapid ideological change under de-Stalinization and completely transformed the ideological bent of their lectures every few months, cycling quickly through criticism of communist practice in the name of communist orthodoxy to criticism of communism itself, to championing socialist ideals, to democracy, and, finally, to liberalism.

Children of Communist leaders and children of prewar Communists usually were in the scout team. Their parents wanted them to be brought up in the communist spirit. Before the authorities could check the growing criticism of the system within the teams, Kuroń's reeducated disciples had managed to join official organizations for older youth. In the late 1960s the rebels further extended their activities to the university, where they asked aggressive and critical questions at meetings held by official organizations. Some sought to create their own discussion clubs affiliated with the university.

One of the best-known opposition youth groups was organized in the latter 1970s by the teenage leader Aleksander Hall—another member of Poland's first post-Communist cabinet. It is the only group I know of to start from nothing, with no other group as its inspiration. This Gdańsk circle chose a priest to provide guidance: it was not the teacher finding the pupils, but the pupils finding the teacher. The parish hall served as the meeting place. The pupils, on their own initiative, wanted to talk about politics. Why politics? Probably life itself schooled them. They had seen with their own eyes the massacre of rioting strikers at Gdynia in December 1970.

Young people were the most active of the Oppositionists, frequently meeting for talks that lasted all night. They were enthusiastic and devoted. Since the latter 1970s, they have organized discussions at universities and collected signatures on protest letters. Operating printing machines and traveling to distant towns was work for the young. I stress their critical role no more than do most Oppositionists. Adults were often helpless, their methods of political struggle beside the point.

There was no visible generation gap: the many activists under 30 or so worked well together with the few older activists probably because leadership was drawn from the older generation. The Opposition thus served to unite and strengthen cadres which had grown up before Stalinism, with others who had gone to school after the war, and with those who knew Stalinism only from tales. With very few significant exceptions, the generation that grew up under Stalinism remained passive for life.

The political trials of the late 1960s, during First Party Secretary Władysław Gomułka's rule, played an important role in bringing political resistance together. Through the trials, victims made new contacts. Those persecuted befriended one another and kept up their friendships after being released. The authorities later would adopt different tactics to diminish such opportunities.

Under First Party Secretary Edward Gierek in the 1970s, Oppositionists were seldom jailed. As a rule, young would-be underground organizers were simply beaten up at the police station. Authorities tried to isolate the Opposition, purging its members from jobs, harassing their contacts, and preventing even their most apolitical publications. Yet the Opposition was able to help provide for the material needs of the dismissed colleagues; and just because pushed by the authorities to the margins of public life, the Opposition found it easier and more necessary to integrate itself, to pass from a loose constellation of circles to a tighter informal organization.

Such leaders and organizers as Jacek Kuroń, who worked to organize the active Opposition, have almost never been employed—both from their choice to concentrate on political activity and from the difficulties placed in the way of their finding lawful employment. Those who rose to leadership tended to be well enough off not to have to work or worry more than usual about material needs; they had the option of being supported by their families and could devote full time to political discussion and involvement. Many leaders inherited apartments from their parents or lived with them throughout adulthood. Those who lacked this luxury were much more dependent on the state and state employment: it was easy for the authorities to punish young activists who came to work in Warsaw by stripping them of their jobs and denying them the right to live there. Thus the authorities intentionally condemned them to dislocation and severance from their entire world—the Opposition.

The Opposition *środowisko* was very tight: it was like family to the lonely and isolated of an atomized society, a redoubt to those with a sense of constant danger. The Opposition often served as a physical nest—a familiar apartment, a well-loved cafe—reinforcing the strongest ties, more important than any political differences. But entrance into the opposition *środowisko* was not easy and was little dictated by political beliefs alone: one had to have the right contacts to be accepted by the right people.

Members were imprisoned in the opposition *środowisko* by the absence of rich life outside it. They could not live any other life, and that is why they easily surrendered to the stern discipline of Opposition authorities. When I first met people in the Opposition, I was shocked at the hierarchical quality of its relationships. Its structure and activities resembled those of a closed religious sect. It was a milieu with much more hierarchy than non-Opposition milieus: everyone knew who was most important, whose opinion counted most, who was less important, and who didn't count at all. The hierarchical nature of the Opposition *środowisko* stemmed from its being organized along the single dimension of politics. Those outside Opposition circles lived in a much more complicated world, their lives not flattened along this one axis. Thus the elitist Opposition had the tremendous advantage over simple, normal people who also had some political views and were sometimes discontent. Theirs was the advantage of singlemindedness and the authority of obsession so often conceded to communist groups in non-communist societies. Others were busy with their families and work and did not discuss politics day in, day out, year upon year. In private contact, the Oppositionists crushed their discussion partners, often with brutal and nasty techniques.

Few organizations can confine themselves to words alone. At those times when the Opposition believed it necessary to go beyond talk, it was faced by the difficult issues of choosing and timing its initiatives. No longer was it a question of public defiance and martyr-making arrest, but of undertaking objectives that would endure longer-term success. The Opposition set out to realize different ideas at different times: a campaign, for instance, of protest letters which by signing one could lose one's job or one's passport. Protest letters came in two forms: mass documents to be signed by as many people as possible and elite letters where it was a privilege to be called upon to sign. Or again, there was a period when Opposition activity was limited to observing historically significant holidays—attending anniversary celebrations and church services occasioned by a patriotic event or a nationally glorious memory.

Beyond Talk

Important changes took place after 1976. After years of endless discussion, new people began rallying specifically to defend protesting workers. The Opposition organized a legal and material assistance bureau to help those imprisoned or thrown out of work following the strikes and riots at Radom and the Warsaw Ursus tractor factory. Some of the newcomers matter-of-factly preferred direct action to talk for talk's sake (as they characterized the earlier Opposition). But I emphatically believe that we should not underestimate the significance of those long early years of repetitive discussion. Without this talkative Opposition, there could not have been a movement of practical social activity. The earlier Opposition initiated such activity although it was carried on by others with operational temperament, for whom there had been no place in the earlier movement.

The Opposition's activities were not confined to assisting the families of jailed workers. The underground publishing house NOWA was founded in 1977, the first and largest of the independent houses. To date it has published more than a thousand books.

In communist countries, science often is a sphere of relative freedom, offering the opportunity of "internal emigration" for those who do not adjust well to the System. Scientists are not required by their superiors to show up for work on a daily basis—ideal for the system's rebels. Thus many prominent Oppositionists such as Mirosław Chojecki, founder of NOWA, were state-employed scientists.

In the late 1970s, the Opposition started to undertake specific practical activities, in which the participants, many of them new to the movement, became ever better organized with each operation. The creation of a system of production and distribution of underground materials played a special part in this. Printing became the most specialized and professional calling since the printing equipment was the only truly underground resource of considerable value. It was crucial that only a small number of dependable people be entrusted with it to avoid disclosure, and equally essential that printers be prepared to toil for weeks without leaving the premises so as to limit outside contacts. They were well paid for contending with such difficulties and dangers. Thus was formed a new Opposition elite, and it became fashionable among young urbanites to work as printers.

Other tasks were done either on a voluntary basis or for a small wage. Larger teams bound the printed pages into books, new friends and acquaintances often being invited to help. New contacts were made through distribution. Books were transported to storage places and then dispersed in batches of several dozen, to private apartments whose owners sold them to friends and neighbors—activities that posed no worse threat than police detention and confiscation of the contraband.

The circulation of underground papers in the late 1970s proved to be important later when Solidarity, in which the Opposition was very influential, emerged in 1980–81. One reason for this was the Opposition's political experience, experience dramatically lacking in the emerging social movement. Another reason was that early readers of the underground press, including Lech Wałęsa himself, were better informed because of their reading and were becoming leaders in Solidarity. These leaders sought the help and experience of the Opposition that had so markedly shaped their thinking. Nevertheless, many Solidarity rank-and-file, as well as local leaders, distrusted and resented the closed character of the intellectual elite Opposition.

The Opposition had always been a social milieu—a środowisko—a source of social life and economic survival. The emergence of Solidarity as a legal organization created a structure of formal relations and groups within the general movement and, for a short time, somewhat separated the środowisko from the political functions of the Opposition. Thousands of new people entered the movement. But long-standing informal contacts and groups still ran deep in decision making, allocation of goods and resources, and in the structure of influence. These contacts were forced underground to become supremely important with the imposition of martial law and the outlawing of Solidarity in 1981. New activists whose political experience began with Solidarity created a political-social środowisko of the old Opposition type wherein political and social life and contacts compounded under pressure within the same medium. Nor have such informal entities as środowiska by any means disappeared with the re-legalization of Solidarity and its entry into government, but continue as major political players, exerting considerable influence and issuing in formal groups and political parties.

16

The Opposition and Money

TADEUSZ WRÓBLEWSKI

> Portuguese, Turkish, and Swedish packages played no
> small part. The coffee, tea, and sardines contained in
> them entered the bellies of the bigger financial climb-
> ers, thereby increasing the budgets of many intelli-
> gentsia families. Let us add to this the significant sums
> that were pumped in from London for political reasons,
> particularly to Warsaw, but were distributed according
> to quite different priorities.
>
> —Kazimierz Wyka, 1945

The title of this paper clearly defines its subject: how the Polish
Opposition acquired and spent money.[1]

Opposition activities require money, technical equipment, and
materials. Those who want to publish independent books or periodicals have to buy, or be given, machines, paper, and ink, and pay
the authors, translators, editors, reviewers, printers, typesetters, and
distributors. Sometimes they also need tape recorders and type-
writers, or even cars, computers, or video cameras. And anyhow,
people who devote their time to opposition activities need an income.

The Opposition's main source of financial support was the West.
Donations came from inspired individuals, from subscriptions, trade
unions, social and political organizations, as well as from corporations, Polish emigré organizations, and government bodies such as
substantial grants from the U.S. Congress.

Once there is money and an Opposition able to draw upon at
least some full-time professional activists for whom the money has
been raised, the question arises: What to do with it? How might the
Oppositionists "earn" that money?

A great part, perhaps most of it was spent on general social projects, for example, aid for workers harassed and victimized by the communist state. In 1976, after strikes and street riots in Radom and Ursus were ruthlessly crushed by the Gierek government, Polish intellectuals created the Committee for Defense of the Workers to raise funds in Poland and in the West to furnish material and legal aid to the victims. Thus began the institutionalized Opposition.

Although this was the Opposition's ultimate objective, it is worthwhile to remember that those who carry out such lofty and noble ends are still human beings like the rest of us, who need money to live.

Payment for articles, books, reviews, and sometimes interviews published in the West provided Oppositionists with much needed income. Some received awards; others were granted lucrative Western scholarships or fellowships. Activists had many opportunities to earn money at home by working for independent papers and publishing houses (that paid in złoty) or working for Western correspondents (for dollars) as translators or fixers. Finally, an activist might be a full-time, salaried employee of underground Solidarity or an underground paper, or for an Opposition agency such as the Helsinki Watch Committee, the *Krytyka* and *Głos* quarterlies, or other independent firms.

Some Oppositionists were more equal than others. Well-known activists had many more opportunities to earn money than their less famous colleagues. Such genuinely eminent figures as Adam Michnik and Jacek Kuroń (cabinet members in the first post-Communist government) could live comfortably from selling their views in the form of paid interviews with foreign press agencies. Indeed, such people had many more offers than they could accept. Western journalists worked for Western editors, who had only a vague idea about the situation in Poland, and thus always demanded the same names. Such Oppositionists often had to turn down intrusive Western correspondents.

The rewards for Oppositionists' utterances could not always be measured in plain cash. Often they did not charge for an interview but accepted a bottle of good whiskey or an invitation to dinner in the best restaurant. They became accustomed to this. Such transactions became commonplace elements in their lifestyle, emphasizing their exalted position vis-à-vis less prominent friends. Even if the requests for such interviews stemmed from an interviewee's place in Opposition or Solidarity organizations, he accounted the income private business and kept it, even when what he said differed little from what his lower-ranking colleagues might have said. This reinforced the interviewee's reputation and with it his chances of further lucrative contacts. It created an elite of opinions, and also helped to create a *financial* elite.

There were many "jobs" for people with average talents (or with average positions, which did not necessarily mean the same thing). Many women served as secretaries. Men often worked as printers in underground publishing firms, which paid very well in comparison to average state salaries. Both men and women were managers, drivers, book dealers, and lecturers.

A prominent Oppositionist dealing with the second rank of Western journalists often put up some semblance of affront at the offer of payment for an interview: or he again might accept the gift, making it clear that he was doing so only to show that he does not take the interviewer seriously. The payment, often a bottle of whiskey, was purely symbolic. The absence of such a bottle did not diminish his budget: his real source of income was well-remunerated articles and interviews for large newspapers, or a permanent "contract" with friendly media such as the Polish-language broadcasting stations in the West.

Less prominent Oppositionists expected payment, however small. They were happy to be offered a carton of Marlboros, although they would try to accept it in ways that would not compromise their dignity. The difference between prominent Oppositionists and their more obscure colleagues was that, in dealing with journalists, the former were fully in charge of the situation and could demand or refuse payment at whim, or indeed decline to be interviewed altogether. But the latter were proud to be interviewed under any circumstances. They wanted to safeguard their dignity but also to receive money.

The Opposition was not altogether centralized. Individual organizations tried independently to obtain money without the knowledge and approval of others. The best way to do this was to make a quest in person, while visiting the West. It was much easier if one had contacts with Polish emigrés or representatives of emigré organizations. Sometimes all that it took was a certain amount of courage and determination. While visiting the United States, for example, an activist from an important Opposition group lobbied a few dozen American organizations and foundations for financial support for work back home—and allegedly raised about $1 million.

This was as much as the U.S. Congress granted to Solidarity in the late 1980s. Money raised by her could be controlled to a much smaller extent.

The distinction between monies and goods designated for individual and for collective use was never clear. Some Opposition organizations were more formal than others. Exact bookkeeping was often deemed impossible for security reasons, and the activists' own money easily got mixed with the "company" money. Generally speaking, the less formalized the organization, the less clear the division between personal and organizational funds.

The extremes are exemplified by the contrast between Solidarity of the legal period, paying fixed salaries to full-time employees, keeping books and having them audited, and Solidarity on the run under martial law, deprived of any opportunity to pursue formal procedures. Private and collective funds melted into one—as did the Opposition's finances until August 1980. Each professional Oppositionist had to determine what portion of the funds in his hands was to be spent on private needs. For example, whether to dine say, in a cheap or a more expensive restaurant.

More important, however, was the way that the distinction between his private life and his activities springing out of the "cause," for which he received money, became less and less easy to establish, particularly during martial law. The very ability of a prominent Solidarity activist to keep hidden was a victory in itself for the cause. Whoever was coming up with the money was not interested in an exact accounting. And so, things such as printing leaflets and having lunch in a good restaurant (or a bad one if it so happened) became no more than different items on the same budget.

It was also rather difficult at times to determine whether an activist was honored with some prize from abroad for his personal, individual achievements or on behalf of the group and the cause he represented. Did, for example, the Nobel Peace Prize simply honor the undoubtedly heroic Lech Wałęsa or also millions of less famous, more deprived, more easily suppressed workers across a defiant nation? In some cases a contributor earmarked the money for a common, opposition purpose, in others he did not. One may presume that the recipient kept some part of it for himself.

The situation was different in legal Solidarity, where people were paid for their work, just as in any more humdrum enterprise. Equality is commonly applauded in Poland, but putting egalitarian rhetoric into practice is much more complicated. Poles, at least those who founded Solidarity in 1980–81, were not egalitarian in the essential sense of the word. They were ready to pay more for good work and for "due" dignity (i.e., that genuine dignity that develops out of the common judgment of the people and thus differs from the usurped "dignity" of communist apparatchiks). They were ready, for example, to set the salary of the president of the Warsaw chapter of Solidarity at triple the average member's salary. They endorsed the slogan "the better you work the better you get paid." On the other hand, they were almost unanimously against the diversification of incomes under the official grade system: at first glance an expression of egalitarian views, but in fact a repudiation of "communist privileges" rather than a vote for any sort of authentic egalitarianism.

Less prestigious Oppositionists could make a good living working for foreign correspondents. Many people working for press agencies came from opposition circles. For one thing, hard-currency income, even though typically much lower than the pay for comparable work abroad, was still much higher than the salary paid by "ordinary" employers. For example, an acquaintance who worked part-time for a Western correspondent received $75 a month, then the equivalent of about four average monthly salaries. This was a substantial return for relatively little work: providing information about the latest events over the telephone and helping the correspondent, who was on the road a lot, when he happened to be in Poland. Nor is it unimportant that such a person shared in the relative luxury of his employers. Working with them he dined in five-star hotel restaurants, drank expensive alcohol, and smoked imported cigarettes. His employer often gave him alcohol and cigarettes as presents, which he could share with friends who had no such connections with such prestigious foreigners. "I had dinner in the Victoria [until several years ago Poland's most expensive hotel] last night," he could brag. "Not too good, I'm afraid."

It is also significant that such a person is close to the heart of political events. He has the opportunity to meet people like Lech Wałęsa, Bronisław Geremek, Jacek Kuroń, Adam Michnik, and on the other hand, Communist leaders Mieczysław Rakowski or Wojciech Jaruzelski, to witness Solidarity rallies, negotiations, and demonstrations. Even if he had never been a political activist, but was, for example, an unemployed English teacher, he entered the circles of the Opposition "big shots," often making friends among them.

Nepotism entails supporting those "close" to one: in the case of the Opposition, friends from the "organization." It is they who got the prestigious, well-paying jobs. But if they themselves were promoted or saw their close friends being promoted they insisted that this was strictly on merit. A prominent Oppositionist with responsibility for allocating the organization's funds, sought out his close friends as work colleagues at usually prestigious, well-paid jobs, even if secretive.

An Oppositionist who has earned a lot of money in such ways may buy his son an apartment. This is a gift of lifelong financial and social significance, as housing is extremely expensive in Poland. In some areas there is a waiting list of up to 20 years for state apartments. Likewise, the daughter of a prominent Oppositionist may be granted an attractive foreign scholarship and other opportunities for travel and contacts because of her mother's eminence. Such inheritance of advantages is looked down upon among Opposition activists.

The Opposition offers the opportunities it is given to close friends. But don't others do this? Perhaps all of us? Most probably, yes: but an Oppositionist often has special advantages. He can earn a Western income without leaving Poland. The unnaturally high exchange rate of the dollar, a result of the isolated economy, makes a Pole who goes to work in the West, however meager his job, a rich man if he spends his money in Poland. His financial advantages are multiplied if he performs highly skilled work.

But an Oppositionist doesn't have to leave Poland for these rewards. Staying in Poland is much better than having to work illegally in the West, where the cost of supporting oneself, given currency ratios, is so much greater. An Oppositionist has these advantages without being separated from his family and without living in poor conditions to maximize what he can bring back.

Furthermore, a *gastarbeiter* [guest worker] performing menial tasks does nothing he can be proud of. Abroad, he is at the bottom of the social ladder and, if illegal, has to avoid the police, who, not him, are in the right. In Poland, on the contrary, an Oppositionist is morally right, and even if he risked imprisonment and the "niceties" of being arrested, having his apartment searched, and books confiscated, he received compensatory prestige and social standing. And his life was much more interesting. Last but not least, he still got the dollars.

But a certain discord arises from the moral tension between being an Oppositionist and the income it brings. What is the reaction of those outside the Opposition?

Critics of the Opposition emphasize the issue of money, a motif that has permeated the official propaganda for years. The propaganda storyline is rather simple. The Opposition's aims are not so noble as their pronouncements. They do not care much for freedom, equality or brotherhood of Poles or the working class, they do not care much for the public good, nor the public itself. All they care for is their own good, hypocritically presented as that of the community.

Such propaganda asserts that the Oppositionists are not just ordinary people. They either come from Stalinist apparatchik circles and thus lack anything in common with the people; or, on the other extreme, are too devoted to "bourgeois" patterns of thinking which are foreign and not egalitarian and therefore have nothing in common with the people either.

Further, the Opposition is said to be multiply connected to the Western powers, especially their main "representative," the CIA, which is quite willing to pay for the luxurious Opposition lifestyle. What they get in return is the opportunity to promote their (not our) aims.

The Opposition and its supporters have two principal responses to such arguments. Most often they try to avoid them, perhaps suggesting that anyone who tries to talk about the foreign origins of the Oppositionists' wealth unintentionally or otherwise supports the regime. They concentrate on the Opposition's achievements, instancing the unquestionable profits from publishing independent magazines, providing foreign media such as RFE-RL, VOA, and BBC with information. When an Oppositionist receives a prize, his colleagues point to the spectacular success of the common cause—"our interest." They do not talk about money, although deep inside they might envy the recipient.

We are dealing with human beings. Everywhere standing, prestige, and opportunities are connected to money. Society accepts this system of rewards. When being active in the Opposition entailed high risks of repression and long imprisonment, public opinion was quite willing to forgive the more well-known activists their relatively luxurious lives. During martial law many of the activists in hiding received more aid from their countrymen than they needed. And nobody envied them.

Western involvement and support were crucial to the survival of the Opposition. But what was vital to the Polish Opposition was to all but a very few in the West a matter of at most secondary, if intermittently fascinating, importance. Audiences and readerships, and the journalists and media who served them, and politicians and trade unionists, all craved a degree of familiarity of certainty: this operated to produce a recognized elite abroad, and with it an elite of opinion, which did not completely speak for the unconsenting nation (which many in the West have found to their surprise in the past year and a half); and with all this, a very real economic elite.

NOTES

1. The matters discussed here characterize the period from the beginning of the organized Opposition in the early 1970s to the "round table" talks that legalized the Opposition in the spring of 1989, always excepting the 16 months of legal Solidarity activity in 1980–81.

The Communist Party

The book thus far has depicted a social process whose very existence and endurance acted upon the society as a whole, gathering momentum through the postwar years and culminating in the Communist Party's collapse. It is clear why the Party merits quick burial: a process of erosion over the past 20 years has undercut its power base, recruitment, and ability to renew its authority. Antoni Sułek of the Institute of Sociology at Warsaw University shows how the Party, having long served as an instrument of upward mobility, was increasingly unable to ensure social status and material comfort for its members. It lost its capacity to mobilize society from the top downward to secure representation at the bottom. Simultaneously, the Party changed its demographic structure, dissolving into a weary mass of pensioners from a more vigorous epoch.

Skilled workers, technicians, and those among the intelligentsia not employed by the state administration, economy, or political organizations left the Party. Contributor Jacek Kurczewski has styled these groups the "new middle class," contending that communist society produced its own new middle class composed of educated and skilled people whose aspirations were cut short by the *nomenklatura* barrier. This barrier made it impossible for a non-Party member, and to a degree for a rank-and-file Party member, to influence his work conditions, neighborhood, and to participate in political life.

Ironically, the same "new middle class" that left the Party has also deserted Solidarity over the past ten years. The political institutions connected with Solidarity—its trade union, government, the (OKP)[1] parliamentary caucus, and Citizens' Committees—have failed precisely where Communist organizations failed, becoming ineffective as instruments of upward mobility and authority. In 1991, Solidarity faces a situation similar to that of the Party in 1980.

NOTES

1. *Obywatelski Klub Parlamentarny*, the Citizens' Parliamentary Club, is Solidarity's caucus in the senate and in parliament.

17

Farewell to the Party

ANTONI SUŁEK

Only now are we paying the price of the Occupation.   —Kazimierz Wyka, 1945

During the 1970s there was a continuous upward trend in the number of Party members: from 2.3 million members in 1971 to 3.1 million in 1979.[1] The pace of increase was not even: slow during the
first half of the decade, like an avalanche in the second. This rapid
rise was the Party's reaction to workers' protests against the price
rises of 1976. The authorities had first resorted to force, then rolled
back the increases, but made no changes in the personnel and policies of the team in power. Instead, the authorities turned to an enormous propaganda campaign of counter-recruitment to the Party.
    The propaganda was intended to transform unrest brought about
by the price increases into a victory for the authorities, and the
massive recruitment was to strengthen the Party without changing
its policies. Recruitment continued until summer 1980. One hundred
thousand new candidates became Party members during the first
half of that year. In 1981 the Party itself noted that one reason for
its weakness was precisely this massive, insufficiently selective influx
of new members.
    This extraordinary increase broke down spectacularly in the sum-
mer of 1980. The wave of strikes and subsequent founding of Solidarity, the economic collapse and internal crisis of the Party itself,
and finally the introduction of martial law, caused a rapid, serious,
and permanent shrinking of membership, to which two fundamental
processes contributed: a decrease in the number of candidates and
a much more dramatic outpouring of resignations. Two much lesser
phenomena supplemented these: expulsions for attitudes and activ-

ities contrary to Party guidelines and the dropping from the rolls of members for inactivity or failure to keep dues current.

Between the first strikes of summer 1980 and the IXth Extraordinary Congress in July 1980, the Party decreased by 300,000; between the IXth and the Xth Congress of 1986, by 780,000. The Party's membership, even offset by recruiting, fell by 35 percent from its 1980 level, and an even greater percentage when we treat as a ratio of those who could leave the Party without fear of losing their positions (executives and eminences within the *nomenklatura*) or their jobs altogether (the army and police). Although 46,000 of the 1980 membership were expelled, the vast majority—650,000 to 700,000—left the Party on their own volition.

Among those stricken, voluntarily or otherwise from the rolls, the most numerous were those who had entered in the latter 1970s— young people and workers. Officially, the leadership found some consolation in claiming that those people who left the Party had joined it "by accident." But even Party publications admitted that, in fact, "a considerable number of those who left the Party were active individuals, motivated by social interest, prepared to work in their own *środowisko*, regarded as an authority in their *środowisko*" and "at the same time a lot of passive lightweights remained in the Party."[2]

By the mid-1980s the Party had somewhat managed to slow attrition. Other data indicate that in 1985, for the first time since 1980, the number of those admitted exceeded that of those who left; and membership slowly started to grow. Despite this growth, however, the 1988 membership (2,132,000) was comparable to that of 1968–69, in effect going back to the level of 20 years earlier. Another, not less telling proof of shrinking Party membership is that in the years 1979–1988, the percentage of Party members in the adult population dropped from 12.2 to 8.0.

This powerfully implies a decline of the Party's prestige and of the legitimacy of its rule in Poland: a suggestion justified by research studies carried out by the government's Center for Social Opinion Research.

First, examinations of the prestige of public institutions found the Communist Party consistently receiving very low ratings in public opinion polls. When at the outset of 1988 people were asked: "In your opinion, do Communist Party activities serve society well and do they comply with society's interests?" the Party received more negative than positive evaluations. During the month of strikes in

August that led to Solidarity's legalization, 27 percent of Poles surveyed answered "yes" and 52 percent "no." In May 1989, just before
the Party's electoral defeat, the respective numbers were almost the
same: 29 percent and 53 percent.[3] The Party ranked at the very
bottom of the institutional prestige scale. Even the police came considerably higher.

Second, the Party's leading role was the most frequently ques-
tioned systemic principle of the Polish People's Republic, although
it lay at the heart of real socialism—socialism as it really functioned.
In August 1984, only 22 percent of Poles were of the opinion that
the majority of society accepted the principle, and 34 percent were
of the opinion that the majority rejected it and would like to change
it. This ratio is much lower than indicators of acceptance of other
principles the Party invokes to legitimize its rule: 65 percent of Poles
believed that the majority of the population accepted that "the
means of production" should be under state ownership; 53 percent
affirmed "the leading role of the working class," and 29 percent Poland's "alliance with the Soviet Union and other socialist countries."

Third, only 35 percent of respondents in the same survey affirmed
the doctrine that "decisions and solutions should be the domain of
the Communist Party—the progressive political power of society,"
while more than 80 percent favored having the *Sejm*—the Polish
Parliament—make such decisions, or favored holding general ref-
erendums on important issues.

The Party's Changing Face

The Communist Party was faced with a well-known unsolvable
dilemma: on the one hand, it strove for an even representation
among all social groups, this being justified by its role in mobilizing
the society for socialist goals, while on the other hand, it wanted to
be the "vanguard of the working class," as justified by its ideology.
Party pronouncements often combine these contradictory directions
in one sentence: "a proportional development of Party membership
[among all social groups]" and "winning over the workers and peasants in particular."[4] For this reason Party statistics treated as a set-
back not only that there was a decline in the number of members
generally, but also that there was a drop in the percentage of workers
(and peasants), and an increase in the percentage of the intelligentsia
and non-manual employees.

Following the workers' protests in the second half of the 1970s, the Party implemented a program to improve its class composition and in particular to increase the percentage of workers. From 1976 to 1979 the percentage of professionally active workers among Party members increased from 41.8 percent to 46.2 percent, while the percentage of non-manual employees dropped from 41.8 percent to 33 percent. The years that followed brought about an undeniable reversal in this trend.

It is difficult to describe these changes precisely, since the comparability of statistical data published is limited. Retired people constituted an increasingly greater part of Party membership, their percentage reaching 14.8 percent in 1982, but the way in which data are compiled had changed from considering retirees a separate group to counting them according to their previous occupations. The numbers and percentages of retired people as well as of professionally active workers, non-manual employees, and peasants can, however, be estimated roughly conceding with a realistic margin of risk. Namely, it is possible to assume that beginning in 1978 the ratio of retired people in the Party increased at approximately the same pace as in the entire adult population. Although it may also be assumed that the proportion of retired people was similarly distributed in relation to those professionally active in different categories of the Party, there is no evidence for this. We may thus estimate that, in 1988, the proportion of retired people in the Party reached about 20 percent and that, of Party members, 30 percent were workers, 42 percent non-manual employees and 7 percent peasants.

The Party's membership crisis has been overwhelmingly concentrated among its working class members. From 1978 to 1988, the number of workers in the Party declined by about 700,000, from 1,340,000 to about 640,000, and their percentage among Party members dropped from 46 percent to about 30 percent, the lowest level ever after the war. Two factors caused this decline. First, of those who returned their Party membership cards between the summer of 1980 and the IXth Congress in July 1981, 72 percent were workers, and the proportion was similar in the years that followed. Second, among all those joining the Party, there were few workers—only 44 percent between 1981 and 1985. In 1978 about 16 percent of all workers were Party members, as contrasted with only about 8 percent in 1988. The Party authorities found it particularly painful that their greatest loss of strength came among workers in heavy industry. Workers traditionally have been the Party's biggest base of support, and authorities always emphasized this as justifying the Party's policies.

By the late 1980s we knew that the Polish United Workers' Party was losing the working-class character of its social base. It was not so easy to determine what character it was taking on. Before the events of 1989 made such numbers irrelevant, published statistics indicated that in the years 1978 to 1988, "employees in non-worker posts" had strengthened their position. Their number fell only by about 150,000, from 1,049,000 to around 900,000, and their percentage among all Party members increased considerably as a result of the mass exodus of workers, from 35.8 percent to 42 percent. However, this aggregate statistical category is diverse and does not facilitate more precise conclusions, including as it does "employees in managerial posts, posts requiring specialized training of a high or secondary level of professional education, as well as administrative posts where people are engaged in office and economic assistance work," and certainly the army and police also.

A more detailed analysis of this category of Party members shows that in 1978 to 1988, there was a net loss of at least 50,000 engineers and technicians—20 percent of all engineers and technicians; 27,000 teachers—18 percent of all teachers; 3,000 medical doctors—20 percent of all physicians; 35,000 economists, planners, and accountants—28 percent of the total number; 12,000 agriculture and forestry service specialists—32 percent of the total; and 2,000 scientists—11 percent of all scientists. The statistics for 1988 include pensioners in the occupations in which they previously were engaged, and thus show the losses in each category as, on average, about one-fifth smaller than they in fact are. Unfortunately, the published statistics do not separate those exercising political power, and those occupying managerial posts do not constitute a separate category in their assigned professional group: managers in industry are not distinguished from the overall category of engineers and economists, school administrators are not distinguished from teachers, or foremen from manual workers. It is, however, possible to assume that the outflow (to be more precise, the net loss) from the Party was extremely selective: those occupying managerial and leadership posts did not leave the Party on anything like so substantial a scale as those employed in more subordinate posts.

This assumption is supported by the results of other studies. In 1987 still almost 900,000 out of the 1.2 million managerial and leadership posts were held by members of the Party.[5] This means that half of the professionally active Party members were involved in management—from industry to the army, from prime minister to foreman. During the first half of the 1980s, 87 percent of one of the regional power elites examined were Party members,[6] and in 1986, 72 percent of the directors of industrial enterprises held membership.[7] From 1973 to 1986, the percentage of Party members among the higher officials of the central state and economic administration fell by only 2 percent—from 90 to 88 percent.[8]

Apart from the specialists mentioned previously, there also were to be found about half a million "others"—"employees working in non-worker positions," not further defined by official statistics. In 1988, there were even more of these than in 1976, and their percentage in the Party had increased from around 15 percent to about 23 percent. Who were these mysterious "others"?

To a considerable degree, they were members of various apparatuses through which the political leadership and central technocracy administered the society: employees of the Party apparatus of coercion, of the judicial system and propaganda; functionaries in the state economy and bureaucracy who have undergone some type of "education other than economic, technical or agricultural" that we noticed earlier. Legal-administrative education, for example, was popular as a path to management. In 1988, the Party employed 13,500 so-called political employees (apparatchiks).[9] More than 100,000 army officers and other professional soldiers were Party members; political leadership of the army was reserved for the Party, and the army was the supreme guarantor of the "constitutional order."

The police also figured as a political arm of the Party. Some 75 percent of all those employed in active-duty positions in "internal affairs" (125,000) belonged, and the percentage is even higher in the Security Service.[10] Despite the fact that they are state officials, only here do the employees vow "faithfully to serve the Party." In 1984 70 percent of public prosecutors[11] and in 1987 48 percent of judges (but as many as 83 percent of judges on the Supreme Court) were members.[12] We do not have any membership data for the propaganda apparatus, but it is sufficient to note that the Party owned an enormous press consortium that issued about 90 percent of all Polish daily newspapers and 75 percent of weeklies, and was therefore the employer of the great majority of journalists.

These data support the thesis that the one social group that strengthened its position in the Party during its lattermost supremacy was the ruling elite, embracing people engaged in conducting and servicing Party-State rule.

This process of change—in the Party's composition and its evolution from a Party of the working class into one of the ruling class—can be interpreted in two ways. There has been a significant change in the class character of the Party, which until the mid-1950s, was at least numerically dominated by workers. The Party took care of their interests more than it did in its decline, developing social services, building cheap housing, greatly extending access to education. By the mid-1980s it was difficult to assert that such a policy existed. In a study conducted over the first half of the decade, 62 to 65 percent of the workers surveyed stated that "at the workplace, the Party takes care mainly of the interests of those working in administrative-bureaucratic posts" and that "the activities of the Party are influenced more by the interests of employees of the militia, army, Party apparatus, office workers and directors than those of manual workers."[13]

But it can also be argued that these changes in the membership base of the Party constituted not so much a significant change in its character but a disclosure of its true nature, an interpretation for which historical circumstances speak persuasively. The Polish Workers' Party, predecessor of the late fallen Party, did not gain power after the war through the support of the masses that it organized. It was, rather, undeniably a minority party owing its power to Soviet support. At the beginning, the Party organized a ruling apparatus, and only afterwards did it set out to recruit a broader base of support. In fact, factories never were true Party bastions. That role was reserved for the "institutions of authority" (state administration, courts, army, and police).

The persistent pervasiveness of Party membership among the upper levels of management and employees of different apparati, while members drawn from the remaining social groups poured out of the Party, brought about a huge disproportion between Party membership among the ruling class and among other social strata. Conspicuous by their departure were skilled workers and technicians and those among the intelligentsia not employed by the state administration, economic, or political organizations. It was precisely these groups that constituted that crucial estate that sociologist Jacek Kurczewski styles the "new middle class."[14]

This parallel alienation among skilled workers and those intelligentsia independent of the ruling elite gave rise to Solidarity, which sociologist Jan Pakulski has aptly classified as an "anti-partocratic" movement.[15] And again, as life seeped back in the latter 1980s, it was in these groups that we most frequently found sentiments of challenge toward the political order. In "Poles '84," the most important political-attitude study of the past years, these groups proved to be the only ones in which dissent dominated over acquiescence. Unable to articulate their political interests within the realm of the Party and of institutions under Party control, the groups nevertheless knew their support or at least assent to be fundamentally necessary to bring about the reforms that the authorities were seeking to implement. The second part of the sentence containing the main conclusions of the research cites this explosive antinomy that tore open Pandora's box a few years later: "People on whom those in power could 'count' often do not want reform, while people who want reform give no political support to those in power.[16]

The Aging of the Party

During the first half of the 1950s, the Party was demographically youthful. In 1954–55 about 15 percent of its members were under 25, and only 17 percent were over 50. Following the October 1956[17] turning point, the percentage of members of age 25 or younger fell to 6.8 and afterwards fluctuated only slightly. The recruitment campaigns that followed the student demonstrations of March 1968 and the upheavals of 1976 targeted not only workers but youth also; even older students in secondary schools were recruited. Thus, during 1977 to 1978, the percentage of members from age 18 to 25 increased from 5.7 percent to 7.8 percent. The percentage increase of older age groups was more systematic—a function of the aging of the Party. Approximately 23 percent of Party members were 50 or older in 1978.

The age structure of the Party changed rapidly after August 1980. It was aging steeply now, as the young people left, or would not join. In 1978 the number of Party members 50 or older and 30 or younger were equal at around 23 percent; in 1988 there were almost 6 times as many over 50 as under 30 (36.3 percent and 6.4 percent, respectively)—a change stemming mainly from the Solidarity and martial law period, but the Party went on graying even in quieter times. In 1981 the average age of Party members was 43.6; in 1987 it was up to 46.

It is possible to treat changes in the Party's age structure from 1978 to 1988 in terms of the membership rate of different age groups: the higher the age, the smaller the ratio of decline. In the age group 18–29, this fell by a factor of three quarters, from 8.6 percent to 2.1 percent, while in the age group above 60 it even increased, from 4.7 to 6.1 percent.

The Party disappeared from the university student milieu years before it evacuated the ministries. At the beginning of 1987, only 879 university students in all Poland were members. In 1988 Warsaw University, the country's largest institute of higher education, could boast just 58 members out of 16,500 students. In all Cracow's institutions of higher education taken together, just 34 Party members were to be found among 35,000. Some institutions of higher education had no student members whatsoever. What a contrast with the not-so-distant 1970s when 50,000 students and 100,000 youth activists joined each year.

Over the tumultuous 1980s, the Party made energetic attempts to attract young people and, up to a point, even succeeded. Of the 122,600 members who joined in 1982–1985, 52 percent, or 64,000, were under 30, figures so far below even replacement level that the toll exacted by the aging process became even more apparent.

This had two significant consequences: it undermined the control the Party sought to exert over the younger generation. Aging already had hindered the Party from penetrating the milieu from which it found itself excluded, such as young workers, students, and the young intelligentsia. Before it was elbowed aside, it simply was running short of an officer corps through which it could govern. The anxiety expressed by the head of the Department of Personnel Policy of the Party Central Committee was radically justified: "What is going to happen in 10 to 15 years? How are we to train the basic forces and personnel reserves, managerial and intellectual elites with a socialist outlook?"[18] He did not have to confront the problem.

Second, the aging of the Party left the younger generation too weak to do much to articulate the Party's political consciousness, or indeed to represent its cohort's own interests through the Party. The Party lumbered along, continuing to favor the orientation and interests of the settled or even outgoing generation. Generational differences in Poland at that moment had unusually deep political resonances. The "Poles '84" study showed a clear relationship between age and intensity of attitudes contesting the political order: among people born before the Second World War, only 19 percent were "contesters," while among those born after 1950, there were already 31 percent.[19] Age differentiation was a significant determinant of Poles' construction of social reality, thorough research studies confirmed.[20] Different social experiences of the "old" and "young" form the backbone of these differences. Elders, less well educated, could remember the "social advancement" of the early People's Republic, Stalinism, and total indoctrination. The latter, better educated, freer from fear, more politically sophisticated, and with a sense of possibility leaking in from outside, could look at the system from the outside and felt powerfully the barriers that stood between them and free debate, blocking their influence on public matters.

This second generation, "children of People's Poland," who left the Party in the tidal wave of 1980–82 and remained underrepresented in the Party down to its fall, realized needs for participation elsewhere—in Solidarity. The generational profile of Solidarity is well known: the union that emerged in 1980 was most popular in the age group around 30, and half of its leading activists were born after the war. Let it suffice to add to these already familiar facts one small but meaningful detail: a comparison of the age of delegates at certain regional meetings of Solidarity with that of the IXth Party Congress in 1980. Sixty-eight percent of the Congress delegates were 40 years old or over, while 64.5 percent of their Solidarity counterparts were no more than 40. Only 2 percent of the Congress delegates were under 30; at Solidarity meetings 23 percent of delegates fell between 18 and 30.[21]

By 1988, the Party was to a greater degree than ever before made up of people well situated in life and of higher status: this proletarian radical Party drawn most conspicuously from the ruling authorities or those who directly served them.

The social position of Party members was bound to influence their ideas, opinions, and political preferences, and it did. Analysis conducted throughout Poland by the Center for Social Opinion Research during the first half of the 1980s confirmed this.[22] In 1984–85, more Party members than non-Party members evaluated their material situations as being decidedly better. Moreover, they also considered the country's economic situation to be better and held that during the past two years the material conditions of the population in general had improved. They were much more frequently optimistic in assessing the economic perspective and believed that the crises would soon end, largely through the government's efforts.

Their optimism exceeded that of others even to a greater degree when it came to their anticipations of evolution of the political situation at home and in the Eastern bloc as a whole. A considerable majority of Party members spoke highly of the Polish People's Republic's achievements, held it to be a democratic country and supported the internal policies of the authorities. They had high hopes for parliamentary elections and said they would vote in them. They defended the authorities' right to limit civil liberties in the name of "realizing State goals," and denied the Church any right to make "political statements." The psychopolitical profile of Party members becomes even sharper when they are compared, not with the general population of non-Party members, but with those of Solidarity members in 1980–81.

So we find that Party members were decidedly better adjusted in their thinking to the political and economic status quo than the rest of society. However, we also learn that in what now so clearly seems an age of transition, the opinions of the ruling elite were *not* the ruling opinions.

The phenomena presented here help us understand the direction of the regime's policies. The Party was, after all, a channel of articulation for the values and interests of its membership. The interests of a considerable majority of which, the influential Party members especially, were concerned with preserving the Party's political monopoly in the State and centralized control over the economy.

To clarify yet further, the persistent blocking of political and economic reforms was caused not only by Party members' political interests and ideological notions, but also by their passivity and long-formed habits. These psychological factors—often also related to age—gave rise to great fear of change, whatever its nature or direction.

By the end of the 1970s, the Party had evolved into a Party of those settled in life, secure in society, and comfortable with the system. This greatly weakened the Party's ability to "mobilize" society—to garner support and to wield influence. It failed to develop any skill in attracting, let alone representing, other social groups—those among the "unofficial" intelligentsia not connected to the authorities, skilled workers, youth and particularly students, the young intelligentsia and young workers. Indeed, the possibility of authentic participation in public life for these latter groups was systematically blocked. To a greater degree than other groups, they withdrew from public life or tried to satisfy their interests outside the Party and the system of institutions which it controlled.

Years ago, I predicted that these groups would find fresh possibilities for articulating their values and representing their interests through independent trade unions, associations, and political parties within the framework of the new political order that one could see emerging like a volcanic island from beneath the cold, exhausted sea of late communism. They did so. Life and the will to experiment have reasserted themselves.

NOTES

1. Author's note: Most of the statistical data presented in this chapter come from or were calculated from the following sources: *Rocznik Statystyczny* (Statistical yearbook), 1967–1989; *Rocznik Polityczny i Gospodarczy* (Yearbook of politics and economics), 1977–1988; *IX Nadzwyczajny Zjazd PZPR* (The IXth Congress of the Polish United Workers' Party) (Warszawa: Książka i Wiedza, 1987). Data from other sources are cited in the text.

2. Author's note: Mirosław Karwat and Włodzimierz Milanowski, "Dylematy Budowy Siły Partii" (Dilemmas of building the party), *Nowe Drogi*, no. 5, 1983.

3. Author's note: These data were provided by the government's Center for Social Opinion Research (CBOS) in "Opinia Społeczna o PZPR w Badaniach CBOS w Latach 1984–1989" (Social opinion about the Polish United Workers' Party in the Research Center for Social Opinion Research from 1984 to 1989), January 1990.

4. Author's note: *X Zjazd PZPR* (The Xth Congress of the Polish United Workers' Party), Report of the Central Committee.

5. Author's note: An interview with Edward Erazmus of the Polish United Workers' Party Academy of Social Sciences, *Rada Narodowa*, March 5, 1988.

6. Author's note: Jacek Wasilewski, "Social Processes of Regional Power Elite Recruitment," *Sisyphus*, vol. 5, 1989.

7. Author's note: Marek Kozak, "Typowe Drogi Zawodowe Kadry Kierowniczej" (The typical career paths of the professional management cadre), *Biuletyn CBOS*, no. 2, 1987.

8. Author's note: Jacek Wasilewski, "Wzory Rekrutacji Elit Władzy w Polsce w Latach Siedemdziesiątych i Osiemdziesiątych" (Patterns of recruitment of the Polish ruling elite in the 1970s and 1980s), *Kultura i Społeczeństwo*, nos. 3–4, 1989.

9. Author's note: An interview with Zygmunt Czarzasty, Secretary of the Central Committee of the Polish United Workers' Party (PZPR), *Polityka*, January 28, 1989.

10. Author's note: An interview with Czesław Staszczak, Deputy Minister of Internal Affairs, *Trybuna Ludu,* October 7, 1988.

11. Author's note: Ryszard Walczak, *Sprowowanie Kierowniczej Roli Partii w Sądach i Prokuraturze Polski Ludowej* (The performance of the leading role of the Party in the court system of the Polish People's Republic) (Warszawa: Polish United Workers' Party Academy of Social Sciences, 1987), p. 429.

12. Author's note: Jan Szarych, *Sędziowie i Sądy w Polsce w Latach 1918–1988* (Judges and courts in Poland from 1918 to 1988) (Warszawa: Ministry of Justice, 1988), p. 121.

13. Author's note: Leszek Gilejko and Przemysław Wójcik, eds., *Położenie Klasy Robotniczej w Polsce* (The situation of the working class in Poland) (Warszawa: Polish United Workers' Party Academy of Social Sciences, 1987), 5:429.

14. Author's note: Jacek Kurczewski, "The Old System and the Revolution," *Sisyphus,* vol. 3, 1982.

15. Author's note: Jan Pakulski, "Social Movements in Comparative Perspective," in *Research in Social Movements, Conflict and Change,* vol. 10 (Greenwood, Conn.: J & I Press, 1988).

16. Author's note: Władysław Adamski et al., "Poles 1980–1984: Dynamics of Social Conflict and Consensus," *Sisyphus* 5:258, 1989.

17. Bloody food riots in October 1956 brought down the fading Stalinist regime and brought to power the "new Communism" of Gomulka.

18. Author's note: *Trybuna Ludu,* June 15, 1988.

19. Author's note: Władyslaw Adamski, ed., *Polacy '84: Dynamika Konfliktu i Konsensusu* (Poles '84: The dynamics of conflict and consensus) (Warszawa: University of Warsaw, 1986), p. 597.

20. Author's note: Mirosława Marody et al., *Polacy '80* (Poles '80) (Warsaw: University of Warsaw Institute of Sociology, 1982), pp. 303–312.

21. Author's note: Elżbieta Kaczyńska, "Les Candidates et les Elus au Congres de Solidarite: Aspects Demographiques," *Sociologie du Travail,* no. 3, 1982.

22. Author's note: *Członkowie Partii a Inne Segmenty Opinii Społecznej* (Party members and other segments of social opinion) (CBOS, 1985).

About the Contributors

WOJCIECH ARKUSZEWSKI, a physicist by training, is Vice-President of the National Solidarity Committee, NSZZ, of the Solidarity trade union. He is a close aide to former Prime Minister Tadeusz Mazowiecki, Arkuszewski's elder by 20 years and his mentor for more than two decades.

JERZY CHŁOPECKI, a sociologist at the Teacher's College in Rzeszów, works as a journalist for the newspaper *Prawo i Życie* (*Law and Life*).

ELŻBIETA FIRLIT teaches sociology at the Central School of Planning and Statistics (SGPiS) at its branch in the city of Rzeszów.

PIOTR GLIŃSKI, a sociologist at the Polish Academy of Sciences in Warsaw, pioneered research on Poland's private entrepreneurship and informal exchange system.

TERESA HOŁÓWKA is an associate professor of logic at Warsaw University's Institute of Philosophy and a writer who recently published a book critically portraying life in the United States. She worked for three years as a catechism teacher in a high-rise suburban parish.

KAZIMIERZ JANCARZ, a parish priest since the late 1970s in the politicized town of Nowa Huta near Cracow, was engaged in the Christian University of Workers. Recently he was transferred to a remote parish.

STEFAN KAWALEC is General Director of the Ministry of Finance. A mathematician by training, Kawalec's research ranges from a report on "The Democratic Opposition in Poland" growing out of his underground activities with workers, to studies of state enterprises. After release from a martial-law prison cell he worked closely with Leszek Balcerowicz, Poland's Minister of Finance, at the Central School of Planning and Statistics (SGPiS).

ANDRZEJ KŁOCZOWSKI is a Dominican Father, prominent in Catholic intelligentsia circles. An art historian before he took his vows, Kłoczowski later studied philosophy of religion. He has served his order for 30 years, heads the seminary in Cracow, and has become a kind of guru to young Dominicans.

JACEK KURCZEWSKI is Vice-President of the Solidarity Central Citizens' Committee and member of the High Parliamentary Tribunal. He also directs the Institute of Applied Social Sciences at Warsaw University. He is an expert on organizational questions relating to voluntary associations and political groups.

BARBARA LEWENSTEIN, a lecturer in sociology at the Institute of Applied Social Sciences at Warsaw University, studies Polish religious and political groups.

MAŁGORZATA MELCHIOR, an assistant professor at the Institute of Applied Social Sciences at Warsaw University, works on questions relating to social identity.

ILONA MORZOŁ is a journalist writing for the culture page of Poland's most widely circulated newspaper, *Gazeta Wyborcza*. She is originally from the Katowice area.

MICHAŁ OGÓREK, the husband of Ilona Morzoł and also a journalist, writes for the weekly *Przegląd Tygodniowy* (*The Week in Review*), where he specializes in social problems.

WOJCIECH PAWLIK, an assistant professor at the Institute of Applied Social Sciences at Warsaw University, studies Poland's informal exchange system and also lifestyle, confession, and rationalization as they pertain to Polish Catholicism.

JOANNA ŚMIGIELSKA, a lecturer in sociology at the Institute of Applied Social Sciences at Warsaw University, specializes in rural sociology.

ANTONI SUŁEK is an associate professor at the Institute of Sociology at Warsaw University and Secretary of the Polish Sociological Association (PTS).

ADAM SZOSTKIEWICZ is culture and religious editor of the influential Catholic weekly, *Tygodnik Powszechny*, the same Cracow publishing and social circle from which former Prime Minister Tadeusz Mazowiecki drew identity. Szostkiewicz was interned during martial law. He served as press secretary for Mazowiecki and his political party, ROAD, during the 1990 presidential campaign.

PIOTR SZWAJCER, a sociologist interned during martial law, directs the huge, formerly underground, NOWA publishing house. He also is President of the Independent Publishing Association.

"TADEUSZ WRÓBLEWSKI" is the pseudonym for a known Opposition activist under Communism who wishes to remain anonymous for purposes of this book.

KAZIMIERZ WYKA (1910–1975) participated in the literary and underground resistance under German occupation, belonging to the same wartime intellectual circle as Nobel laureate poet Czesław Miłosz. In 1945 Wyka founded the influential monthly *Twórczość* (*Creativity*), and in 1948 was a co-founder of the Institute for Literary Research, a prominent intellectual center at the Academy of Sciences in Warsaw. He directed the Institute from 1953 to 1970 and later retired to Cracow.

Index